T0336179

Organizational and Technological Implications of Cognitive Machines:
Designing Future Information Management Systems

Farley Simon Nobre
Innovation Technology Enterprise, Brazil

Andrew M. Tobias
University of Birmingham, UK

David S. Walker
University of Birmingham, UK

INFORMATION SCIENCE REFERENCE

Hershey · New York

Director of Editorial Content:	Kristin Klinger
Development Editor:	Julia Mosemann
Director of Production:	Jennifer Neidig
Managing Editor:	Jamie Snavely
Assistant Managing Editor:	Carole Coulson
Typesetter:	Jennifer Henderson
Cover Design:	Lisa Tosheff
Printed at:	Yurchak Printing Inc.

Published in the United States of America by
IGI Publishing (an imprint of IGI Global)
701 E. Chocolate Avenue
Hershey PA 17033
Tel: 717-533-8845
Fax: 717-533-8661
E-mail: cust@igi-global.com
Web site: http://www.igi-global.com

and in the United Kingdom by
IGI Publishing (an imprint of IGI Global)
3 Henrietta Street
Covent Garden
London WC2E 8LU
Tel: 44 20 7240 0856
Fax: 44 20 7379 0609
Web site: http:/www.eurospanbookstore.com

Library of Congress Cataloging-in-Publication Data

Nobre, Farley Simon, 1971-
  Organizational and technological implications of cognitive machines : designing future information manage-ment systems / by Farley Simon Nobre, Andrew M. Tobias and David S. Walker.
      p. cm.
  Includes bibliographical references and index.
  Summary: "This book addresses the possible implications of cognitive machines for current and future organi-zations"--Provided by publisher.
  ISBN 978-1-60566-302-9 (hardcover) -- ISBN 978-1-60566-303-6 (ebook)
  1. Knowledge management. 2. Organizational learning. 3. Capability maturity model (Computer software) I. Tobias, Andrew M. II. Walker, David S. (David Stanley), 1941- III. Title.
  HD30.2.N63 2009
  658.4'038011--dc22
                                    2008040205

British Cataloguing in Publication Data
A Cataloguing in Publication record for this book is available from the British Library.

All work contributed to this book is original material. The views expressed in this book are those of the authors, but not necessarily of the publisher.

To our families and to all the people who encourage education in the world.

Table of Contents

Section III:
Cognitive Machines

Section VI:
Implications and the New Organization

Section VII:
General Conclusions

Foreword

Historically, organizations have evolved due to economic, social, and political worldwide contexts within human history. A new stage of development after the Industrial Revolution subsequently followed and many contributions from multidisciplinary studies and theories have been added since the beginning of the 20th Century especially in new emerging global organizations.

In these processes organizations have provided people with higher capabilities for information processing and uncertainty management in complex environments. In such a perspective, information has always been a core and strategic element for organizations. Nevertheless, it was only with continuous advances in information science and technology along with new organizing forms that emerged from the middle of the 20th Century that organizations have developed systems for improving capacities of computation and information management.

This book represents some contribution to a disciplined theory on organizational cognition, whose main purpose comprises to understand and to improve the computational capacity of the organization along with its ability for knowledge management. It touches upon three key elements of cognition: Man, Machines, and Processes. The first is concerned with humans in organizations. The second is concerned with new agents that participate in organizations through high levels of automation. The third is concerned with the processes that provide the organization with cognition, and thus with the capability to learn, to pursue goals and to achieve results.

What is unique in this book is that among the participants of the organization it includes the concept of cognitive machines – which are new agents necessary, when we need to extend the human boundaries of computational capacity along with knowledge and uncertainty management to more advanced models of cognition and information processing in organizations.

In addition, the authors put forward new challenges and new perspectives to the understanding of the participation of cognitive machines in organizations. The book also addresses the possible implications of cognitive machines for current and future organizations. From all these diverse backgrounds, it outlines the concept of new organizations with structures and processes of computational organizational management networks.

There is no doubt that the management and technology principles of the past and the present have contributed with brilliantly successful applications in many areas of organizations and society. But these successes should not obscure the fact that the world is changing, that new organizational and technological systems - such as Organizational Cognition, Cognitive Machines, and Computational Organization Management Networks (COMN) - are becoming reality, and that systems that have proved to be successful in the past may not provide the right tools for addressing the problems of the future.

The research presents new insights and alternatives for national and international organizations and it can be used for academic and practical functions in the diverse areas of business administration, management, social sciences, information systems, psychology, informatics, engineering, and computer science. This work represents a milestone along the new avenues of exploration in this vital area of management and technology activities. A future based on Utopia rather than Armageddon might now be possible.

Professor Michael Czinkota
McDonough School of Business
Georgetown University
Washington – USA
August 2008

Professor Michael R. Czinkota works in the international marketing field at Birmingham and at Georgetown University. He served in the U.S. government as deputy assistant secretary of commerce and as head of the U.S. delegation to the OECD industry committee in Paris, and was a partner in a fur trading firm. Aside from more than 100 articles on export management and trade policy, his key books are International Marketing *(8th edition) and* International Business *(7th edition) and* Mastering Global Markets. *He is on the board of governors of the Academy of Marketing Science, on the international board of the American Management Association and on the international marketing board of the American Marketing Association. He has been awarded several honorary degrees.*

Preface

This book is largely the result of research undertaken in the University of Birmingham, UK, and in the Humboldt University of Berlin in between 2001 and 2005. It also embraces extensive research that has been carried out and published in a number of research papers by the authors elsewhere, and papers presented at conferences internationally. Its contents can be taught in undergraduate and graduate courses which span the social sciences, business administration, computer sciences, and engineering.

From a macro perspective, this book is about organizations, cognitive machines, and the environment. It is concerned with the relations between them. It relies on the premise that the technology of cognitive machines can improve the cognitive abilities of the organization; it also relies on the proposition that an increase in organizational cognition reduces the relative levels of uncertainty and complexity of the environment with which the organization relates. Moving further, such a proposition opens new perspectives to the study of the implications of cognitive machines for organizations, especially organizational design, behavior, cognition, learning, and performance. From all these concepts, this book proposes new organizations whose structure and processes are based on computational organization management networks and whose main participants (or agents) comprise cognitive information systems and cognitive machines.

From a micro perspective, this book is concerned with theories of organizational cognition and cognitive machines. It proposes concepts towards a theory on organizational cognition which contribute to improve the capability of the organization to manage and to process information. It also proposes the design and analysis of cognitive machines and it investigates the participation of these machines in dysfunctional conflicts resolution in organizations. It introduces premises and propositions about organizational cognition, cognitive machines, and the participation of these machines in organizations.

It assumes that cognition involves processes which provide individuals, groups, and organizations with the ability to learn. It focuses on premises and propositions about organizational cognition rather than organizational learning. Therefore, special attention is given to the implications of cognitive machines for organizational cognition. Its content is chronologically described in the following.

Firstly, it presents a broad overview on key concepts of organizations and technology in order to provide the reader with the scope of the main disciplines of this research.

Secondly, it presents rationale for, and it proposes principles towards a theory about organizational cognition. The new concepts describe relations between organizations and the environment, and they are based on principles of contingency theory, administrative behavior (decision-making and bounded rationality), open systems, socio-technical systems, organizational learning, and computational organization theory. In such a perspective, the organization is viewed as a cognitive system whose cognitive processes are attributes of the participants within the organization and the relationships or social networks which they form. These cognitive processes are supported by the goals, technology, and social structure of the organization. Moreover, organizational cognition is also influenced by inter-organizational processes and thus by the environment. The participants within the organization comprise agents in the form of humans and cognitive machines, and they are supposed to act in the name of the organization.

Additionally, it presents a methodology of organization design in order to support the choice of strategies which increase the degree of cognition of the organization and thus its ability to manage and to process information. It selects the technology and the participants in the organization as the elements of design since they comprise cognitive machines.

Thirdly, it presents the design and analysis of a framework of cognitive machines. The design comprises theories of cognition and information-processing systems, and also the mathematical and theoretical background of fuzzy systems, computing with words, and computation of perceptions. According to the theory of levels of processing in cognition, it advocates that the ability of these machines to manipulate a percept and natural concepts in the form of words and sentences of natural language provides them with high levels of symbolic processing, and thus with high degrees of cognition. Hence, they mimic (even through simple models) cognitive processes of the human mind. The analysis of these machines comprises theories of bounded rationality, economic decision-making, and conflict resolution along with perspectives about their participation in the organization. From the results of the analysis it advocates that such machines can solve or reduce intra-individual and group dysfunctional conflicts which arise from decision-making processes in the organization, and thus they can improve the cognitive abilities of the organization.

Fourthly, this book provides evidence by indicating the alignment of its premises and propositions with results of an industrial case study. Its central point of contribution is concerned with the development of approaches and measures to evaluate the degree of organizational cognition. For this purpose it looks carefully at three complementary activities.

The first activity is about processes of organizing. It presents an evolutionary process improvement model - The Capability Maturity Model - which was implemented in the organization of study. In this part, we contribute by defining correlations between measures of organization process improvement and degree of organizational cognition. Among the measures of process improvement are included organization process maturity, capability, and performance. From such correlations, we also derive conclusions about the association between organizational cognition and organizational learning.

The second activity is about the evaluation of the process of organizing and it proposes the design of a management control system which performs the tasks of measurement, analysis, and control of the organization process performance. The computation of process performance indexes is performed by a cognitive machine which is engineered with criteria of analysis and design.

The third activity is concerned with data analysis, results, and conclusions about the industrial case study. In this part, findings indicated that improvements in the level of organization process performance were correlated with improvements in the level of organization process maturity. Such improvements received major contributions from The Capability Maturity Model guidelines. Additionally, improvements in the levels of organization process performance and maturity were associated with improvements in the degree of organizational cognition. These improvements could be measured in two ways. Firstly, on an integer scale [1, 5], which indicated the level of organization process maturity associated with the degree of organizational cognition. Secondly, on a real scale [0, 10] which indicated the level of organization process performance correlated with the level of organization process maturity, and thus associated with the degree of organizational cognition. A very important implication and contribution of these correlations is that they open new directions to the development of methods to assess, to evaluate and to measure the degree of organizational cognition from appraisal methods of The Capability Maturity Model, and also from other organization process improvement models. We also outline the main contributions and limitations found with the implementation of The Capability Maturity Model in the organization of study.

Macro results of the industrial case study showed that the Capability Maturity Model (CMM) provided the organization with improvements in its process maturity level. However, despite improving engineering and management processes for complex software projects at the technical level in the organization, the progress of the CMM in those areas of higher hierarchical levels (such as managerial and institutional levels) was slow and poor due to lack of commitment of the organization to the CMM policies at those higher layers.

Fifthly, it contributes by outlining the implications of cognitive machines for organizations and it derives concepts of new organizations. It analyses the impact of cognitive machines on organizational design and on the elements of the organization which subsume goals, social structure, technology, participants, inducements, and contracts. It also examines limitations of past and current manufacturing organizations and it proposes new features for their future through perspectives of management, socio-technology, and organizational systems theory. From these perspectives, it introduces the concept of customer-centric systems - which represent a new organizational production model with capabilities to manage high levels of environmental complexity, to pursue high degrees of organizational cognition, to operate with high levels of mass customization, and to provide customers with immersiveness. From all this background, and most important, this book proposes the definition, the structure and the processes of Computational Organization Management Networks (COMN) which are new organizations whose principles of operation are based on the concepts of Organization Functional Layers, Hierarchic Cognitive Systems along with those of Telecommunications Management Networks of the International Telecommunication Union. Structured with functional layers and the cognitive roles which range from technical and managerial to institutional levels of analysis, and also equipped with technological, operational, managerial and business processes, the concept of Computational Organization Management Networks (COMN), as proposes in this book, plays an important part in the developments of future organizations where cognitive machines and Cognitive Information Systems (CIS) – that is information management systems with high degrees of cognition, intelligence and autonomy - are prominent actors of governance, automation and control of the whole organization. Additionally, it introduces the concept of immersive systems in order to provide the new organization with the capability of immersiveness.

The authors hope that their contributions in this book will provide signposts for future research and at the same time provide practical guidelines for practicing managers in today's competitive global markets.

Dr Farley Nobre, Dr Andrew Tobias & Prof. Dr David Walker
August 2008

Acknowledgment

This book is partly the result of PhD research undertaken by Dr Farley Nobre at The University of Birmingham and in The Humboldt University of Berlin between 2001 and 2005, sponsored by CNPq, an Institution of the Ministry of Science and Technology of Brazil. The book also draws upon current and recent research by Andrew Tobias and David Walker of The University of Birmingham, on organizational structures. We are indebted to CNPq and to both Universities for providing a distinguished research environment for its completion.

We would like to thank the staff of The Humboldt University of Berlin for the services and resources provided by them during Farley's stay in that University in the period between October 2002 and July 2003. In particular, we are indebted to Professor Hans-Dieter Burkhard and Dr. Gabriela Lindemann from the School of Computer Science for their kind reception of Farley and his introduction to the Artificial Intelligence Research Group, SOCIONICS project, seminars and courses. We also would like to thank Prof. Dr. D. Demougin, Dr. D. Kübler, and Dr. C. Helm for their lectures on organizations and behavioural economics at the School of Economics and Business Administration of The Humboldt University of Berlin.

Our scientific acknowledgements are also due to both Prof. L.A. Zadeh and Prof. H.A. Simon (in memory) due to their important contributions to most of the multi-disciplinary fields (spanning from artificial intelligence, cognition and decision analysis to systems theory and organizations) which shaped this book.

We also are very pleased to thank all the IGI Global staff due to their attention and services provided, and special thanks go to Julia Mosemann who continuously advised on this publication.

Section I
Introduction to the Book Context

The last thing one knows when writing a book is what to put first.
Blaise Pascal (1623-1662).

Section I presents a general picture of this book and it consists of Chapter I only.

Chapter I explains the scope and domains of this book and it presents the motivations for this research. It overviews key concepts of the main disciplines which form its body and it describes the problems to be addressed and the solutions to be designed.

Chapter I
General Introduction

ORGANIZATIONS

The Genesis of Organizations

The practice of organizing is ancient, but formal study of organizations is relatively new. The search for knowledge on organizations through scientific methods of investigation has received increasing attention since the beginning of the 20th century. Such investigations have found enough maturity and formality to constitute a new discipline known today as organization theory.

Principles of organizations evolved with ancient and medieval civilizations, and developed and matured after the Industrial Revolution in Europe in the 18th century and latterly in the United States of America in the 19th century. Such a transformation flourished gradually after the apogee of the Renaissance in Europe which was marked by a period of revolution in thinking, supported by religious, economic, social and political changes (Wren, 1987).

The Role of Organizations of Today

Organizations of today need to be continuously analysed, designed and redesigned on a disciplined and periodical basis. Organization theory constitutes both analysis and design of organizations; it comprises processes of organizing the parts in order to provide efficacy and efficiency[1] to the whole.

Organizations integrate people, technology and goals into a coordinative social structure in order to cope with the environment. The environment includes information; technology; people like consumers and stakeholders; other organizations like buyers and suppliers; and networks of organizations, institutions, market regulators and the whole economy (Milgrom and Roberts, 1992; and Scott, 1998). The environment also comprises cultural values and natural resources.

Information plays the foremost role in organizations of today since the elements of the organization are contingent upon it. Therefore, organizations have a major task of processing information similarly to a cognitive system with abilities to sensing, filtering and attention, storing and organizing knowledge, problem solving, decision-making and learning (Reed, 1988). Additionally, in order to pursue intelligent behaviour, organizations have to possess peripheral[2] skills for passing information to the environment. This process of responding and acting complements the previous cognitive stages. Furthermore, information provides the basis for the assertion that organizations shape the environment, and the environment also shapes organizations.

Studies on organizational learning and knowledge management are presented in (Dierkes et al, 2003); and on organizational intelligence, and organizations resembling information processing systems and distributed computational agents are presented in (Blanning and King, 1996; Carley and Gasser, 1999; and Prietula et al, 1998). However, a formal study which relates organizations with concepts of cognition and learning (innovation) was previously proposed in (March & Simon, 1958; and Simon, 1997b). This research asserts that cognition involves processes that provide individuals, groups and organizations with the ability to learn. Therefore, it focuses on premises and propositions about organizational cognition rather than organizational learning.

Tracing back to the industrial revolution, organizations have gradually shifted attention from the conception of corporation of physical structures with agglomeration of people (and machines) to the concepts of processes of organizing[3], information processing systems (Rousseau, 1997; and Sims et al, 1993) and learning (Dierkes et al, 2003). Therefore, as important as managing themselves, organizations of today have to manage the environment.

The Importance of Organizations

Organizations affect people's lives daily. They provide people with goods, services, well-being, wealth, status, social structures (of normative and behavioural parts), power, etc. Social norms can be conducted by consensus, charisma, legitimacy or force. However, organizations can also provide people with control over others - and thus they can stimulate pathologies (Scott, 1998).

Moreover, people spend much of their time in contact with organizations, as consumers, stakeholders, employees, managers, etc. Hence, people shape organizations. In a broader sense, the economic, social and political facets of local and global cultures shape organizations, and organizations also influence and change them over time.

Organizations exist worldwide in the form of manufacturing and service industries, public and private firms, profit and non-profit institutions, and they include trade and labour unions, schools and universities, armies, churches, hospitals and prisons. IBM, Rolls-Royce, Ford, NEC, British Airways, Banco do Brasil and Lloyds Bank - to name but a few of them - are examples of firms. The formal integration of European markets under the aegis of the European Union is an example of a trading organization.

TECHNOLOGY

The Genesis of Technology

Similarly to organizations, technology has provided the history of human evolution and development with major contributions (Gordon, 2000; Dosi et al, 1992; and Nobre, 2003d). Technology emerges from the ability of humans to search and to manage knowledge, and to transform it into ends (which can be ends by themselves or other means used to achieve more complex goals). Hence, technology is synonymous with means deliberately employed by humans to attain practical outcomes. Therefore, technology encompasses knowledge, and also tools, practices, processes and even other technologies (Kipnis, 1990; and Richter, 1982).

The Role of Technology in Organizations of Today

The domain of technology in organizations encompasses different levels of analysis and distinct elements of application. Analysis ranges from technical, managerial, institutional to worldwide systems, and elements vary from machines to normative and regulative processes.

As stated before, information is the foremost resource used by organizations to cope with the environment, and vice-versa. Hence, technology plays a distinguished role in connecting the flow of information between them. It provides means for the interaction between organizations and the environment, and thus for the exchange of goods, services, people and other resources.

Organizations of today are synonymous with processes of organizing and their functioning resembles a cognitive system with the ability to manage information and to learn. In such a perspective, technology contributes to organizations by providing them with additional means which support them to carry out complex cognitive tasks (Simon, 1977 and 2002).

The Importance of Technology for Organizations

Organizations expand what people can achieve, and **technology** expands what organizations can do. By integrating these premises, it can be stated that organizations and technology together extend people's capability to achieve more complex goals (Nobre, 2005).

Over the last two centuries, technology has provided organizations with brilliant contributions and with effects on their political, social and economic contexts. Great inventions - to name but a few of them - are those of electricity, including both electric light and electric motors; internal combustion engine, as largely employed in transport systems; petroleum, natural gas, and various chemical, plastics and pharmaceutical processes; communication systems, including the telegraph, telephone, photography, radio and television; urban sanitation infrastructure and indoor plumbing; and medicines, including antibiotics (Gordon, 2000). Such advances can also include modern wireless communication systems, computers and internet.

Technology infiltrates both organizations and the environment and it provides them with prominent means to cope with each other. Therefore, organizations shape their environment mainly through the use of technology, and the environment also shapes organizations through similar means.

GENERAL SYSTEMS THEORY

The Genesis of General Systems Theory

General systems theory emerged during the first half of the 20th century paved by the need for a new approach to the unification of sciences, and thus for interdisciplinary concepts, principles, models and laws. It developed as a scientific discipline to deal with principles of organized wholes, including living, nonliving, natural and artificial systems (Bertalanffy, 1968; and Buckley, 1968). It received major contributions from the domains of cybernetics (Wiener, 1948, 1954 and 1961), communication theory (Shannon and Weaver, 1963), game theory (von Neumann and Morgenstern, 1944; and Gul, 1997) and systems analysis (Zadeh and Polak, 1969). Moreover, it got additional insights from principles of complexity (Klir and Folger, 1988; Simon, 1996; and Stacey et al, 2000), organization and entropy (Rapoport, 1986; and Sundarasaradula et al, 2006), open systems and homeostasis (Bertalanffy, 1962), self-organizing systems (Ashby, 1968), world and system dynamics (Forrester, 1961 and 1973).

The Role of General Systems Theory

The preponderant characteristic of general systems theory concerns its generality devoted to the study of abstract and mathematical properties of systems, regardless of their physical nature (Zadeh, 1962). Therefore, the major idea with general systems theorists has been the investigation of isomorphism of concepts, laws and models among various fields spanning from life, earth and natural to social sciences. Hence, useful transfers have been done from one field to another. This has encouraged researchers to develop unified theories (Bahg, 1990; Boulding, 1966 and 1978; Grinker, 1956; and Miller and Miller, 1990), and also mathematical and qualitative models for the formulation and derivation of principles which are supposed to be applicable to systems in general (Klir, 1969 and 1972; and Zadeh and Polak, 1969).

Despite such an effort, a gap remains when analysis moves from nonliving to living systems (Buckley, 1968; and Zadeh, 1962). This gap exists because the laws which govern these two classes of systems are different. Additionally, living systems are generally more complex than nonliving systems. Nevertheless, new approaches have emerged in order to provide alternative tools for the analysis and design of systems of higher levels of complexity (Bond and Gasser, 1988; Weiss, 1999; and Zadeh, 1973, 1997, and 2001).

The Importance of General Systems Theory for Organizations

General systems theorists have provided organizations with new perspectives of analysis and design (Khandwalla, 1977; and Scott, 1998). Among their main contributions are the concepts of open systems, self-regulation and hierarchical systems.

Open systems constitute a perspective derived from models of biological phenomena (Bertalanffy, 1968). Shortly speaking, the open system perspective provides the organization with the definition of a system of interdependent parts interacting with an environment which can be constituted by other organizations or systems (Silverman, 1970). Through interaction with its environment, the organization can evolve towards an increase of order and complexity (Bertalanffy, 1962). Such a phenomenon is considered essential to its survival and it provides the organization with the capability of self-maintenance on the basis of a throughput of resources from its environment.

Self-regulation is a principle derived from the broad field of cybernetics (Wiener, 1961), and also from the phenomena of homeostasis within living systems (Bertalanffy, 1962). Self-regulation means the ability of a system to maintain its steady states by sensing and by responding to its environment. Self-regulating systems encompass processes which work according to some artificial or natural law of behaviour, and they are supported by the principle of feedback. Therefore, they play a fundamental role in control theory, and thus in management control of organizational processes (Anthony, 1984), administrative decision-making (Simon, 1982a), organization design (Haberstroh, 1965), organizational change (Sundarasaradula et al, 2005) and adaptive learning cycles of learning organizations (Daft & Noe, 2001).

The conception of hierarchic systems is derived from analyses of living systems (Bertalanffy, 1962; and Miller & Miller, 1990), and also from principles of hierarchy of complex systems (Boulding, 1956; and Simon, 1996). Through this conception, organizations are viewed as systems composed of multiple subsystems, and also systems contained in larger systems called supra-systems. In such a way, organizations can be investigated under different perspectives which span from technical and managerial to institutional levels of analysis (Scott, 1998).

General systems theory influences this research with the domains of unification and isomorphism[4] along with the concepts of open systems, self-regulation, hierarchic systems and complexity.

THE NATURE OF THEORY OF ORGANIZATIONS

Sections II, III and IV comprise concepts, premises and propositions towards a theory about organizational cognition, cognitive machines and the participation of cognitive machines in organizations respectively. However, in order to propose concepts towards a theory of any subject we first need to define what we mean by theory. Appendix A provides a definition of theory and its components. Moreover, it introduces a process of theorizing as applied to this book; it presents different approaches to the study of organizations and it defines criteria of choice of research methods. Appendix A concludes by explaining the approaches which were chosen to the study of organizations within this book.

The Domain of Theory of Organizations

Theories of organizations fall into the domain of social sciences and they have received most of their contributions from the disciplines of economics, sociology, psychology, politics, management, philosophy and anthropology. Nevertheless, mathematics, engineering and most recently computer science have played prominent roles in the analysis and design of organizations. They provide organization scientists with tools which support accurate and economic analysis, but also with new theoretical and practical outcomes (Cyert & March, 1963; Gilbert & Troitzsch, 1999; Prietula et al, 1998; Simon, 1957 and 1982a; and Starbuck, 1965).

Natural sciences, encompassing physics, biology and chemistry, provides knowledge of theories, principles and laws which are largely derived from the nature through human discoveries. Instead, social sciences derive most of their theories, principles and laws from human and societal behaviour. Therefore, the use of scientific methods for the understanding of people behaviour and cognition constitutes an important part in the social sciences and thus in organizations (March & Simon, 1993).

A Comparative Approach: Theories of Natural vs. Social Sciences

This book assumes that differences between theories of natural and social sciences reside not only in the properties and structure of their elements of study, but most importantly in the abilities of these elements. The former refers to physical, biological and chemical attributes, and the latter means abilities to cognition, intelligence and autonomy.

The main elements of social systems are humans and networks of people, and thus organizations and networks of organizations. Such systems possess high degrees of cognition, intelligence and autonomy which are distributed among their individuals and among their relationships. On the other hand, the elements of, and the relationships with, physical, biological and chemical systems - including all the objects and organisms of the ecological system, but excluding the man - are less complex than those found in social systems if we consider that they have lower degrees of cognition, intelligence and autonomy (if any in most of the cases).

Therefore, the nature of a theory of organizations resides in principles of human behaviour and cognition.

RATIONALE FOR A NEW THEORY ON ORGANIZATIONS

Organization theory has reached the 21st century as a formal and mature discipline, supported by rigorous contributions received from the beginning of the 20th century, and mainly from the last fifty years (Cyert & March, 1963; Dierkes et al, 2003; Galbraith, 1977 and 2002; March, 1965; March & Simon, 1993; Milgrom & Roberts, 1992; Pugh, 1997; Scott, 1998; and Simon, 1997b). The literature about organization theory has provided distinct, complementary and common perspectives of organizations. The publications encompass books which cover different writers of organizations (Pugh & Hickson, 1997), diverse types of organizations (McKinlay, 1975; and March, 1965), prominent comparative studies of different classes of organizations (Blau & Scott, 1963), and also references that broadly survey literature results (Hodge, et al 2003; and Scott, 1998).

However, organizations and the environment change over time. Not only change their structure and processes of functioning, but also change the perspectives that researchers have about them over periods of time. Hence, we need to review theories of organizations which relate to the current problem analysis in order to find a better solution design. Therefore, this book comprises the selection of diverse perspectives on organizations in the literature and also the unification[5] of their concepts towards a new theory. Special attention is given to the schools of administrative behaviour, decision-making and bounded rationality (March & Simon, 1993; and Simon, 1997a and 1997b), systems theory (open systems) (Buckley, 1968; and Khandwalla, 1977), socio-technical systems (Trist, 1981), contingency theory (Galbraith, 1977 and 2002), organizational learning and knowledge management (Dierkes et al, 2003), computational organization theory (Carley & Gasser, 1999) and also to the perspectives of rational, natural and open systems (Scott, 1998).

THE SCOPE OF THE BOOK

The Domain of Organizational Cognition: Principles and Theory

First, this book focuses on the general picture of organizations pursuing high degrees of cognition in order to reduce the relative levels of uncertainty and complexity of the environment. Therefore, it does not discriminate organizations by their type and purpose (i.e. profit or non-profit industries, public or private institutions, manufacturing and service firms, unions, armies, schools, and so on); nor by their size (number of employees and divisions); nor by their geographical location (east-west); and nor by their age (old-mature or young-immature).

It defines relations between organizations and the environment under perspectives of organizational cognition. Such relations are presented in the form of premises and propositions and they include definitions of intelligence, cognition, autonomy and complexity of organizations, along with environmental complexity and uncertainty. Such premises, propositions and definitions form concepts of a theory on organizational cognition and they support the perspective of organizations pursuing high degrees of cognition.

Additionally, the domain of organizational cognition includes a methodology of organization design that comprises strategies to: - increase the degree of cognition of the organization and also to reduce the relative level of complexity of the environment. The technology and the participants in the organization are selected as the elements of design because they comprise cognitive machines. These machines can be classified as special types of information technology systems and they can act in the name of the organization by playing cognitive roles.

The Domain of Cognitive Machines: Principles and Design

Second, this book focuses on technologies which contribute to create (even simple) models of human cognition. The process of conception and engineering of cognitive machines through proper technologies is effective in the sense that these machines are deliberately designed to carry out complex cognitive tasks in organizations.

Special attention is also given to the definitions of principles of cognitive machines and also of concepts of cognition, intelligence, autonomy and complexity for machines.

Proceeding further, this book presents the design of a framework of cognitive machines.

The design of the framework of cognitive machines comprises theories of cognition and information-processing systems (Bernstein, et al 1997; Newell and Simon, 1972; and Reed, 1988) and also the mathematical and theoretical background of fuzzy systems (Zadeh, 1965, 1973 and 1988), computing with words (Zadeh, 1996a and 1999) and computation of perceptions (Zadeh, 2001). Additionally, by considering the theory of levels of processing in cognition (Reed, 1988), this book advocates that the ability of these machines to manipulate a percept and concepts in the form of words and sentences of a natural language provides them with high levels of symbolic processing, and thus with high degrees of cognition. Hence, they mimic (even through simple models) cognitive processes of the human mind.

The Domain of Cognitive Machines in Organizations: Analysis

Third, this book provides analyses of cognitive machines and perspectives about their participation in organizations through theories of bounded rationality, economic decision-making (Simon, 1997a) and conflict resolution. From the results of the analyses it advocates that such machines can solve or reduce intra-individual and group dysfunctional conflicts which arise from decision-making processes in the organization, and thus they can improve the cognitive abilities of the organization (Nobre, 2005).

Additionally, it focuses attention to the definition of relations between organizations and cognitive machines, and also between organizations (within cognitive machines) and the environment. Such definitions are presented in the form of premises and propositions which also include contractual relationships between the cognitive machine, its designer and the organization.

The Domain of the Implications of Cognitive Machines

Fourthly, this book outlines the implications of cognitive machines for organizations and it analyzes their impact upon the elements of the organization in order to derive a picture of future organizations. For such a purpose, the concepts of organization design, goals, social structure, participants, technology, inducements and contract, among other elements, are reviewed with the perspective of cognitive machines in the new organization.

The Domain of the New Organization

Fifthly, this book advocates that the scope of the new organization comprises high levels of automation in order to pursue the necessary capabilities to govern, to coordinate and to control cognitive tasks in the technical, managerial, institutional and worldwide levels of the whole enterprise. This is into such a complex technological domain and perspective that we need to concentrate efforts in the design and engineering of machines and information management systems with high degrees of cognition, intelligence and autonomy.

Moreover, the new organization needs to be organized and equipped with structure and processes which provide it with the capabilities to pursue high degrees of organizational cognition. This is into such an organizational domain that we propose the concept of Computational Organization Management Networks (COMN) – which are new organizations structured with functional layers and cognitive roles that range from technical and managerial to institutional levels of analysis, and also equipped with technological, operational, managerial and business processes. The concept of Computational Organization Management Networks (COMN) plays an important part in the developments of future organizations where cognitive machines and Cognitive Information Systems (CIS) are prominent actors of governance, automation and control of the whole organization.

MOTIVATIONS FOR THIS RESEARCH

A Theory of Organizational Cognition

The perspective of organizations as **cognitive systems** was put forward by March and Simon (1958 & 1993) and later this was extended by other researchers to the study of organizations as distributed computational agents (Prietula et al, 1998). In such a perspective, individuals have bounded rationality abilities and the organization can extend their limitations to the achievement of more complex goals - e.g.

limitations of knowledge, memory and information processing, attention, communication, coordination, decision-making, problem-solving and learning (Carley & Gasser, 1999; and Simon, 1997a and 1997b).

This research supports such a perspective and it focuses on the general picture of the organization pursuing cognition as a necessary feature for its survival, development and achievement of complex goals. Therefore, it introduces a theory about organizational cognition which relies on the proposition that an increase in the degree of cognition of the organization reduces the relative levels of uncertainty and complexity of the environment with which the organization relates.

What makes this study distinct is the way it connects cognitive machines with the organization, and in particular with organization design and with the topic of intra-individual and group dysfunctional conflicts which arise from decision-making processes in organizations.

Organizational Cognition and Organizational Learning

Briefly, organizational learning is a multi-disciplinary field which is concerned with the management and creation of knowledge in organizations (Dierkes et al, 2003). It comprises perspectives of psychology, management, sociology, biology, philosophy, anthropology, history, economics and political science.

This book is about organizational cognition and it assumes that cognition comprises processes which provide individuals, groups and thus organizations with the ability to learn, to make decisions and to solve problems. It relates to the field of organizational learning through the perspective of cognitive psychology. In the field of psychology research, cognition is one of the approaches to the study of theories of learning (Lefrançois, 1995).

Therefore, this book contributes to the field of organizational learning by introducing concepts about organizational cognition - along with cognitive machines and their participation in organizations.

Bringing Cognitive Machines Closer to Organizations

Machines of today are coming to play an increasing role in organizations as cognitive agents and decision-makers. Such machines are emerging to participate and to act in the name of organizations (Nobre, 2005). Nevertheless, despite being investigated mainly by the literature of engineering and computer science, the subject of machine intelligence and cognition has not received enough emphasis by organization theorists. One of the obvious reasons is that social scientists have little background (and thus knowledge) on the subject of artificial intelligence, computer science, electrical and electronics engineering, among other technological sciences. The other reason is simply the reverse, i.e. technological scientists have little knowledge on organizations and social sciences, and thus they usually apply their engineering, mathematical and computational tools in problems of technical systems.

This book represents an effort to connect the area of organizations with the **technology** of cognitive machines (and vice-versa) in different ways of contributions. Firstly, by presenting a theory on organizational cognition along with a methodology of organization design which comprises cognitive machines as an important element of choice; secondly, by presenting the design of a framework of cognitive machines which can reduce intra-individual and group dysfunctional conflicts which arise from decision-making processes in the organization; thirdly, by analysing these machines through the concepts of bounded rationality, economic decision-making and conflict resolution; and lastly by applying a cognitive machine in the adaptive learning cycle of an organization whose purpose is the analysis, decision and management control of the performance of large-scale software projects.

This book also contributes by providing initial and important steps in order to set up definitions about the roles, responsibilities and relationships between the cognitive machine, its designer and the organization.

Cognitive Machines and Conflict Resolution in Organizations

Processes of decision-making involve trade-offs among alternatives which are characterized by uncertainty, incomparability and unacceptability, and hence they lead organization's participants to both intra-individual and group dysfunctional conflicts (March & Simon, 1993). The former conflict arises in an individual mind. The latter type arises from differences among the choices made by two or more individuals and groups in the organization.

Intra-individual and group dysfunctional conflicts also reflect the bounded ability of human sensory organs and brain to resolve details (Zadeh, 2001). Hence, these conflicts cannot be managed and solved with incentive and reward systems. Such cognitive and information constraints are synonymous with bounded rationality (March, 1994; March & Simon, 1993; and Simon, 1982b, 1997a, and 1997b).

Focusing on this problem, this book contributes by designing a framework of cognitive machines which can reduce or solve such conflicts.

Cognitive Machines, Bounded Rationality and Economic Decision-Making

The cognitive machines as designed within this book are analyzed through theories of bounded rationality and economic decision-making. From the results of the analyses it advocates that such machines can solve or reduce intra-individual and group dysfunctional conflicts in the organization, and thus they can improve the cognitive abilities of the organization.

Therefore, this book also contributes by putting such machines in the contexts of bounded rationality and economic decision-making along with conflict resolution.

Cognitive Machines, Mental Models and Organizations

If we assume that the cognitive roles in the world of organizations, as fulfilled by agents, have performance and outcomes which can be attributed to either humans or machines, without any distinction, then we are ready to consider machines as members of organizations which act in the name of them similarly to people[6].

This book acknowledges that there is much more work and research to take before we can build machines with similar levels of cognition to humans. Nevertheless, it recognizes that important steps have been given with the advancements in computer, artificial intelligence and cognition research from the middle of the 20th century.

Proceeding further with such steps, this book presents the design of a framework of cognitive machines. Such a design comprises theories of cognition and information-processing systems (Bernstein, et al 1997; and Newell and Simon, 1972), and also the mathematical and theoretical background of fuzzy systems (Zadeh, 1965 and 1973), computing with words (Zadeh, 1996a and 1999) and computation of perceptions (Zadeh, 2001). Additionally, based on the theory of levels of processing in cognition (Reed, 1988), this book advocates that the ability of these machines to manipulate a percept and concepts in the form of words and sentences of a natural language provides them with high levels of symbolic processing, and thus with high degrees of cognition. Hence, they mimic (even through simple models) processes of the human mind.

Unification of Organizational and Technological Theories

This book also contributes by connecting theories of bounded rationality of Herbert Simon (Simon, 1997a and 1997b) with the theories of fuzzy systems of Lotfi Zadeh (Zadeh, 1973 and 1999) in order to justify advantages of the participation of cognitive machines in organizations. The connections are derived by explaining why cognitive machines can extend limits of knowledge (lack of information) and limits of information processing and management (lack of cognition and computational capacity) of humans when participating in organizations.

Such a background is regarded as an important contribution of this investigation – i.e. to connect theories and results of these two brilliant researchers.

Application: An Industrial Case Study

This book provides evidence that indicates the alignment of its premises and propositions with results of an industrial case study. In this part, its central point of contribution is concerned with the development of approaches and measures to evaluate the degree of organizational cognition.

Measurements of Organizational Cognition

Organizational cognition involves a set of processes that provide the organization with the capability to learn, to solve problems and to make decisions. Consequently, we also believe that organizational cognition provides organizations with improvements in their technical, managerial, institutional and business processes. Therefore, in this book, and specifically in the industrial case study, we develop approaches and measures to evaluate the degree of organizational cognition. For this purpose we associate concepts, practices and results of organization process improvement with organizational cognition.

Therefore, this book also contributes by outlining new directions to the development of approaches to assess, to evaluate and to measure the degree of organizational cognition from appraisal methods of organization process improvement models.

Implications of Cognitive Machines and the New Organization

Investigations on the implications of cognitive machines for organizations contribute to the analysis of organizational change and to the design of new organizations. This book provides analyses about the impact of cognitive machines on organizational design and upon the elements of the organization - comprising goals, social structure, inducements and contracts, technology and participants. Therefore, it contributes with this background and it touches upon the concept of future organizations.

Proceeding further in such a direction of analyses, it examines limitations of past and current manufacturing organizations through perspectives of management, socio-technology and organizational systems theory; and thus it contributes by proposing the concept and features of a new model of organizational production system with capabilities to manage high levels of environmental complexity, to pursue high degrees of organizational cognition, to operate with high levels of mass customization, and to provide customers with immersiveness.

From this background, it advocates that the new organization has to be equiped with high levels of automation in order to pursue the necessary capabilities to govern, to coordinate and to control cognitive tasks in the whole enterprise.

Proceeding further and most important, this book contributes by deriving and by proposing the definition, the structure and the processes of Computational Organization Management Networks (COMN) which are new organizations whose principles of operation are based on the concepts of Organization Functional Layers, Hierarchic Cognitive Systems along with those of Telecommunications Management Networks of the International Telecommunication Union. Structured with functional layers and the cognitive roles which range from technical and managerial to institutional levels of analysis, and also equipped with technological, operational, managerial and business processes, the concept of Computational Organization Management Networks (COMN) plays an important part in the developments of future organizations where cognitive machines and Cognitive Information Systems (CIS) are prominent actors of governance, automation and control of the whole enterprise.

SUMMARY

Chapter I provided a general picture of the book. It explained the scope of the book and the motivations for this research.

It began by introducing key concepts of organizations, technology and general systems theory that play an important part within the book proposal. Most importantly, it showed how much these multidisciplinary areas of research complement each other. It also discussed the nature of theories of organizations and it presented rationale for a new theory on organizations.

The main domains of study of the book were classified by:

a. Organizational Cognition: Principles and Theory
b. Cognitive Machines: Principles and Design
c. Cognitive Machines in Organizations: Analysis
d. Implications of Cognitive Machines
e. The New Organization

REFERENCES

Anthony, R .N., Dearden, J., & Bedford, N. M. (1984). Management Control Systems. Richard D. Irwin, Inc.

Ashby, W. R. (1968). Principles of the Self-Organizing System. In W. Buckley (Ed.), Modern Systems Research for the Behavioral Scientist (pp. 108-118). Aldine Publishing Company.

Bahg, C. (1990). Major Systems Theories Throughout the World. Behavioral Science, 35 (2), 79-107.

Bernstein, D. A. et al (1997). Psychology. Houghton Mifflin Company.

Bertalanffy, L. von, (1962). General System Theory: A Critical Review. General Systems, VII: 1-20.

Bertalanffy, L. von, (1968). General system theory: foundations, development, and applications. Allen Lane.

Blanning, R. W., & King, R. K. (1996). AI in Organizational Design, Modeling, and Control. IEEE Computer Society Press.

Blau, P. M., & Scott, W. R. (1963). Formal Organizations: A Comparative Approach. Routledge.

Bond, A. H., & Gasser, L. (1988). Readings in Distributed Artificial Intelligence. Morgan Kaufmann Publishers, Inc.

Boulding, K. E. (1956). General Systems Theory: The Skeleton of Science. Management Science, 2, 197-208.

Boulding, K. E. (1966). The Impact of the Social Sciences. Rutgers University Press.

Boulding, K. E. (1978). Ecodynamics: A New Theory of Societal. Evolution. SAGE Publications.

Buckley, W. (1968). Modern Systems Research for the Behavioral Scientist. Aldine Publishing Company.

Carley, K. M., & Gasser, L. (1999). Computational Organizational Theory. In G. Weiss (Ed.), Multiagent Systems: A Modern Approach to Distributed Artificial Intelligence (pp. 299-330). The MIT Press.

Cyert, R. M., & March, J. G. (1963). A Behavioral Theory of the Firm. 1st Ed. Blackwell Publishers.

Daft, R. L., & Noe, R. A. (2001). Organizational Behavior. Harcourt, Inc.

Dierkes, M., Antal, A. B., Child, J., & Nonaka, I. (2003). Handbook of Organizational Learning and Knowledge. Oxford University Press.

Dosi, G., Giannetti, R., & Toninelli, P. (1992). Technology and Enterprise in a Historical Perspective. Oxford University Press.

Forrester, J. W. (1961). Industrial Dynamics. The MIT Press.

Forrester, J. W. (1973). World Dynamics. The MIT Press.

Galbraith, J. R. (1977). Organization Design. Addison-Wesley.

Galbraith, J. R. (2002). Designing Organizations - An executive guide to strategy, structure, and process. Jossey-Bass.

Gilbert, N., & Troitzsch, K. G. (1999). Simulation for the Social Scientist. Open University Press.

Gordon, R. J. (2000). Does the New Economy Measure up to the Great Inventions of the Past? The Journal of Economic Perspectives, 14(4), 49-74.

Grinker, R. R. (1956). Towards a Unified Theory of Human Behavior: An Introduction to General Systems Theory. Basic Books Inc.

Gul, F. (1997). A Nobel Prize for Game Theorists: The Contributions of Harsanyi, Nash and Selten. The Journal of Economic Perspective, 11(3), 159-174.

Haberstroh, C. (1965). Organization Design and Systems Analysis. In J. March (Ed.), Handbook of Organizations (pp. 1171-1211). Rand McNally & Company.

Hodge, B. J., Anthony, W. P., & Gales, L. M. (2003). Organization Theory - A Strategic Approach. Prentice-Hall.

Khandwalla, P. N. (1977). Design of Organizations. Harcourt Brace Jovanovich.

Kipnis, D. (1990). Technology and Power. Springer-Verlag New York Inc.

Klir, G. J. (1969). An Approach To General Systems Theory. Van Nostrand Reinhold Company.

Klir, G. J. (1972). Trends in General Systems Theory. John Wiley & Sons.

Klir, G. J., & Folger, T. A. (1988). Fuzzy Sets, Uncertainty, and Information. Englewood Cliffs, N.J: Prentice Hall.

Lefrançoies, G. (1995). Theories of Human Learning. Brooks Cole Publishing Company.

March, J. G. (1965). Handbook of Organizations. Rand McNally & Company.

March, J. G. (1994). A Primer on Decision Making: How Decisions Happen. The Free Press.

March, J. G., & Simon, H. A. (1958). Organizations. 1st Ed. John Wiley & Sons, Inc.

March, J. G., & Simon, H. A. (1993). Organizations. 2nd Ed. John Wiley & Sons, Inc.

McKinlay, J. B. (1975). Processing People: cases in organizational behaviour. Holt-Blond Ltd.

Milgrom, P., & Roberts, J. (1992). Economics, Organizations & Management. Prentice-Hall Inc.

Miller, J. G., & Miller, J. L. (1990). Introduction: The Nature of Living Systems. Behavioral Science, 35 (3): 157-163.

Neumann, J. von, & Morgenstern, O. (1944). Theory of Games and Economic Behavior. Princeton University Press.

Newell, A., & Simon, H. A. (1972). Human Problem Solving. Prentice-Hall.

Nobre, F. S., (2003d, July) Organizations and Technology - Past, Present and Future Perspectives. Seminar presented for the Artificial Intelligence Research Group of the Department of Computer Sciences in the Humboldt University of Berlin. Johann von Newmann-Haus, Berlin.

Nobre, F. S. (2005). On Cognitive Machines in Organizations. PhD Thesis. University of Birmingham / Birmingham-UK. 343 pages. Birmingham Main Library. Control Number: M0266887BU.

Prietula, M. J., Carley, K., & Gasser, M. (1998). Simulating Organizations: Computational Models of Institutions and Groups. AAAI Press / The MIT Press.

Pugh, D. S. (1997). Organization Theory: Selected Readings. Penguin Books.

Pugh, D. S., & Hickson, D. J. (1997). Writers on Organizations. Penguin Books.

Rapoport, A. (1986). General Systems Theory: Essential Concepts & Applications. Abacus Press.

Reed, S. K. (1988). Cognition: Theory and Applications. 2nd Ed. Brooks-Cole Publishing Company.

Richter, M. N. (1982). Technology and Social Complexity. State University of New York.

Rousseau, D. M. (1997). Organizational Behavior in the New Organizational Era. Annual Review of Psychology, 48, 515-546.

Scott, W. R. (1998). Organizations: Rational, Natural, and Open Systems. Prentice Hall, Inc.

Shannon, C. E., & Weaver, W. (1963). The Mathematical Theory of Communication. University of Illinois Press.

Silverman, D. (1970). The Theory of Organizations. Heinemann.

Simon, H. A. (1957). Models of Man: Social and Rational. John Wiley & Sons.

Simon, H. A. (1977). The New Science of Management Decision. Prentice-Hall, Inc.

Simon, H. A. (1982a). Models of Bounded Rationality: Economic Analysis and Public Policy. Vol. 1. The MIT Press.

Simon, H. A. (1982b). Models of Bounded Rationality: Behavioral Economics and Business Organization. Vol. 2. The MIT Press.

Simon, H. A. (1996). The Sciences of the Artificial. 3rd Ed. The MIT Press.

Simon, H. A. (1997a). Models of Bounded Rationality: Empirically Grounded Economic Reason. Vol.3. The MIT Press.

Simon, H. A. (1997b). Administrative Behavior: A Study of Decision-Making Processes in Administrative Organizations. The FREE Press.

Simon, H. A. (2002). Organization theory in the age of computers and electronic communication networks. In M. Augier & J.M. March (Ed.), The Economics of Choice, Change and Organization - Essays in Memory of Richard M. Cyert (pp. 404-418). Edward Elgar.

Sims, D., Fineman, S., & Gabriel, Y. (1993). Organizing & Organizations: An Introduction. SAGE Publications.

Stacey, R. D., Griffin, D., & Shaw, P. (2000). Complexity and Management - Fad or radical challenge to systems thinking? Routledge.

Starbuck, W. H. (1965). Mathematics and Organization Theory. In J.G. March (Ed.), Handbook of Organizations (pp. 335-386). Rand McNally & Company.

Sundarasaradula D., Hasan H., Walker D. S., & Tobias A. M. (2005). Self-Organization, Evolutionary and Revolutionary Change in Organizations. Strategic Change, 14 (7), 367-380.

Sundarasaradula D., Hasan H., Walker D. S., & Tobias A. M. (2006). Formal Organizations: How Classical Thermodynamics can help us to understand them. International Journal of Business Research, 6(3), 1-14.

Trist, E. L. (1981). The Evolution of Sociotechnical Systems as a Conceptual Framework and as an Action Research Program, in Andrew Van de Ven and William Joyce (Ed.), Perspectives on Organization Design and Behavior, pp.19-75. New York: Wiley-Interscience.

Turing, A. M. (1950). Computing Machinery and Intelligence. Mind - A Quarterly Review of Psychology and Philosophy, LIX (236), 433-460.

Weiss, G. (1999). Multiagent Systems – A Modern Approach to Distributed Artificial Intelligence. The MIT Press.

Wiener, N. (1948). Cybernetics. 1st Ed. The MIT Press.

Wiener, N. (1954). The human use of human beings: cybernetics and society. 2nd Ed. London.

Wiener, N. (1961). Cybernetics or control and communication in the animal and the machine. 2nd Ed. The MIT Press.

Wren, D. A. (1987). The Evolution of Management Thought. 3rd Ed. John Wiley and Sons.

Zadeh, L. A. (1962). From Circuit Theory to System Theory. Proceedings of the IRE, 50: 856-865.

Zadeh, L. A. (1965). Fuzzy Sets. Information and Control, 8: 338-353.

Zadeh, L. A., & Polak, E. (1969). System Theory. McGraw-Hill.

Zadeh, L. A. (1973). Outline of a New Approach to the Analysis of Complex Systems and Decision Process. IEEE Transactions on Systems, Man, and Cybernetics, 3(1), 28-44.

Zadeh, L. A. (1988). Fuzzy Logic. IEEE Computer, April, 83-92.

Zadeh, L. A. (1996a). Fuzzy Logic = Computing with Words. IEEE Transactions on Fuzzy Systems, 4(2), 103-111.

Zadeh, L. A. (1997). The Roles of Fuzzy Logic and Soft Computing in the Conception, Design and Development of Intelligent Systems. In Nwana & Azarmi (Ed.), Software Agents and Soft Computing: Towards Enhancing Machine Intelligence (pp. 183-190). Springer.

Zadeh, L. A. (1999) From Computing with Numbers to Computing with Words – From Manipulation of Measurements to Manipulation of Perceptions. IEEE Transactions on Circuits and Systems, 45(1), 105-119.

Zadeh, L. A. (2001). A New Direction in AI: Toward a Computational Theory of Perceptions. AI Magazine. Spring, 73-84.

ENDNOTES

[1] Efficacy regards the attainment of goals and efficiency concerns the economic use of resources in order to satisfy such goals. It does not mean that these concepts are restricted to the perspective of rational systems since natural systems also encompass specific and multiple goals. For a review on rational, natural and open systems we recommend the reading of Appendix C.

[2] Peripheral is not synonymous with marginal. Instead, it denotes the broader structural features of organizations at the managerial and institutional levels (Scott, 1998).

[3] A corporation is synonymous with an entity organized to pursue goals and to provide goods and services; and the concept of organizing refers to the processes used to make the goods and services possible. Hence, organizing is synonymous with social networks, management and entrepreneurship, cognition and behaviour.

[4] Isomorphism concerns the use of common concepts and approaches to the respective analysis and design of distinct problems and solutions for organizations. Therefore, it is synonymous with economy of resources.

[5] Unification requires analysis of the various parts of the whole and also design for their integration.

[6] This analysis is comparatively similar to the classical imitation game of Alan Turing (Turing, 1950), where a machine and a human are placed in rooms apart from a second human being, referred to as the interrogator. Through a terminal of textual communication, the interrogator is asked to distinguish the computer from the human being solely on the basis of their answers to questions asked over this device. If the interrogator cannot distinguish the machine from the human, then, Turing argues, the machine may be assumed to be intelligent.

Section II
Organizational Cognition

The difficulty lies, not in the new ideas, but in escaping the old ones, which ramify, for those brought up as most of us have been, into every corner of our minds.

John Maynard Keynes (1883-1946)

Section II introduces concepts towards a theory of organizational cognition whose initial lines of contribution were first touched on (Nobre, 2005, 2004b, 2004a, and 2002c). It comprises Chapters II and III and its background is largely influenced by:

a. The concept of uncertainty, as introduced by the school of contingency theory (Galbraith, 1973, 1977, and 2002).
b. Theories of bounded rationality and cognitive processes in organizations, as introduced by the school of administrative behaviour and decision-making (Simon, 1947; March & Simon, 1993; March, 1994; and Simon, 1997a and 1997b).
c. The concepts of open systems and complex hierarchic systems, as introduced by the school of general systems theory (Buckley, 1968; Khandwalla, 1977; and Simon, 1996).
d. Computational organization theory, as proposed in (Carley & Gasser, 1999).

In summary, Chapter II presents rationale for a theory on organizational cognition.

Chapter III introduces principles, definitions, premises, and propositions towards a theory of organizational cognition.

Chapter II
Rationale for Organizational Cognition

INTRODUCTION

This chapter presents rationale for a theory of organizational cognition on the basis of contingency theory and bounded rationality concepts. According to the bounded rationality theory (Simon, 1947, 1982a, 1997a, and 1997b), this book advocates that organizations have limitations of knowledge management and computational capacity.

A theory of organizational cognition is important and necessary when we decide to design organizations with higher capabilities of information processing and uncertainty management. In such a way, organizational cognition is a discipline which contributes to improve the computational capacity of the organization and its ability for knowledge management. Moreover, the theory of organizational cognition as proposed in this book, plays an important part, and introduces a new perspective, in the analysis of the relations between the organization, its elements and the environment.

Assuming such core rationale, this chapter introduces a methodology to support the choice of strategies of organization design which either reduces the amount of information that the organization needs to process, or increases the degree of cognition of the organization. The alternative of design that provides an increase in the degree of organizational cognition is the one selected from such a methodology. Moreover, technology and participants (both including cognitive machines) are the elements of design that we choose in order to improve the degree of cognition of the organization – that is in order to improve the organization capability of information processing and uncertainty management.

PRELIMINARIES OF BOUNDED RATIONALITY AND CONTINGENCY FOR ORGANIZATIONS: COGNITION VS. UNCERTAINTY

This section reviews some of the key concepts of contingency theory which play an important part in this chapter. It also comprises perspectives of the bounded rationality theory (Simon, 1997a and 1997b) for organizations – specially the perspective of organizations with limitations of knowledge and computational capacity.

The Organization and the Environment

Contingency theory has demonstrated through comparative studies and large scale empirical research that organizations are contingent upon the environment. This means that (Galbraith, 1973):

- "There is no one best way to organize."
- "Not all the ways to organize are equally effective."

Therefore, organization design is contingent upon the environment

Scope of the Environment

The environment comprises levels of analysis which can range from technical to institutional aspects (Scott, 1998). The technical aspect is synonymous with task environment and the organization is viewed as a production system which transforms materials and services from inputs into outputs. In telecommunication companies for instance, there might be divisions for product innovation and research, marketing, systems engineering and design, testing and production. Each division has specific task environments (Nobre & Volpe, 1999; and Volpe & Nobre, 2000). The institutional aspect of the environment is broader than the technical since it is concerned with the cultural factors along with the belief, normative, regulative and political systems shaping the organization. The perspective of the organization and the environment raging from technical and managerial to institutional and worldwide levels of analysis is presented in some latter stages in the next chapter.

Uncertainty: Lack of Information and Limits of Cognition

Contingency theory has also defined uncertainty as the variable which makes the organization contingent upon the environment. Hence, organization design, and thus organizational choice, depends on the concept of uncertainty.

Briefly, uncertainty is concerned with (Nobre, 2005):

i.   Lack of information, which leads the organization to unpredictability of outcomes.
ii. And, insufficiency of cognitive abilities for general information-processing.

The former, lack of information, implies that (Galbraith, 1977):

Definition 2.1: Uncertainty is the difference between the total amount of information that the organization needs to have in order to perform a task, and the amount of information that the organization has already possessed.

The latter, insufficiency of cognition, implies that:

Definition 2.2: Uncertainty is also the difference between the degree of cognition that the organization needs to have in order to perform a task, and the degree of cognition that the organization has already possessed.

These two approaches to uncertainty complement each other and thus we propose that:

Proposition 2.1: The greater the amount of information that the organization needs to have in order to perform and to complete a task, the greater is the degree of cognition that the organization needs to have in order to process and to manage this information for task execution and completion.

Figures 2.1 and 2.2 illustrate such concepts of uncertainty using symbolic scales of measurement.

Therefore, the question to be answered in the next sections is: - what to do in order to reduce the level of uncertainty that the organization confronts and needs to manage?

Figure 2.1. Uncertainty as lack of information

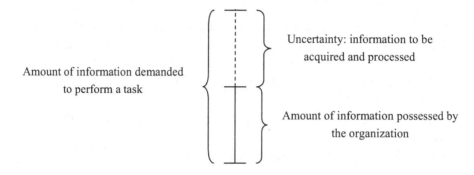

Figure 2.2. Uncertainty as lack of cognition

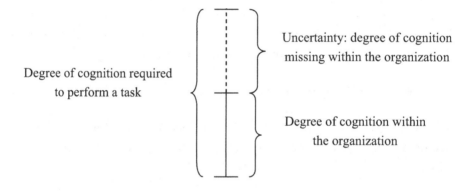

THE ROLE OF ORGANIZATION DESIGN IN ORGANIZATIONAL COGNITION

Organization design is concerned with the choice of organizing models which provide the organization with the ability to cope with the level of uncertainty of the environment with which the organization relates. It comprises constraint variables and cost-benefit analysis.

Additionally, while the amount of information that the organization needs to have in order to perform a task depends upon the environment with which the organization relates[1], the degree of cognition of the organization depends upon the choice of its elements. Nevertheless, the choice of the organization elements also depends upon the environment. Consequently, organization cognition is also contingent upon the environment.

Strategies of Organization Design

Organizing models vary according to the choice of the elements of the organization. The behaviour and the cognitive abilities of the organization are contingent upon the selection of its goals, social structure, participants and technology.

The choice of the elements of the organization, and thus organization design, can proceed in two ways:

i. Firstly, it can be concerned with the choice of models of organizing which reduce the amount of information that the organization needs to acquire, to process and to manage in order to perform and to complete tasks.

ii. Secondly, it can be concerned with the choice of models of organizing which provide a growth in the degree of cognition of the organization. Therefore, this option improves the capability of the organization to acquire, to process and to manage information in order to perform and to complete tasks.

According to the literature, the first option - i.e. reduction of the amount of information - can be achieved with the strategies for creation of slack resources (i.e. reduction of performance), environmental management (which concerns the organization attempting to influence and to modify the environment, rather than changing its elements) and creation of self-contained tasks (which causes reduction in division of work and thus in the demand for coordination of different tasks). The second option - i.e. the increase in the degree of organizational cognition - can be achieved with strategies of investment in information-processing and management systems, along with creation of lateral relations (which is concerned with the de-centralization of decisions) (Galbraith, 1977). This book supports the perspectives of both strategies and it presents a methodology of organization design in order to choose one among them.

We anticipate that, from such a methodology, the strategy of investment in information processing and management systems is the one we select in order to lead the organization to improve its cognitive abilities, and in particular, its ability to make decisions.

Methodology of Organization Design

- **Motivations:** The methodology presented here represents a guide to support decision-makers in the choice of strategic alternatives for:

i. Reducing the amount of information that the organization needs to process.

ii. And, increasing the cognitive abilities of the organization.

The selection of one strategy involves trade-offs among these options. Therefore, this methodology is used to justify the choice of one among these strategic alternatives of organization design.

We anticipate that the strategy which is concerned with the increase in the degree of cognition of the organization is the one chosen and used through out the book. Technology and participants are the selected elements of organization design since they comprise cognitive machines. This book assumes that these machines can participate and act in the name of organizations like decision-makers.

- **Methodology:** The methodology is illustrated in Figure 2.3. The dotted lines symbolize the dynamic interaction between the elements of the organization and a change in one element affects the others. The arrows indicate a path to the process and cycle of design. It begins with the goals and it proceeds through the social structure, technology and participants in the way of a continuous process of analysis, design and redesign.
- **Environment:** Before changing and designing the elements of the organization, we can try to manage the environment with which the organization relates in order to reach equilibrium between the organization capabilities and the environmental complexity.

Environmental management is concerned with the tasks in the organization that attempts to influence and to control the environment, rather than to change the organization elements (Galbraith, 1977). Environmental management requires that the organization performs additional cognitive tasks. It includes extra practices of: acquisition and selection of information from the market; knowledge management;

Figure 2.3. Methodology of organization design

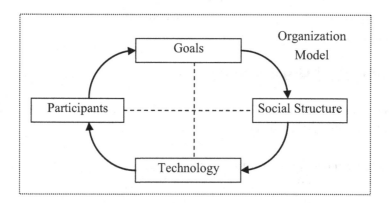

decision-making and problem-solving. Hence, despite attempting to reduce information, this alternative demands additional cognitive abilities from the organization in order to perform new tasks in the environmental level and to process additional information. Therefore, this alternative can demand a higher degree of cognition from the organization and thus investments in information processing systems.

- **Goals:** In the design of the organization, goals come first because they provide direction to the organization (Galbraith, 2002). Goals and sub-goals support the organization, its parts (units and divisions) and its participants with the process of attention[2] (March & Simon, 1993; and Reed, 1988), hence they provide the organization with focalization, reduction of amount of information, and thus reduction of uncertainty. Therefore, in this case, reduction of uncertainty is a result of goal and sub-goal specification.

The design and redesign of goals of the organization also play important tasks in the Creation of Slack Resources – which is concerned with the reduction in the level of the organization performance (Galbraith, 1977). Consequently, there is a reduction in the amount of information that the organization needs to manage. This alternative can be implemented by redesigning the goals of the organization and by relaxing some of the performance criteria that the organization must attend. It comprises a review of the strategic planning of operations management and production systems in the organization. Among the actions that the organization can take in order to reduce complexities of its performance criteria include: reduction of output diversity (i.e. by decreasing the variety of products and the customization level); increase project's schedule and time-to-market[3]; increase resources of budget and production cost; reduction of agility, flexibility, quality and reliability; among other actions. These alternatives will have some implications such as lack of credibility with customers, reduction of market share[4], loss of competitive advantage, and reduction of profitability for the organization. This book assumes that the alternative for creation of slack resource, in the context presented here, is undesirable and unacceptable for organizations of today operating in competitive markets.

- **Social Structure:** After the completion of the strategic planning and the specification of goals, we need to design a social structure in order to support the implementation and the achievement of the organization goals.

The design and redesign of the social structure have some implications for the organization which comprise:

i.   Reduction or growth in the amount of information that the organization needs to process and to manage for task execution and completion.
ii.   And, growth or reduction in the degree of cognition of the organization.

Social structure is synonymous with the anatomy and the physiology of the organization. It comprises organizational methods such as division of work, departmentalization, span of control and specialization; vertical and lateral processes, rules and decision programs; hierarchy of authority, centralization and decentralization; reward systems; and activities such as the creation of self-contained tasks and lateral relations. These concepts and their implications for the design of organizations are well explained in (Galbraith, 2002; and Scott, 1998) and they have been used by designers in order to find satisfactory results for the organization. In this context, which repeats along the book, the term "satisfactory" is synonymous with "satisficing" as defined in (Simon, 1997a).

Social structure also plays a fundamental part in the creation of management policies in the organization which subsume processes of organizational learning, innovation, sustainable competitive advantage, human resources and intellectual capital management, among others.

The methodology of organization design and redesign continues in the following stages with the selection of technology and participants.

•   **Technology:** Information overflows the structure of organizations of today (Galbraith, 2002). The functioning of the organization depends upon its degree of cognition which provides the organization with abilities to sensing and perceiving, filtering and attention, storing and organizing knowledge, problem solving, decision-making and learning. Therefore, it is important to choose the technologies which can support the organization with processes and systems that contribute to improve the cognitive capabilities of the organization.

In this book, the technology of cognitive machines is the selected element of design in order to improve the degree of cognition of the organization, and thus to reduce the level of environmental uncertainty and complexity. Particular attention is given to decision-making processes.

•   **Participants:** The participants in the organization are the main agents who provide the organization with cognition. Their cognitive, physical, temporal, institutional and spatial limitations are supported by: the social networks which they form; the organization goals and sub-goals which support them in the process of attention; and also the structure of the organization which provides them with managerial and coordinative processes.

The participants in the organization have cognitive and emotional processes which influence and shape the organization behaviour. Therefore, the selection of participants plays an important part in the survival and development of the organization. However, recruitment and reward systems (with inducements that motivate the participants), along with training programs, are processes that the organization must also design in order to succeed through its goals.

Therefore, in this book the participants in the organization are also chosen as additional elements of design. Particular attention is given to the participation of cognitive machines in the organization.

At this early stage, we emphasize that the focus of the book is to give attention to cognitive processes in the organization and therefore we leave emotional processes for further research.

SUMMARY

Chapter II presented core rationale for organizational cognition on the basis of contingency theory and bounded rationality concepts.

A theory of organizational cognition is important and necessary when we decide to design organizations with higher capabilities of information processing and uncertainty management. In such a way, organizational cognition is a discipline which contributes to improve the computational capacity of the organization and its ability for knowledge management.

Assuming such rationale, this chapter introduced a methodology to support the choice of organization design strategies which either reduces the amount of information that the organization needs to process, or increases the degree of cognition of the organization. The alternative that provides an increase in the degree of organizational cognition was the one selected from such a methodology. Moreover, technology and participants (both including cognitive machines) were the elements of design that we chose in order to improve the degree of cognition of the organization – i.e. in order to improve the organization capability of information processing and uncertainty management.

From this perspective, we derived some definitions and conclusions:

i.   Organizations are contingent upon the environment which comprises technical and institutional aspects.
ii.   Organization design depends on the concept of uncertainty which encompasses lack of information and limits of cognition.
iii. Organization models vary according to the choice of the elements of the organization.

iv.   The behaviour and the cognitive abilities of the organization are contingent upon the selection of its goals, social structure, participants and technology.
v.   Organizational cognition is contingent upon organization design.
vi.   And, organization cognition is contingent upon the environment.

Moreover, it was proposed that:

Proposition 2.1: The greater the amount of information that the organization needs to have in order to perform and to complete a task, the greater is the degree of cognition that the organization needs to have in order to process and to manage this information for task execution and completion.

The theory of organizational cognition as proposed in this book also plays an important part, and introduces a new perspective, in the analysis of the relations between the organization, its elements and the environment. This additional contribution is presented in the next chapter.

REFERENCES

Galbraith, J. R. (1973). *Designing Complex Organizations*. Addison-Wesley.

Galbraith, J. R. (1977). *Organization Design*. Addison-Wesley.

Galbraith, J. R. (2002). *Designing Organizations - An executive guide to strategy, structure, and process*. Jossey-Bass.

March, J. G., & Simon, H. A. (1993). *Organizations*. 2nd Ed. John Wiley & Sons, Inc.

Nobre, F. S., & Volpe, R. (1999). SEI-CMM Implementation at the NEC Brasil S.A. *Proceedings of the International Conference on Software Technology: Industrial Track* (pp. 45-72). Curitiba, Brazil.

Volpe, R., & Nobre, F. S., *et al* (2000). The Role of Software Process Improvement into TQM: An Industrial Experience. *IEEE Proceedings of the International Engineering Management Conference* (pp. 29-34). Albuquerque-NM, USA.

Nobre, F. S. (2002c, November). *Organisational Systems: Towards A Unified Theory*. Seminar presented for the Artificial Intelligence Research Group of the Department of Computer Sciences in the Humboldt University of Berlin. Johann von Newmann-Haus, Berlin.

Nobre, F. S. (2004a). Analysis and Design of Organizational Systems: Towards a Unified Theory. *The 1ˢᵗ Conference of the Association of Brazilian Post-graduate Students and Researchers in the United Kingdom (ABEP)*. Proceeding: 52. Oxford Centre for Brazilian Studies, Oxford-UK.

Nobre, F. S. (2004b, November). *Analysis and Design of Organizations - Towards a Theory of Organization Cognition*. Seminar presented at the Birmingham Business School / Centre for International Business and Organization Research (CIBOR). Birmingham-UK.

Nobre, F. S. (2005). On Cognitive Machines in Organizations. *PhD Thesis*, 343 pages. University of Birmingham. Birmingham Main Library. Control Number: M0266887BU. Birmingham-UK.

Reed, S. K. (1988). *Cognition: Theory and Applications*. 2ⁿᵈ Ed. Brooks-Cole Publishing Company.

Scott, W. R. (1998). *Organizations: Rational, Natural, and Open Systems*. Prentice Hall, Inc.

Simon, H. A. (1947). *Administrative Behavior: A Study of Decision-Making Processes in Administrative Organization*. New York, NY: Macmillan.

Simon, H. A. (1982a). *Models of Bounded Rationality: Economic Analysis and Public Policy*. Vol.1. The MIT Press.

Simon, H. A. (1997a). *Models of Bounded Rationality: Empirically Grounded Economic Reason*. Vol.3. The MIT Press.

Simon, H. A. (1997b). *Administrative Behavior: A Study of Decision-Making Processes in Administrative Organizations*. The Free Press.

(Wikipedia) *The Free Encyclopaedia*. http://en.wikipedia.org

ENDNOTES

[1] This level of environment involves the organization's output diversity (e.g. diversity of goals, products, services, markets, customers, geography, etc.) and level of performance (e.g. strictness of criteria of quality, time and budget constraints, etc.).

[2] The process of attention plays the role of directing and focusing certain mental efforts of the organization's participants to enhance perception, performance and mental experience during task execution. This is done when the organization

provides specific sub-goals of lateral and vertical relations for its participants and units.

[3]   In commerce, time to market (TTM) is the length of time it takes from a product being conceived until its being available for sale (Wikipedia's online dictionary).

[4]   Market share, in strategic management and marketing, is the percentage or proportion of the total available market or market segment that is being serviced by a company (Wikipedia's online dictionary).

Chapter III
A Theory of
Organizational Cognition

INTRODUCTION

Chapter III introduces definitions, premises, and propositions towards a theory of organizational cognition. It proposes principles about organizational cognition and thus it clearly distinguishes organizational cognition from the concept of organizational learning. It outlines the concept of hierarchic levels of cognition in organizational systems and thus it proposes cognition as an important element of the organization. It presents new definitions on organizations, environment along with the relations between them through cognitive perspectives. Such definitions include concepts of intelligence, cognition, autonomy, and complexity for organizations. It derives a definition of environmental complexity and it proceeds by introducing propositions about the relations between organizational complexity and environmental complexity. While the former is synonymous with organizational cognition, the latter is synonymous with environmental uncertainty.

BACKGROUND, CRITICAL VIEW AND ADVANCEMENTS

Organizational cognition is a discipline which has its foundations based on multidisciplinary research areas that span from social sciences, economics, business administration, management, sociology, political science, anthropology, philosophy, psychology, information systems, cognitive sciences and computer sciences to some other areas that play an important part in organizational studies such as organizational behaviour and organizational theory (Nobre, 2005).

The subject of organizational cognition has been touched in the literature after advancements in the discipline of organizational learning which has received important and diverse contributions from distinct researchers (Argyris & Schon, 1978; March & Olsen, 1975; and Senge, 1990).

Multidisciplinary studies on organizational learning and knowledge management are presented in (Dierkes *et al*, 2003); and on organizational intelligence, and organizations resembling information processing systems and distributed computational agents are presented in (Blanning & King, 1996; Carley & Gasser, 1999; and Prietula *et al*, 1998). However, a formal study which relates organizations with concepts of cognition and learning (innovation) was previously and firstly proposed in (Simon, 1947; March & Simon, 1958; and Simon, 1997b).

Nevertheless, despite some connections in between organizational learning, knowledge management, organizational intelligence and organizational cognition, this latter subject has began to receive more attention only from the beginning of the 21st Century, with some book publications. The Lant and Shapira's book for example (Lant & Shapira, 2001) presents a collection of chapters on the subject of cognition and its impact on organizational studies. Contributors to their book chapters include famous researchers such as James March and Willian Starbuck. However, despite providing the literature with a set of chapters that introduce many perspectives on the general subject of organizational cognition, Lant and Shapira's book does not give a concise definition of organizational cognition. Moreover, and most important, it does not make a clear distinction of the concept of organizational cognition from those of organizational learning, knowledge management, among other related terminologies which have been used through an interchangeable way in most of the literature on these subjects. Another publication which does not clearly distinguish these terms is the book of Iandoli and Zollo (2007). Additionally, while most of the books available in the literature have focused more on cognitive processes of management, in this book we are more concerned with the cognitive processes of the organizational structure which is composed by the goals, technology, social structure and participants of the organization.

Proceeding further, what makes our book distinct is that we provide a set of principles, definitions, premises and propositions towards a theory of organizational cognition. We clearly derive definitions on organizational cognition and we also distinguish it from organizational intelligence, organizational complexity, organizational autonomy and organizational learning. This new background on organizational cognition plays an important part in the study of organization design, in the relations between the organization and the environment, and in the analysis of the implications of cognitive machines for organizations. Moreover, in Part V, on the industrial case study, we contribute by outlining new directions to assess, to evaluate and to measure the degree of organizational cognition.

Therefore, our book also comprises new insights for future research on organizations.

TEN PRINCIPLES OF ORGANIZATIONAL COGNITION

The ten principles proposed in this section form the basis for all definitions, premises and propositions about organizational cognition as presented in this book. Such principles are introduced in the following:

1. Organizational cognition is concerned with the processes which provide agents and organizations with the ability to learn, to make decisions and to solve problems.
2. A theory of organizational cognition is important and necessary when we decide to design organizations with higher capabilities of information processing and uncertainty management.
3. Organizational cognition is a discipline which contributes to improve the computational capacity of the organization along with its ability for knowledge and uncertainty management.
4. The main agents of organizational cognition are the participants within the organization and the social networks which they form.
5. Cognitive processes are supported by the goals, technology and social structure of the organization. Moreover, organizational cognition is also influenced by inter-organizational processes and thus by the environment.
6. The cognition of the organization can also be represented as a matter of degree whose level depends on the choice of models of organizing.
7. The choice of organizing models, and thus organization design, plays a fundamental role in organizational cognition.
8. The capability of the organization for information processing, knowledge and uncertainty management, task execution, and management of complexities of the environment, depends on its degree of cognition.
9. The degree of cognition of the organization depends upon the choice of its elements, and the choice of the organization elements depends upon the environment. Consequently, organization cognition is contingent upon the environment.
10. Organizational cognition supports knowledge management[1] and organizational learning[2] with processes that contribute to improve continuously the elements, the competitive advantage, and the results of the organization. This contribu-

tion comprises improvements in the equilibrium between the participants' motives and the organizational goals; customer satisfaction; and organization profitability.

HIERARCHIC LEVELS OF COGNITION IN ORGANIZATIONAL SYSTEMS

Studies of complex systems and their classification through hierarchical levels of complexity are proposed in (Boulding, 1956; and Simon, 1996). In these studies, a system is defined as a large number of objects together with relationships between them and between their attributes (or properties). The parts, elements or objects which form the systems vary from being very simple to very complex in structure, and from being highly stable to highly dynamic and variable in their interaction. Moreover, each system of higher complexity level incorporates the features of those below it.

In such a context, this book asserts that differences between complex systems reside not only in the properties and structure of their elements, but most importantly in the abilities of these elements. The former - i.e. properties and structure - refers to physical, biological and chemical attributes, and the latter - i.e. abilities - means cognition, intelligence and autonomy.

Therefore, by analysing the Boulding's typology of systems (Boulding, 1956), where he classified systems according to their levels of complexity, we conclude that the higher the system complexity, the higher its degree of cognition, intelligence and autonomy. The next paragraphs present the Boulding's classification of systems which are enumerated in the order of growth of levels of complexity:

1. Frameworks: systems comprising static structures, such as the arrangements of atoms in a crystal or the anatomy of an animal.
2. Clockworks: simple dynamic systems with predetermined motions, such as the clock and the solar system.
3. Cybernetic Systems: systems capable of self-regulation in terms of some externally prescribed set point or target, such as a thermostat.
4. Open systems: systems capable of self-maintenance based on a through-put of resources from their environment, such as living cells.
5. Blueprinted-growth systems: systems that reproduce not by duplication but by the production of seeds or eggs containing pre-programmed instructions for development, such as the egg chicken system.
6. Internal-image systems: systems capable of a detailed awareness of the environment in which information is received and organized into an image or

knowledge structure of the environment as a whole. Animals function at this level.

7. Symbol-processing systems: systems that possess self-consciousness and are capable of using language. Humans function at this level.
8. Social systems: systems comprising agents functioning at level 7 who share a common social order and culture. Organizations operate at this level.
9. Transcendental systems: systems composed of the absolutes and the inescapable unknowable.

According to the above typology of systems, levels 1 to 3 include the physical systems whose structures are highly rigid, constrained and limited. Levels 4 to 6 encompass the biological systems. Levels 7 to 8 comprise the human and social systems. Moving from levels 1 to 8, systems become progressively more complex and their structures become somewhat less rigid and constrained, and the connections between the interacting parts become relatively loose, where less constraint is placed on the behaviour of one element by the condition of the others (Scott, 1998). Additionally, and most importantly, from levels 1 to 8, systems grow in their levels of cognition, intelligence and autonomy. Level 9 is beyond our imagination.

The main elements of social systems are humans and networks of people, and thus organizations and networks of organizations. Such systems possess high degrees of cognition, intelligence and autonomy which are distributed among their individuals and among their relationships. On the other hand, the elements of, and the relationships with, physical, biological and chemical systems - including all the objects and organisms of the ecological system, but excluding the man - are less complex than those found in social systems if we consider that they have lower degrees of cognition, intelligence and autonomy (if any in most of the cases).

Therefore, we can state that cognition plays a fundamental part in organizations, and that the nature of organizations reside in principles of human behaviour and cognition.

ATTRIBUTES OF THE ORGANIZATION AND THE ENVIRONMENT

The concepts derived for the variables in this section represent a synthesis and an extension of some definitions provided within the literature. Cognition and complexity of organizations and machines, and relative complexity of the environment, are the principal concepts to be addressed in this section. The concepts of intelligence and autonomy of both organizations and machines and their relations to cognition and complexity are also introduced.

Organizational Intelligence

- **Concept of Intelligence:** Intelligence is a general mental ability (Schmidt & Hunter, 2000), which depends on general cognitive and emotional abilities (Goleman, 1994).

Intelligence depends on two complementary processes which are evoked by abstract or physical stimuli: they are rational and emotional processes.

Rational process or rationality is the ability to follow procedures for decision-making and problem-solving in order to achieve goals (Simon, 1997a). Rational behaviour is synonymous with intelligence when it leads someone to good outcomes (March, 1994). Hence, the closer the outcome to the optimal solution, the more intelligent is the rational behaviour. Additionally, rational processes are contingent upon the cognitive limitations of humans, and thus they are better represented by the concept of bounded rationality (Simon, 1982b).

Emotional process[3] is less procedural than rationality and it is purposeless in the context of achieving goals. However, researchers have shown that emotions play an important part to motivate, direct and regulate actions in the service of goal pursuit (Bagozzi, 1998; Keltner & Gross, 1999; and Keltner & Haidt, 1999). Emotional behaviour is synonymous with intelligence when it represents the ability to excel in life - it includes self-awareness, self-discipline, self-motivation, impulse control, persistence, empathy, zeal, social deftness, trustworthiness and a talent for collaboration. Moreover, on the one hand, emotions influence cognitive tasks such as attention, learning, decision-making and problem-solving (Goleman, 1994). On the other hand, cognitions are in the service of emotions (Plutchik, 1982) - like in the processes of stimulus interpretation and environment evaluation.

Therefore, intelligence is contingent upon cognitive and emotional processes. Hence, intelligence comprises two complementary elements:

Definition 3.1: Intelligence

Rational Intelligence: is the ability to use cognitive processes in learning[4], decision-making and problem-solving.

Emotional Intelligence: is the ability to use emotional and cognitive processes in order to understand ourselves (i.e. intra-personal intelligence) and relate with others (inter-personal or social intelligence).

In this book, we focus more on the subject of cognitive processes rather than emotional processes; and the concept of bounded rationality is adopted rather than rationality in its classical sense (Simon, 1997a). Nevertheless, the cognitive machines introduced in the next chapters have the capability to manipulate a percept and concepts represented in the form of words, propositions and sentences of a natural language; and such concepts can involve representations of emotions. Linguistic descriptions of emotions include attributes of feelings like happy, sad, angry, etc. Hence, the processes of the cognitive machine can also manipulate complex symbols of emotions.

- **Intelligence of Organizations:** Organizations also have intelligence which is provided by their internal elements - i.e. participants, social structure, technology and goals.

The participants within the organization can provide it with intelligence according to the concept of intelligence.

The social structure of the organization has normative and behavioural parts. The normative structure provides the organization with rational processes (March & Simon, 1993; and Scott, 1998), and thus with rational intelligence. Complementarily, the behavioural structure can provide the organization with emotional processes (Fineman, 1993), and thus with emotional intelligence.

The technology within the organization can provide it with means which improve its cognitive abilities for learning, decision-making and problem-solving. This comprises information search, attention, representation and organization of knowledge, memory expansion and communication.

Goals and sub-goals provide the organization with focalization and direction. They can support the organization, its units and its participants with the process of attention (March & Simon, 1993). When viewed as means, sub-goals direct the organization to more complex goals at upper levels. Hence, goals provide the organization with criteria of choice.

Organizational Cognition

Like perception and emotion, cognition is viewed as a process throughout this book. In fact, cognition comprises a set of processes - e.g. attention, knowledge organization, decision-making and problem-solving - which form together the human cognitive system. In such a way, degree of cognition is synonymous with the level of elaboration and integration of such a set of processes.

Organizations resemble cognitive systems when they present abilities and processes for sensing, perceiving, filtering and attention; storing and organizing knowledge; problem solving, decision-making and learning. Such processes are evoked by internal and external stimuli to the organization. Like humans, organizations have relations to the environment.

The perspective of organizations as lateral and vertical distributed cognitive agents was firstly touched upon in the work of March and Simon (1958 and 1993). Later, it was further extended in the work of Carley and Gasser (1999). This book adopts the same perspective and it views the structure of the organization resembling a nexus of cognitive agents and processes organized with lateral and vertical relations. Such cognitive agents are the participants within the organization (i.e. humans and cognitive machines) and they can also represent a department, a division or a general unit of the organization. They have channels of communication between them which attend the social structure and the protocols of the organization.

In a broad sense, cognition develops in order to increase the probability of humans to survive (Plutchik, 1982). Similarly, organizational cognition plays the same role.

- **Human vs. Organizational Cognition:** Human cognition is part of a natural system and hence it is not a man-made system. Therefore, the brain and thus the cognitive abilities of humans are more or less unchangeable.

On the other hand, organizational cognition is part of an artificial system[5] and hence it is designed and a man-made kind. Moreover, it involves living (e.g. humans) and non-living (e.g. machines) forms. Therefore, the cognitive abilities of organizations can be changed and improved through the process of organization design. Organizational cognition is contingent upon the goals, social structure, participants, technology and the environment of the organization.

- **Organizational Cognition vs. Intelligence:** This subsection concludes by presenting premises about organizational cognition, degree of organizational cognition and by relating organizational cognition to intelligence:

Premise 3.1: Organizational cognition comprises a set of processes similarly to those which form the human cognitive system - e.g. processes of attention, knowledge organization and decision-making.

Premise 3.2: The degree of cognition of the organization is contingent upon the level of elaboration and integration of its associated cognitive processes.

Proposition 3.1: The greater the degree of cognition of the organization, the greater is its chance to exhibit intelligent behaviour.

Organizational Autonomy

Instead of defining autonomy as synonymous with freedom or authority to act, this book regards autonomy as the ability of an organism to act through the use of cognition. Additionally, like cognition, intelligence and complexity, autonomy is a matter of degree. Therefore:

Proposition 3.2: The greater the degree of cognition of the organization, the greater is its autonomy.

Organizational Complexity

This book regards the level of complexity of the organization as contingent upon its degree of cognition. Therefore:

Proposition 3.3: The greater the degree of cognition of the organization, the greater is its ability to solve complex tasks.

The literature has also defined the level of complexity of an organized social system as a function of its number of components, differentiation of its components and interdependence between its components (La Porte, 1975). Despite this definition excluding explicit reference to the complexity of organizations, it only may be related to the social structure of the organization. Furthermore, this definition misses out an important and necessary concept for organizations, the concept of organizational cognition.

Environmental Complexity

The complexity of the environment is contingent upon the level of uncertainty that it represents to the organization. Similarly, the complexity of a task environment is contingent upon the level of uncertainty that it represents to the organization during task execution. Hence:

Proposition 3.4: The greater the level of task complexity, the greater is the level of task uncertainty.

Proposition 3.5: The greater the level of environmental complexity, the greater the level of environmental uncertainty.

Proposition 3.6: The greater the level of environmental complexity, the greater is the level of environmental uncertainty that the organization confronts and needs to manage.

The level of complexity of the environment is relative to the organization with which it interacts. Therefore, distinct organizations (of different degrees of cognition) confront with different levels of uncertainty even when they operate in a common environment or execute a common task.

ORGANIZATIONAL COGNITION AND THE ENVIRONMENT

On Cognition vs. Complexity (and Uncertainty)

Firstly, a synthesis of premises is presented to support the propositions introduced in the following.

Premise 3.2: The elements of the organization - i.e. goals, social structure, participants and technology - support the organization with cognitive processes such as filtering and attention, storing and organizing knowledge, problem solving, decision-making and learning.

Premise 3.3: The complexity of the organization is contingent upon its degree of cognition.

Therefore, we propose that:

Proposition 3.7: The higher the level of complexity of the organization, the higher is its degree of cognition.

Proposition 3.8: The higher the degree of cognition of the organization, the lower is the relative level of environmental complexity.

Firstly, proposition 3.7 assumes by definition that the higher the level of complexity of the organization, the higher its degrees of cognition. Secondly, proposition 3.8 does not mean that the level of complexity of the environment reduces, but that such a level of complexity is relatively reduced when compared to the growth in the level of complexity of the organization. Therefore, by associating propositions 3.4 to 3.8, we state that:

Proposition 3.9: The lower the relative level of environmental complexity, the lower is the relative level of environmental uncertainty that the organization confronts and needs to manage.

Similarly, proposition 3.9 states that the level of uncertainty in the environment is relatively reduced with an increase in the degree of cognition of the organization. Therefore, the next theorem can be deduced from the previous chain of propositions:

Theorem 3.1: The higher the degree of cognition of the organization, the lower is the relative level of environmental complexity and uncertainty that the organization confronts and needs to manage.

DEFINITIONS OF THE ORGANIZATION

This section proposes definitions of organizations which are complementary to each other.

Organizations as Distributed Cognitive Agents

The definition of organizations introduced in this section represents a synthesis of concepts. The most influential perspectives are those presented in (March & Simon, 1958; Scott, 1998; and Carley & Gasser, 1999).

Firstly, organizations are assemblages of distributed agents. Agents are classified as natural or artificial, and living or nonliving. Humans are natural-living agents, while machines are artificial-nonliving ones.

Secondly, organizations pursue a coordinative system rooted into a social structure which is composed by normative and behavioural parts. Coordinative systems of distinct organizations have different degrees of centralization and decentralization.

Thirdly, organizations pursue goals. The conception of goals varies from individual to organization levels and also from technical, managerial and institutional to worldwide levels. The meaning of goals can range from the perspectives of rational, natural to open systems. Additionally, the strategy of satisfice[6] which attempts to meet criteria for goal adequacy, rather than goal optimization, is better applied to the organization since agents lack the cognitive resources to maximize. The cognitive, physical, temporal, institutional and spatial limitations of agents are presented in Appendix C.

Lastly, organizations are open systems, and therefore they pursue the skills of sensing from, and responding to the environment.

In conclusion, organizations are assemblages of distributed and interacting agents with a coordinative system. They are supposed to satisfy goals, and they have relations with the environment. In such a context, the term "satisfy" is synonymous with "satisfice" as defined by Simon (1997a).

- **Agents of Organizational Cognition:** Cognitive processes are attributes of the participants within the organization and the relationships or social networks which they form. These cognitive processes are supported by the goals, technology and social structure of the organization. Moreover, organizational cognition is also influenced by inter-organizational processes and thus by the environment. The participants within the organization comprise humans and cognitive machines and they are supposed to act as decision-makers in the name of the organization.

- Characteristics of the Organization

i.   The members of organizations are cognitive agents and they include decision-makers as proposed in (March & Simon, 1993; and Simon 1997b).

ii.   Processes of decision-making involve trade-offs among alternatives which are characterized by uncertainty, incomparability and unacceptability, and hence they can lead organization members to intra-individual conflict. Additionally, members of groups in organizations differ in their perceptions and goals, and thus they can disagree in their decisions causing group conflicts (March & Simon, 1993).

iii. The intra-individual and group conflicts which arise in organizations as exposed in (ii) are mainly determined by uncertainties and lack of information, and most importantly by cognitive limitations of humans. Hence, these conflicts cannot be solved by incentive and reward systems[7]. Such cognitive and information constraints are synonymous with bounded rationality (March, 1994; March & Simon, 1993; and Simon, 1982b, 1997a, and 1997b). However, as proposed in Chapter VII, this book also contributes by designing a framework of cognitive machines which can be used to reduce or to solve such conflicts.

iv.   The members of organizations have different perceptions. Such a differentiation is accentuated due to the variety of individual motives[8], but also because of the inequality of distribution of information among the participants in the organization. Therefore, it can lead the participants within the organization to group conflicts (March and Simon, 1993).

v.   The members of organizations have motives which differ from organization goals. Hence, organizations have to motivate them and to provide them with inducements (such as incentive and reward systems) which lead them to participate in organization activities, including decision-making and problem-solving. If satisfactory alignment is found between the organization's goals and its participants' motives (Gibbons, 1998), then organization equilibrium can be achieved (March & Simon, 1993).

vi.   Organizations shape participants' perceptions and behaviour through social structure, technology and goals, and participants shape organizations through their behaviour, emotions, perceptions, motives and cognitive skills.

vii.   The environment shapes organizations (i.e. their social structure, technology, goals, participants and behaviour), through its sources of complexity and uncertainty, but also through information, services, goods, processes and technology.

viii.   Organizations also shape the environment through similar means.

Organizations as Hierarchic Cognitive Systems

The classification of the organization in technical, managerial and institutional levels of analysis was initially proposed by Talcott Parsons (Parsons, 1960). This book borrows and supports his ideas and it also extends them to include a fourth level of analysis named worldwide system. Moreover, these levels of analysis are introduced here in the context of cognitive systems. Their meanings are described by the following paragraphs and Figure 3.1 illustrates the organization under such a perspective.

- **Technical Level:** The technical system is concerned with cognitive tasks and general activities used for the development of goods and services. It comprises people, machines, communication systems and processes. This level depends on information and resources of the environment for the acquisition of new technologies, and also for the acknowledgement of compliance of goods and services with customers' requirements, technical, quality and general standards.

- **Managerial Level:** The managerial system is concerned with cognitive tasks of analysis, design and redesign of the organization. It carries out activities of planning, coordination and innovation in areas such as: goals and strategy; structure (normative structure, specialization, span of control, distribution of authority, departmentalization, etc.); technology and processes[9] (of communication, information processing, decision and control); rewards (incentives and inducements); and human resources (recruiting, training, etc.). Such a

Figure 3.1. The organization levels of analysis

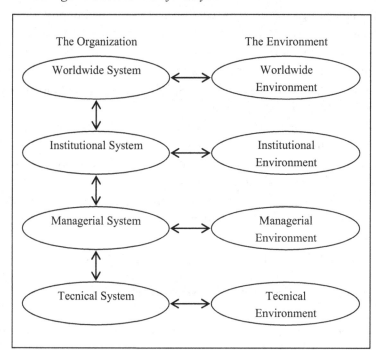

level also needs a channel of communication with the environment in order
to acquire information about incentive and reward systems provided by other
organizations and competitors; to hire new talents; and to select new partnerships with buyers and suppliers for instance. It is also a mediation level
between technical and institutional systems.

•   **Institutional Level:** The institutional system is concerned with cognitive tasks
    used to mediate between the organization and its environment. It comprises
    the understanding of the social, political, cultural and economic contexts of
    the organization's environment. The cognitive tasks at this level shape both
    the technical and the managerial systems, and also the environment (and vice-
    versa). At this level, participants have responsibility to: understand regulative
    processes within the market which constrain the boundaries of action of the
    organization; understand the cultural aspects of the organization and its envi-
    ronment; manage the relationships between the organization and the network
    of organizations which influence upon its business; understand tax rules on
    the transaction of goods and services, labour union rights and structure, etc.;
    set up broader goals and strategies for the organization (like its expansion to
    other geographical locations and markets, delineation of new products and

services, etc.); attract and maintain a body of stakeholders; analyze the wealth of the organization; - to promote partnerships with other organizations; define the percentage of the stocks to be shared within the market; and participate (preponderantly) in the decision processes of design and redesign of the organization.

- **Worldwide Level:** The worldwide system is concerned with cognitive tasks which connect the organization to the world and its globalization system. Such tasks involve the analysis of the implications of organizations, networks and populations of organizations for the social, cultural, economic, political and ecological contexts of the environment. It provides general analysis on the implications of organizations for: the whole economy; the world income distribution; the Gross Domestic Product (GDP) per capita of a country; people's social life, well-being, wealth and health; the global ecosystem, its natural resources, energy demand, and so on. Some prominent studies related to this level of analysis are presented in (Easterlin, 2000; Johnson, 2000; Jones, 1997; Pritchett, 1997; and World Bank, 2003).

Organizations as Complex Systems with Cognition, Intelligence and Autonomy

Definition 3.2: The organization is a special type of dynamic system[10] characterized by a level of complexity C_L which is contingent upon its degree of cognition C_d, intelligence I_d and autonomy A_d.

Axiom 3.1: Considers that C_L is the level of complexity of an organization O_s and that C_d, I_d and A_d are its degrees of cognition, intelligence and autonomy respectively. Moreover, assumes that C_L can be characterized by a function g of parameters C_d, I_d and A_d:

$$C_L = g(C_d, I_d, A_d) \mid 1 \geq C_L, C_d, I_d, A_d \geq 0 \qquad (3.1)$$

C_L, C_d, I_d and A_d are defined in the interval [0,1] since they can be characterized by using the concepts of fuzzy sets and membership functions[11] (Zadeh, 1965). The application of the fuzzy sets theory is encouraged to this definition of organizations because complexity, cognition, intelligence and autonomy are vague and loose concepts in the sense defined by Black (1937 and 1963), and they are also fuzzy in the way defined by Zadeh (1965 and 1973).

Axiom 3.2: In such a way, let us define an organization O_s denoted here by an object u belonging to a universe of discourse U, which contains the all classes of organizations, i.e. $(u_i \in U \mid i=1,...,N)$, for N integer.

Axiom 3.3: Let us define the level of complexity C_L, and the degrees of cognition C_d, intelligence I_d and autonomy A_d as fuzzy sets with their respective membership functions denoted by $\mu_{C_L}(u)$, $\mu_{C_d}(u)$, $\mu_{I_d}(u)$ and $\mu_{A_d}(u) \in [0,1]$, i.e.:

$$C_L = \{u \mid \mu_{C_L}(u) \in [0,1], u \in U\} \qquad (3.2)$$

$$C_d = \{u \mid \mu_{C_d}(u) \in [0,1], u \in U\} \qquad (3.3)$$

$$I_d = \{u \mid \mu_{I_d}(u) \in [0,1], u \in U\} \qquad (3.4)$$

$$A_d = \{u \mid \mu_{A_d}(u) \in [0,1], u \in U\} \qquad (3.5)$$

Therefore, O_s can assume four degrees of complexity, intelligence, cognition and autonomy respectively, where such degrees can be interpreted as degrees of compatibility or membership of O_s to the respective fuzzy sets C_L, C_d, I_d and A_d.
From equation (3.1), it can be stated that:

Definition 3.3: C_L is a function g which can be represented by a t-norm $\cap$ or an s-norm $\perp$ (Dubois & Prade, 1985), i.e.:

$$C_L (\cap) = \{u \mid \mu_{C_L}(u) = \mu_{(C_d \cap I_d \cap A_d)} \in [0,1], u \in U\} \qquad (3.6)$$

$$C_L (\perp) = \{u \mid \mu_{C_L}(u) = \mu_{(C_d \perp I_d \perp A_d)} \in [0,1], u \in U\} \qquad (3.7)$$

COGNITIVE DEFINITION OF THE ENVIRONMENT

This section and the next one are about the environment e, and the relations R_e between the organization O_s and the environment e.

Axiom 3.4: Let us consider an organization O_{s1} with relations R_{e1} to an environment e_1 which has relations R_{e2} to another environment e_2. Therefore, a generic environment e_n of an organization O_{sn} may have relations $R_{e(n+1)}$ to another environment $e_{(n+1)}$, where n is an integer.

Axiom 3.5: Let us define a network N_E constituted by *(n+1)* organizations $O_{s(i=1,...,n+1)}$. Let us also define O_{s2} as the environment of O_{s1} with relations R_{e1} between them, and O_{s3} as the one of O_{s2} with R_{e2}. Therefore, it can be derived that $O_{s(n+1)}$ is the environment of O_{sn} with relations R_{en} between them.

Axioms (3.4) and (3.5) also imply that an environment is relative in the sense that it depends on the position of our analysis on a map of networks of organizations. It also means that the roles of *e* and O_s may be exchanged since an *e* becomes an O_s and vice-versa according to the reference of analysis taken on a map of networks of organizations. Therefore:

Definition 3.4: Similarly to O_s, the definitions (3.2) and (3.3) also apply to the environment *e* (where O_s is replaced with *e*).

COGNITIVE RELATIONS BETWEEN THE ORGANIZATION AND THE ENVIRONMENT

This section complements the definitions of organizations O_s and the environment *e* by introducing different types of relations R_e which can exist between them. It borrows and adapts the approach to the analysis of ecological dynamics presented in (Boulding, 1978) in order to describe the diversity of R_e.

Axiom 3.6: Lets us assume an organization $O_s(t)$ with a set of state variables denoted by *X(t)*, where *t* denotes time. Additionally, let us define the organization performance $P_{Os(t)}$ as a measure of its efficacy and efficiency which are dependent on the behaviour of *X(t)*.

Axiom 3.7: Similarly, let us consider an environment *e(t)* with state variables *Y(t)* and with performance denoted by $P_{e(t)}$, which holds the same assumptions given to $P_{Os(t)}$.

Axiom 3.8: Let us assume that $O_s(t)$ can affect *e(t)* in one of three ways. It may affect it favourably, and hence the relations $R_e(t)$ is cooperative. A rise in $P_{Os(t)}$ will increase $P_{e(t)}$ (i.e. if $P_{Os(t)} \uparrow$ then $P_{e(t)} \uparrow$). Secondly, the relationship $R_e(t)$ may be competitive. A rise in $P_{Os(t)}$ leads to a decline in $P_{e(t)}$ and a fall in $P_{Os(t)}$ to a rise in $P_{e(t)}$ (i.e. if $P_{Os(t)} \uparrow$ then $P_{e(t)} \downarrow$ and if $P_{Os(t)} \downarrow$ then $P_{e(t)} \uparrow$). Thirdly, $P_{e(t)}$ may have no dependence on $P_{Os(t)}$ and therefore a rise or a fall in $P_{Os(t)}$ may have no effect on $P_{e(t)}$ (i.e. if either $P_{Os(t)} \updownarrow$ then $P_{e(t)}(0)$).

Table 3.1. Classes of relationships $R_e(t)$

$R_{(Os \to e)}$ / $R_{(e \to Os)}$	Cooperative $P_{Os(t)}\uparrow P_{e(t)}\uparrow$	Competitive $P_{Os(t)}\uparrow P_{e(t)}\downarrow$	Independent $P_{Os(t)}\updownarrow P_{e(t)}(0)$
Cooperative $P_{e(t)}\uparrow P_{Os(t)}\uparrow$	1	4	7
Competitive $P_{e(t)}\uparrow P_{Os(t)}\downarrow$	2	5	8
Independent $P_{e(t)}\updownarrow P_{Os(t)}(0)$	3	6	9

Table 3.2. Analysis of relationships $R_e(t)$

Cases	Interpretation
1	*Os(t)* contributes to *e(t)* and *e(t)* contributes to *Os(t)*
2	*Os(t)* contributes to *e(t)* but *e(t)* harms *Os(t)*
3	*Os(t)* contributes to *e(t)* but *e(t)* has no effect on *Os(t)*
4	*Os(t)* harms *e(t)* but *e(t)* contributes to *Os(t)*
5	*Os(t)* harms *e(t)* and *e(t)* harms *Os(t)*
6	*Os(t)* harms *e(t)* but *e(t)* has no effect on *Os(t)*
7	*Os(t)* has no effect on *e(t)* but *e(t)* contributes to *Os(t)*
8	*Os(t)* has no effect on *e(t)* but *e(t)* harms *Os(t)*
9	*Os(t)* does not affect *e(t)* and *e(t)* does not affect *Os(t)*

Similar relations can be postulated for the influence of *e(t)* on $O_s(t)$. In this case, new representations have to be derived. Therefore:

Axiom 3.9: Let us denote $R_{(e \to Os)}$ as the relations to the effect of *e(t)* on $O_s(t)$, and $R_{(Os \to e)}$ of $O_s(t)$ on *e(t)*.

The results of all possible combinations are represented in the Table 3.1 and Table 3.2 describes the results of such combinations.

Definition 3.5: Relations R_e are dynamical systems whose attributes can change over time. Examples of attributes applicable to such relations are competition and cooperation. R_e does not guarantee bilateral properties - i.e. the kinds of relations from $O_s(t)$ to *e(t)* as given by $R_{(Os \to e)}$ may differ from the ones given by $R_{(e \to}$

$_{Os}$. Moreover, definitions (3.2) and (3.3) also apply to the concept of relations R_e between O_s and e.

COGNITIVE NETWORKS OF ORGANIZATIONS

An important result derived from axiom (3.5) and definition (3.4) is the concept of networks of organizations as outlined here.

Definition 3.6: A network of *(n+1)* organizations $O_{s(i=1,...,n+1)}$ is a dynamic system denoted by $N_E(t)$ whose relations $R_{e(i=1,...,n+1)}$ change over time.

Relations between organizations and the market change over time. As an example, after the privatization of the telecommunications market in Brazil in the late of 1990's, most of the companies in that environment lost part of their customers, and since then, they had to find new solutions in order to survive (Volpe & Nobre, 2000).

SUMMARY

Chapter III introduced definitions, premises and propositions towards a theory of organizational cognition. It proposed principles about organizational cognition and thus it clearly distinguished organizational cognition from the concept of organizational learning. It outlined the concept of hierarchic levels of cognition in organizational systems and it proposed cognition as an important element of the organization. Chapter III also introduced definitions on organizations, environment along with the relations between them through cognitive perspectives. Such definitions included concepts of intelligence, cognition, autonomy and complexity for organizations. It derived a definition of environmental complexity and it proceeded by introducing propositions about the relations between organizational complexity and environmental complexity. While the former was defined as synonymous with organizational cognition, the latter was defined as synonymous with environmental uncertainty.

From such definitions it was established that:

For **Organizations**:

Proposition 3.1: The greater the degree of cognition of the organization, the greater is its chance to present intelligent behaviour.

Proposition 3.2: The greater the degree of cognition of the organization, the greater is its autonomy.

Proposition 3.3: The greater the degree of cognition of the organization, the greater is its ability to solve complex tasks.

For the **Environment**:

Proposition 3.4: The greater the level of environmental complexity, the greater is the level of environmental uncertainty.

As for the **Environment** and the **Organization**:

Theorem 3.1: The higher the degree of cognition of the organization, the lower is the relative level of environmental complexity and uncertainty that the organization confronts and needs to manage.

This chapter also introduced new characteristics and definitions of organizations. It defined organizations as distributed cognitive agents, hierarchic cognitive systems and complex systems. From such a background it was established that the level of complexity of the organization is contingent upon its degrees of cognition, intelligence and autonomy. It concluded by extending cognitive definitions of the organization to the environment; by presenting definitions of cognitive relations between the organization and the environment; and by defining cognitive networks of organizations.

Therefore, from the background of Part II we state that the theory of organizational cognition as proposed in this book plays an important task, and introduces a new perspective, in the analysis of the relations between the organization, its elements and the environment.

REFERENCES

Argyris, C., & Schön, D. A. (1978). *Organizational Learning: A Theory of Action Perspective*. Addison-Wesley.

Bagozzi, R. P., *et al* (1998). Goal-directed Emotions. *Cognition and Emotion, 12*(1), 1-26.

Bernstein, D. A. *et al* (1997). *Psychology*. Houghton Mifflin Company.

Black, M. (1937). Vagueness: An Exercise to Logical Analysis. *Philosophy of Science, 4*, 427-455.

Black, M. (1963). Reasoning with Loose Concepts. *Dialogue, 2*, 1-12.

Blanning, R. W., & King, R. K. (1996). *AI in Organizational Design, Modeling, and Control*. IEEE Computer Society Press.

Boulding, K. E. (1978). *Ecodynamics: A New Theory of Societal. Evolution*. SAGE Publications.

Bunge, M. (1979). *Treatise on Basic Philosophy. Ontology II: A World of Systems*. D. Reidel Publishing Company.

Carley, K. M., & Gasser, L. (1999). Computational Organizational Theory. In G. Weiss (Ed.), *Multiagent Systems: A Modern Approach to Distributed Artificial Intelligence* (pp. 299-330). The MIT Press.

Dierkes, M., Antal, A. B., Child, J., & Nonaka, I. (2003). *Handbook of Organizational Learning and Knowledge*. Oxford University Press.

Dubois, D., & Prade, H. (1985). A review of fuzzy set aggregation connectives. *Information Sciences, 36*, 85-121.

Dunnette, M. D., & Hough, L. M. (1992). *Handbook of Industrial and Organizational Psychology, 3*. Consulting Psychologists Press, Inc.

Easterlin, R. A. (2000). The Worldwide Standard of Living Since 1800. *The Journal of Economic Perspectives, 14*(1), 7-26.

Elding, D., Walker D. S., & Tobias A. M. (2006). Towards a Unified Model of Employee Motivation. *Strategic Change, 15*(6).

Fineman, S. (1993). *Emotions in Organizations*. SAGE Publications.

Forrester, J. W. (1961). *Industrial Dynamics*. The MIT Press.

Gibbons, R. (1998). Incentives in Organizations. *The Journal of Economic Perspectives, 12*, 115-132.

Goleman, D. (1994). *Emotional Intelligence: Why it can matter more than IQ*. Bantam Books.

Hall, A. D., & Fagen, R. E. (1956). Definition of System. In W. Buckley (Ed.), *Modern Systems Research for the Behavioral Scientist* (pp. 81-92). Aldine Publishing Company.

Iandoli, L., & Zollo, G. (2007). *Organizational Cognition and Learning: Building Systems for the Learning Organization.* Information Science Publishing. ISBN:9781599043135.

Johnson, D. G. (2000). Population, Food, and Knowledge. *The American Economic Review, 90*(1), 1-14.

Jones, C. I. (1997). On The Evolution of the World Income Distribution. *The Journal of Economic Perspectives, 11*(3), 19-36.

Keltner, D., & Gross, J. (1999). Functional Accounts of Emotions. *Cognition and Emotion, 13*(5), 467-480.

Keltner, D., & Haidt, H. (1999). Social Functions of Emotions at Four Levels of Analysis. *Cognition and Emotion, 13*(5), 505-521.

La Porte, T. R. (1975). *Organized Social Complexity: Challenges To Politics and Policy.* Princeton University Press.

Lant, T. K., & Shapira, Z. (2001). *Organizational Cognition: Computation and Interpretation.* Lawrence Erlbaum Associates. ISBN 0805833331.

March, J. G. (1994). *A Primer on Decision Making: How Decisions Happen.* The Free Press.

March, J. G., & Olsen, J. P. (1975). The Uncertainty of the Past: Organizational Learning under Ambiguity. *European Journal of Political Research,* (3), 147-171.

March, J. G., & Simon, H. A. (1958). *Organizations.* 1st Ed. John Wiley & Sons, Inc.

March, J. G., & Simon, H. A. (1993). *Organizations.* 2nd Ed. John Wiley & Sons, Inc.

Minsky, M. (1986). *The Society of Mind.* Picador.

Nobre, F. S., Volpe, R. *et al* (2000). The Role of Software Process Improvement into TQM: An Industrial Experience. *IEEE Proceedings of the International Engineering Management Conference* (pp, 29-34). Albuquerque-NM, USA.

Nobre, F. S. (2005). On Cognitive Machines in Organizations. *PhD Thesis*, 343 pages. University of Birmingham / Birmingham-UK. Birmingham Main Library. Control Number: M0266887BU.

Parsons, T. (1960). *Structure and Processes in Modern Societies.* Free Press.

Paulk, M. C. *et al* (1994). *The Capability Maturity Model: Guidelines for Improving the Software Process.* Addison Wesley Longman, Inc.

Plutchik, R. (1982). A psychoevolutionary theory of emotions. *Social Science Information, 21*, 529-553.

Prietula, M. J., Carley, K., & Gasser, M. (1998). *Simulating Organizations: Computational Models of Institutions and Groups*. AAAI Press / The MIT Press.

Pritchett, L. (1997). Divergence, Big Time. *The Journal of Economic Perspectives, 11*(3), 3-17.

Scherer, K. R. (1982). Emotion as a process: Function, origin, and regulation. *Social Science Information, 21*, 555-570.

Schmidt, F. L., & Hunter, J. E. (2000). Select Intelligence. In E.A. Locke (Ed.), *The Blackwell Handbook of Principles of Organizational Behavior* (pp.3-14). Blackwell Publishers Ltd.

Scott, W. R. (1965). Field methods in the study of organizations. In J.G. March (Ed.), *Handbook of Organizations* (pp.261-304). Rand McNally, Chicago, IL.

Senge, P. (1990). *The Fifth Discipline: The art and practice of the learning organization*. Doubleday, New York.

Simon, H. A. (1947). *Administrative Behavior: A Study of Decision-Making Processes in Administrative Organization*. New York, NY: Macmillan.

Simon, H. A. (1982b). *Models of Bounded Rationality: Behavioral Economics and Business Organization, 2*. The MIT Press.

Simon, H. A. (1997a). *Models of Bounded Rationality: Empirically Grounded Economic Reason, 3*. The MIT Press.

Simon, H. A. (1997b). *Administrative Behavior: A Study of Decision-Making Processes in Administrative Organizations*. The Free Press.

World Bank (2003). *The Little Data Book*. World Bank. ISBN 0-8213-5426-4.

Zadeh, L. A. (1965). Fuzzy Sets. *Information and Control, 8*, 338-353.

Zadeh, L. A. (1973). Outline of a New Approach to the Analysis of Complex Systems and Decision Process. *IEEE Transactions on Systems, Man, and Cybernetics, 3*(1), 28-44.

Zadeh, L. A. (1996a). Fuzzy Logic = Computing with Words. *IEEE Transactions on Fuzzy Systems*, 4(2), 103-111.

Zadeh, L. A. (1999). From Computing with Numbers to Computing with Words – From Manipulation of Measurements to Manipulation of Perceptions. *IEEE Transactions on Circuits and Systems, 45*(1), 105-119.

Zadeh, L. A. (2001). A New Direction in AI: Toward a Computational Theory of Perceptions. *AI Magazine, Spring*, 73-84.

ENDNOTES

[1]   In resume, knowledge Management subsumes a range of practices used by organisations to identify, create, represent, and distribute knowledge for reuse, awareness and learning.

[2]   Shortly speaking, organizational learning is a field within organizational theory that studies learning and adaptive models for organizations.

[3]   Emotional process is synonymous with emotion when viewed as a process, rather than simple states (Scherer, K. R. 1982). One assumes that feeling represents affective and emotional states such as happiness, sadness, anxiety, guilt, fear, jealous, angry, love, etc.

[4]   Learning is the process of making changes in the working of our mind, behaviour and understanding through experience (Bernstein *et al*, 1997; and Minsky, 1986).

[5]   We also understand that organizations may emerge from informal processes (with no design procedures), but if they want to increase their chance for survival and development, they will need to be reviewed through the process of organization design.

[6]   The word satisfice was coined by Herbert Simon (March & Simon, 1958). In resume, satisficing is a decision-making strategy which attempts to meet criteria for adequacy, rather than to identify an optimal solution.

[7]   A tutorial on strategic reward systems is found in (Dunnette & Hough, 1992: 1009-1055).

[8]   A Unified Model of Employee Motivation is presented in (Elding D., Walker D. & Tobias A., 2006).

[9]   Processes of this kind can also involve - to name but a few of them - process improvement models like CMM (Paulk *et al*, 1994), quality procedures like ISO 9000 and 14000, principles of management and production like just-in-time and lean-production, intranet and the knowledge to be shared within the organization, policies for recruiting and hiring agents (participants), procedures for evaluating agents and performance, etc.

[10]   A dynamic system has time-varying interactions (Forrester, 1961). This book views systems as defined in (Bunge, 1987; and Hall & Fagen, 1956). Additionally, it considers the organization as a system with memory - i.e. given the

state of an organization O_s at a discrete time k, then it is assumed that $O_s(k+1) = O_s(k) + O_s(k-1)$.

[11] Fuzzy sets are classes whose boundaries are not clearly defined and hence the transition from membership to non-membership of their elements is gradual rather than abrupt. Examples include the classes of short and tall, young and old, black and white, and poor and rich people. Therefore, the elements v of a fuzzy set A assume degrees of membership $\mu_A(v)$ in A whose values can vary gradually from 0 to 1, in a discrete or continuous way, i.e. $A = \{v \mid \mu_A(v) \in [0,1], v \in V\}$, where V denotes the universe of v. In its broader sense, fuzzy sets theory provides a mathematical background for the representation of information in the approaches to fuzzy logic, computing with words and perceptions (Zadeh, 1973, 1996a, 1999, and 2001).

Section III
Cognitive Machines

Humans have a remarkable capability to perform a wide variety of physical and mental tasks without any measurements and any computations. Familiar examples are parking a car, driving in city traffic, playing golf, cooking a meal, and summarizing a story. In performing such tasks, humans use perceptions of time, direction, speed, shape, possibility, likelihood, truth, and other attributes of physical and mental objects. (Zadeh, L.A. 2001, p.73).

Section III introduces a perspective on cognitive machines whose initial lines of contribution were first touched on (Nobre, 2005; Nobre and Steiner, 2003a and 2003b; and Nobre, 2003e). It includes rationale and motivations for their development, the proposal of concepts and principles about them, and the design of a class of them. Part III comprises Chapters IV, V, and VI and its background is largely influenced by:

a.   Theories of evolutionary and cognitive psychology (Heyes & Huber, 2000; and Simon, 1983); information-processing systems, perception and cognition (Barsalou, 1999; Bernstein et al, 1997; Lefrançois, 1995; Newell & Simon, 1972; and Reed, 1988).
b.   Theories of fuzzy sets (Zadeh, 1965), fuzzy logic (Zadeh, 1973), computing with words (Zadeh, 1996a and 1999) and computation of perceptions[1] (Zadeh, 2001).

In summary, Chapter IV outlines some rationale for cognitive machines by connecting theories of bounded rationality of Herbert Simon with theories of fuzzy systems of Lotfi Zadeh in order to justify advantages of the participation of cognitive machines in organizations.

Chapter V proposes concepts and principles for cognitive machines.

Chapter VI introduces the design of cognitive machines. These machines and their models were chosen in order to increase the degree of cognition of the organization and thus to improve the ability of the organization to perform cognitive tasks such as to make decisions.

Chapter IV
Rationale for
Cognitive Machines

INTRODUCTION

This chapter outlines rationale for cognitive machines. It connects theories of bounded rationality of Herbert Simon with theories of fuzzy systems of Lotfi Zadeh in order to justify advantages of the participation of cognitive machines in organizations. The connections are derived by explaining why cognitive machines can extend limits of knowledge (lack of information) and limits of information processing and management (lack of cognition and computational capacity) of humans when participating in organizations.

UNIFICATION OF ORGANIZATIONAL AND TECHNOLOGICAL THEORIES

The Herbert Simon and Lotfi Zadeh's Theories

This book was influenced by the scientific work of Herbert A. Simon and Lotfi A. Zadeh developed in the period between the middle and the end of the 20th century. Despite having no direct relation to each other, they provided the literature with theories which under the perspective of this research complement each other by contributing important results to the fields of artificial intelligence, cognition, organizations and systems theory[2]. Such a background may be regarded as the first contribution of this investigation – i.e. to connect theories and results of these two brilliant researchers.

Bounded Rationality Theory

Simon was awarded in 1978 with the Nobel Prize in Economics. He received his PhD in Political Science from The University of Chicago in 1943 and among his prominent scientific contributions is the theory of administrative behaviour which comprises the concept of bounded rationality (Simon, 1982a, 1982b, 1997a and 1997b).

The theory of bounded rationality as proposed by Simon represents an important framework for the analysis of human behaviour, cognition and decision processes in organizations. It can also be viewed as a model of cognition and economic decision-making processes which considers the limits of knowledge and computational capacity of humans. However, Simon's theory of bounded rationality was missing alternative mathematical and computational tools which could be used to encapsulate the particularities of his model of human cognition and decision processes in a proper way. This was an important requirement for the development of the field of artificial intelligence – i.e. the need of alternative mathematical and computational approaches for the analysis, design and engineering of systems (machines) whose processes and behaviour are metaphors for, and models of, human cognition and intelligence.

Despite having important advancements since its inception in the early fifties, artificial intelligence has found serious limitations to progress in those areas where problems require approximate (fuzzy) rather than precise (crisp) formulation (Zadeh, 2001). Such areas need alternative methodologies for the representation and manipulation of natural concepts[3] which are characterized by fuzzy boundaries (Nobre, 2005).

Fuzzy Systems Theory

Zadeh received his PhD in Electrical Engineering from The University of Columbia in 1949 and among his prominent scientific contributions are the theories of fuzzy systems (Zadeh, 1965 and 1973), computing with words (Zadeh, 1996a) and computation of perceptions (Zadeh, 1999).

The theory of fuzzy systems represents an important framework with mathematical and computational background for the analysis of complex systems and decision processes – where complex systems is synonymous with systems (such as organizations) whose behaviour is preponderantly influenced by human emotion, cognition and social networks. The theories of computing with words and computation of perceptions are derivations of fuzzy systems and they represent approaches with the necessary elements to encapsulate the particularities of the Simon's model of bounded rationality. These particularities are mainly concerned with limitation of knowledge and computational capacity.

Connection Between the Theories

- **Limitation of knowledge:** Limitation of knowledge is synonymous with lack of information and also with the kind of uncertainty which pervades most of the concepts manipulated by humans. These concepts are called natural concepts and they are characterized by fuzzy boundaries (Bernstein et al, 1997). Moreover, natural concepts form relations in propositions, and clusters of propositions form mental models[4]. In such a way, Zadeh's theories provide the necessary mathematical and computational background for the representation of natural concepts and mental models through complex symbols described by words and sentences of natural language.
- **Limitation of computational capacity:** Limitation of computational capacity is synonymous with the bounded ability of the human brain to resolve details and to solve problems with constraints such as time and cost. Such a limitation requires from humans the search for approximate solutions and satisfactory results rather than precise and optimal outcomes. In such a way, Zadeh's theories provide appropriate elements of approximate reasoning and economic decision-making which are necessary for the manipulation of natural concepts and mental models.

Core Rationale

The connection of these theories forms the core and the "heart" to empower the design of cognitive machines, and also to understand the roles of these machines in organizations. Therefore, we can state that:

Definition 4.1: Cognitive machines are necessary when we need to extend the human boundaries of computational capacity along with knowledge and uncertainty management to more advanced models of cognition or information processing.

Results of the Unification

This book exploits results of the unification of these theories of these two researchers. It put separate pieces of these theories together in order to:

a. Bring the discipline of fuzzy systems and its derivatives (computing with words and computation of perceptions) closer to cognition, resulting in the design of cognitive machines.
b. Investigate the extension the human boundaries of computational capacity along with knowledge and uncertainty management to more advance models of cognition and information processing.
c. Relate cognitive machines with organizations.
d. Introduce cognitive machines as participants in the organization.
e. Use cognitive machines in conflict resolution (i.e. to solve intra-individual and group dysfunctional conflicts).
f. Analyze the implications of cognitive machines for future organizations.

SUMMARY

Chapter IV introduced rationale for cognitive machines. It established important connections between theories of bounded rationality of Herbert Simon and theories of fuzzy systems of Lotfi Zadeh in order to justify advantages of the participation of cognitive machines in organizations. Through such connections we could explain why cognitive machines can extend limits of knowledge (lack of information) and limits of information processing (lack of cognition and computational capacity) of humans when participating in organizations.

Therefore, it was stated that:

Definition 4.1: Cognitive machines are necessary when we need to extend the human boundaries of computational capacity along with knowledge and uncertainty management to more advanced models of cognition or information processing.

REFERENCES

Bernstein, D. A. et al (1997). Psychology. Houghton Mifflin Company.

Nobre, F. S., & Steiner, S. J. (2003a). Perspectives on Organizational Systems: Towards a Unified Theory. Doctoral Consortium on Cognitive Science at the ICCM 2003. Bamberg-Germany, April 09th 2003.

Nobre, F. S., & Steiner, S. J. (2003b). Beyond Bounded Rationality: Towards Economic Decision-Making Machines. Conference on Dynamical Systems Approaches to Cognitive and Consciousness. Proceeding: 31. Switzerland.

Nobre, F. S. (2003e, July). Beyond Bounded-Rationality - Towards Economic Decision-Making Machines. Seminar presented for the Artificial Intelligence Research Group of the Department of Computer Sciences in the Humboldt University of Berlin. Johann von Newmann-Haus, Berlin.

Nobre, F. S. (2005). On Cognitive Machines in Organizations. PhD Thesis, 343 pages. University of Birmingham / Birmingham-UK. Birmingham Main Library. Control Number: M0266887BU.

Reed, S. K. (1988). Cognition: Theory and Applications. 2nd Ed. Brooks-Cole Publishing Company.

Simon, H. A. (1982a). Models of Bounded Rationality: Economic Analysis and Public Policy, 1. The MIT Press.

Simon, H. A. (1982b). Models of Bounded Rationality: Behavioral Economics and Business Organization, 2. The MIT Press.

Simon, H. A. (1997a). Models of Bounded Rationality: Empirically Grounded Economic Reason, 3. The MIT Press.

Simon, H. A. (1997b). Administrative Behavior: A Study of Decision-Making Processes in Administrative Organizations. The Free Press.

Wikipedia. The Free Encyclopaedia. From http://en.wikipedia.org

Zadeh, L. A. (1962). From Circuit Theory to System Theory. Proceedings of the IRE, 50: 856-865.

Zadeh, L. A. (1965). Fuzzy Sets. Information and Control, 8, 338-353.

Zadeh, L. A. (1973). Outline of a New Approach to the Analysis of Complex Systems and Decision Process. IEEE Transactions on Systems, Man, and Cybernetics, 3(1), 28-44.

Zadeh, L. A. (1994). Soft Computing and Fuzzy Logic. IEEE Software, November, 48-56.

Zadeh, L. A. 1996a). Fuzzy Logic = Computing with Words. IEEE Transactions on Fuzzy Systems, 4(2), 103-111.

Zadeh, L. A. (1997). The Roles of Fuzzy Logic and Soft Computing in the Conception, Design and Development of Intelligent Systems. In Nwana and Azarmi (Ed.), Software Agents and Soft Computing: Towards Enhancing Machine Intelligence (pp. 183-190). Springer.

Zadeh, L. A. (1999). From Computing with Numbers to Computing with Words – From Manipulation of Measurements to Manipulation of Perceptions. IEEE Transactions on Circuits and Systems, 45(1), 105-119.

Zadeh, L. A. (2001). A New Direction in AI: Toward a Computational Theory of Perceptions. AI Magazine. Spring, 73-84.

ENDNOTES

[1]   In this book, we understand perception as a process. Perception is the process through which sensations (or sensory information) are interpreted; by using knowledge and understanding of the environment, so that they become meaningful experiences (Bernstein, et al 1997). We also understand that, in his work on a computational theory of perceptions (Zadeh, 2001), Zadeh uses the term "perceptions" with the meaning of a "percept" or a set of "percepts", where a percept represents a class of objects with fuzzy boundaries.

[2]   Simon and Zadeh played a counterpart task in the literature by proclaiming the lack of qualitative and quantitative approaches for coping with complex problems (where human behaviour, emotions and cognition are key factors). In his theory of bounded rationality, Simon called for new approaches which could extend the methods of decision analysis used by economists to a more realistic scenario on human decision-making (Simon, 1982b and 1997a). In his work about systems theory, Zadeh pointed out the need for new mathematics in order to narrow the gap of understanding between the analysis of non-living and living systems (Zadeh, 1962). In this book, we advocate that such a new approach (as proclaimed by bounded rationality and general systems theorists) emerged with the advent of fuzzy systems theory (Zadeh, 1965 and 1973) and its derivatives on computing with words and perceptions (Zadeh, 1996a, 1999 and 2001) along with soft computing (Zadeh, 1994 and 1997).

[3]   Concepts are categories of physical and abstract objects with common properties like the attributes of colour (red, yellow, green, etc), size (small, medium, large, etc), etc. A concept may be regarded as a percept recognized and classified into a category.

[4]   Mental models are descriptions or explanation in someone's mind for how something works in the real world. It is a kind of internal symbol or representation of external reality, hypothesized to play a major role in cognition and decision-making processes (Wikipedia's online dictionary).

Chapter V
Principles of
Cognitive Machines

INTRODUCTION

This chapter presents principles of cognitive machines. It presents definitions of intelligence, cognition, autonomy, and complexity for machines. It proposes a definition of cognitive machines and it presents theories and technologies behind cognitive machines, where the technologies are selected according to some criteria.

HUMANS, COGNITION AND MACHINES

Evolution of Cognition

Organisms of the ecological system have evolved towards the improvement of their abilities and mechanisms for fitness and adaptation in the environment. Among such organisms, human beings are the species that has found the highest probability to survive, to reproduce and to continue evolving and developing.

Such a predominance of humans is a particular privilege provided by the evolution of their brain, emotional and cognitive processes (Heyes & Huber, 2000; and Simon, 1983). Among the results of such a continuous evolutionary path are their abilities to learn, to search information and to organize knowledge, to make decisions and to solve problems. Humans adapt to the environment, but they also change the environment to their own needs. Humans have cultivated agriculture, improved their immunology system, modified natural resources in order to explore energy, created organizations and cities, and developed transport and telecommunications systems, designed machines which mimic their own behaviour, and so on. In such a way, humans have been transferring some of their abilities to systems, and in particular to machines.

Designing Cognition: From Humans to Machines

Perhaps, cognition is the most precious and difficult ability that humans can transfer to artificial (man-made) systems. The design of cognitive processes requires from humans the understanding of their own mind and the implementation of these processes into machines depends on the availability and development of appropriate technologies. This book advocates that scientists still have much research to do in order to engineer cognitive machines which mimic a complex model of the human mind, but it also considers that they have had enough advancement in such a field in order to form a body of knowledge on the engineering of machines with some cognitive abilities (Haikonen, 2003; Luger & Stubblefield, 1998; Newell, 1990; and Zadeh, 2001). Moreover, this book assumes that the birth of the discipline of artificial intelligence in the 1950's was the mark for the beginning of what is called the design of cognitive machines.

However, the terms artificial intelligence and machine intelligence are not used in this book for one main reason:

- Intelligence and intelligent behaviour depends on cognition and emotion. Therefore, and firstly, we should concern the design of cognitive processes in order to provide machines with some intelligent behaviour. Machines with cognitive processes have greater probability to behave intelligently than any other machine.

Figures 5.1 and 5.2 illustrate two different strategies to the design of machines with intelligent behaviour and cognition respectively. The strategy illustrated in the Figure 5.2 is the one adopted in this book.

DEFINITIONS OF MACHINE INTELLIGENCE, COGNITION, AUTONOMY AND COMPLEXITY

The concepts proposed here are derived from the previous definitions of organizational intelligence, cognition, autonomy and complexity.

Figure 5.1. Design strategy with focus on machine intelligence and intelligent behaviour

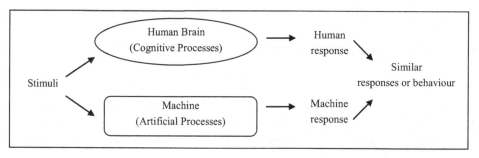

Figure 5.2. Design strategy with focus on machine cognition

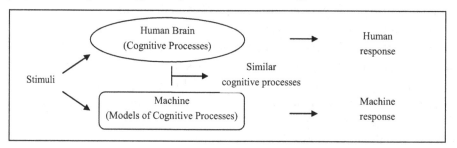

Machine Intelligence

Machine intelligence (Folgel, 2000; and Furukawa *et al*, 1994) and learning (Mitchell, 1997) are all branches of artificial intelligence research (Luger & Stubblefield, 1998). Shortly speaking, machine intelligence is a discipline for the design of machines in order to provide them with intelligent behaviour.

The idea of measures of Machine Intelligence Quotient (MIQ) was touched upon in the work of Zadeh (1996b and 1997). Such an idea is quite reasonable since intelligence is a matter of degree which may be measured in a continuous scale. Moreover, as advocated in the literature, the methodologies of Soft Computing can be used in the analysis and design of high Machine Intelligence Quotient (MIQ) systems (Zadeh, 1994 and 1997) - where MIQ can be defined as a measure of intelligence applied to machines and systems. In such a way, MIQ engineering provides machines with some degrees of intelligence. The definition of MIQ and the criteria and processes to measure it are tasks that are in their beginning of developments, but one primary distinction between rational human intelligence and MIQ is that the first is more or less constant, whereas MIQ changes with time and it is machine-specific (Zadeh, 1997).

However, rather than using the term intelligent machines, this book adopts cognitive machines. The reason for such a new nomination is conceptual. Whether machines can have intelligence or intelligent behaviour depends upon how intelligence or intelligent behaviour is defined. Such a definition requires criteria of intelligence which may be accepted or not according to the researcher's perspective and their academic background.

Machine Cognition

Briefly, machine cognition is one of the disciplines, among others such as artificial intelligence and cognitive sciences, which can be used in the design of cognitive machines. Such machines have a structure which is synonymous with their anatomy, and processes which are synonymous with their physiology and functioning. If the machine structure plays a similar role to the human brain and body (but not necessarily having the same form), the machine processes play a similar role to the human cognitions.

Therefore, the relationship between machine cognition and intelligence can be defined by:

Proposition 5.1: The greater the degree of cognition of the machine, the greater is its chance to exhibit intelligent behaviour.

Machine Autonomy

This book defines machine autonomy similarly to the autonomy of an organism. Hence:

Proposition 5.2: The greater the degree of cognition of the machine, the greater is its autonomy.

Machine Complexity

This book regards the level of complexity of a machine as contingent upon its degree of cognition. Therefore:

Proposition 5.3: The greater the degree of cognition of the machine, the greater is its ability to solve complex tasks.

It is important to observe that organizational complexity and machine complexity are defined as contingent upon cognition. Therefore, the complexity of organizations and machines are synonymous with their cognitions which are processes used to solve complex tasks.

DEFINITION OF COGNITIVE MACHINES

Definition 5.1: Cognitive machines are agents whose processes of functioning are mainly inspired by human cognition. Therefore, they have great possibilities to present intelligent behaviour.

CONTINGENCY FOR COGNITIVE MACHINES

Similarly to the principles of the school of contingency theory for organizations, we can state that cognitive machines are contingent upon the environment. Therefore, they are designed to embody the structure and the processes that most fit them in the environment.

Their structure has not to be a physical body, nor to have any relation or similarity to the anatomy of humans, apart from some robots, but their processes (physiology) are metaphors for human cognition.

We believe, envisage and develop throughout the book the perspective that advancements in cognitive machines will provide them with capabilities to participate in the levels and layers of the whole organization and they mostly will be embodied in the form of software agents.

THEORIES AND TECHNOLOGIES BEHIND COGNITIVE MACHINES

The design of cognitive machines comprises theories and models of cognition along with technologies to engineer them. This section overviews the theories and technologies which support the model of cognitive machines as concerned throughout this book.

Information Processing Theory: A Cognitive Approach

The literature about cognitive psychology has presented different and unified theories on cognition (Newell, 1990), and also theories on the relationship between cognition and perception (Barsalou, 1999). Information-processing theory is the approach selected to the study and design of cognitive processes in this book. This approach uses the computer as a metaphor (or analogy) to simulate and to understand human thinking and processes such as decision-making and problem-solving (Newell & Simon, 1972; Reed, 1988; and Reisberg, 1997). Therefore, this book uses such an approach as a framework to the design of cognitive machines.

The Scope of Design

According to the literature, processes of cognition include sensing and perceiving, pattern recognition, attention, memory, concept formation and attainment, categorization, verbal and spatial knowledge, representation and organization of knowledge, language, thought, comprehension, problem-solving and decision-making (Reed, 1988; and Lefrançois, 1995).

However, this chapter focuses on cognitive processes of:

a. Perception, attention and concept identification;
b. Short-term and long-term memory;
c. Representation and organization of knowledge via categorization;
d. And decision-making.

Therefore, it concentrates efforts in the design of a framework of machines with the cognitive abilities of (a), (b), (c) and (d), and most important, with flexibility and capability to extend their functions to, and to incorporate into their structure, processes of learning. According to this book, these machines are deliberately designed to participate in organizations. They are likely to contribute by reducing or solving intra-individual and group dysfunctional conflicts in organizations.

On Machine Learning and Problem-Solving

Processes of learning and problem-solving are left for further research. However, the disciplines of neural computation (Hertz, 1991), soft computing (Zadeh, 1994), adaptive fuzzy systems (Wang, 1994), evolutionary computation and genetic algorithms (Bäck, *et al*, 2000; and Fogel, 2000), along with genetic programming (Koza, 1992) have demonstrated in the literature to be powerful tools which can aggregate abilities of learning and problem-solving to the cognitive machine framework designed in this chapter.

Machines are Amodal-Symbolic-Processing Systems

Theories of cognition and perception can be classified into modal and amodal-symbol systems (Barsalou, 1999).

- **Modal-Symbol Systems:** In modal-symbol systems, the perceptual states which arise in sensory-motor systems are extracted and selected via the process of attention, and later stored in memory[1] to function as symbols. The structure of these symbols is analogically related to the perceptual states which produced them. On this view, perception and cognition are interdependent processes and they share common parts.
- **Amodal-Symbol Systems:** In amodal-symbol systems, perceptual states are translated or codified into a new representational system of symbols. As a consequence, the internal structure of these symbols is unrelated or only linked arbitrarily to the perceptual states that produced them.

The cognitive machines as considered in this book (like computers) operate as amodal-symbol systems. They require artificial transducers to map perceptual states (e.g. the temperature of a room) to a new base of symbols (which may be represented by numbers like 25°C, words like *warm* and sentences of natural language like *warm but not too warm*).

Figures 5.3 and 5.4 illustrate how modal and amodal-symbol systems function when perceptual states about a car arise in sensory-motor systems. While the perceptual states $(s_{i=1,...,M})$ in the modal-symbol system are mapped to perceptual symbols $(p_{i=1,...,M})$ of analogue internal structure, these same states $(s_{i=1,...,M})$ are mapped to, and thus translated into, new representational structures $(y_{i=1,...,N})$ of functional symbolic systems (Newell and Simon, 1972; and Minsky, 1986). The output arrows at the right side of both figures point out to the activation of new cognitive functions such as memory and decision-making.

Technological Scope of Cognitive Machines

In summary, this book considers classes machines which operate based on, but are not limited to, one or more principles among electrical, mechanical, analogue, digital, optical, biological, hybrid and artificial cognitive-neural signals and processes. Secondly, such machines are made of technologies of computers, communication networks and software programs. Thirdly and most importantly, this book assumes that if these machines are to pursue high degrees of cognition, then they should be governed by the disciplines of fuzzy systems (Klir & Folger, 1988; Klir & Yuan, 1996; Wang, 1994; and Zadeh, 1973), computing with words and computation of perceptions (Zadeh, 1996a, 1999, and 2001) along with soft computing (Zadeh, 1994 and 1997). While the former technologies are synonymous with the anatomy or structure of the machines, the latter technologies (i.e. the disciplines) are synonymous with their physiology, functioning and cognitive processes.

Figure 5.3. Modal-symbol systems

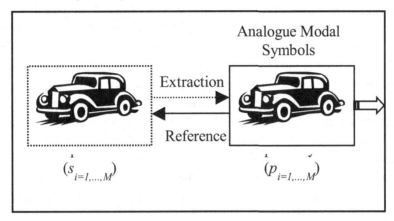

Figure 5.4. Amodal-symbol systems

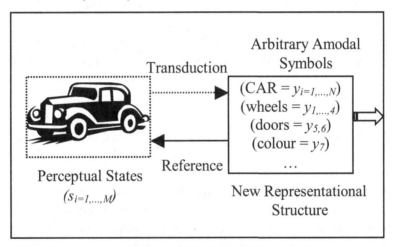

Principal attention is given to the disciplines of fuzzy systems (FS), computing with words (CW) and computation theory of perceptions (CTP). The criteria used to select these disciplines are based on the following pillars (Nobre, 2005):

i.   Firstly, humans have a distinguished ability to perform diversified physical and mental tasks without any manipulation of measurements (Zadeh, 2001) - such as driving in city traffic and summarizing a speech for instance. When performing such tasks, humans use their ability to perceive objects and sounds, to form concepts and to manipulate them. Most of the concepts humans form and reason with have fuzzy boundaries (Bernstein, *et al* 1997; Lefrancois, 1995; and Reed 1988) - e.g. the attributes of colour like *green* and *blue*; the attributes of price like *cheap* and *expensive*; etc. These concepts are often described by words, propositions and sentences of natural language. In such a way, the disciplines of FS, CW and CTP provide the necessary principles to represent percepts and thus concepts through complex symbols in the form of words, propositions and sentences of natural language. Additionally, they also provide mechanisms to manipulate such symbols.

ii.   Secondly, activities of decision-making and general tasks in organizations involve not only numerical information, but also perceptions and emotions, and thus the identification and manipulation of concepts which have fuzzy boundaries – examples of such tasks include the design of organizations, management and recruitment of people, and most of the activities within the technical, managerial, institutional and worldwide levels of analysis of the organization.

iii. Thirdly, the theories and mechanisms of computing with words and computation of perceptions provide a background to the design of machines with the ability to process more complex symbols than other approaches (Zadeh, 1999 and 2001). Therefore, according to the theory of levels of processing in cognition (Red, 1988), such machines can operate at high levels of symbolic processing, and thus they can find high degrees of cognition.

iv.   Fourthly, regarding the discipline of fuzzy systems, it emerged as a new approach to the analysis of complex and decision-making processes such as those found in social systems; and also to provide a bridge between the analysis of man-made (like machines) and living systems (like humans) (Zadeh, 1962, 1965, and 1973).

v.   Fifthly, they are methodologies which complement and extend the approaches to crisp computation to more complex applications where the available information is too imprecise to justify the use of numbers. Moreover, such methodologies are necessary when there is a tolerance for imprecision which can be exploited to achieve tractability, robustness, low solution cost and better rapport with reality (Zadeh, 1999).

vi.   Sixthly, they were developed for the analysis and design of systems which pursue high degrees of machine intelligence quotient (Zadeh, 1996b and 1997).

vii. Lastly, such disciplines have found maturation supported by theories and applications (Pedrycz & Gomide, 1998 and 2007; and Nobre, 2003c).

SUMMARY

Chapter V presented principles of cognitive machines. It introduced definitions of intelligence, cognition, autonomy and complexity for machines. It proposed a definition of cognitive machines and it presented theories and technologies behind cognitive machines, where the technologies were selected according to some criteria.

It was proposed that:

For **Cognitive Machines**:

Definition 5.1: Cognitive machines are agents whose processes of functioning are mainly inspired by human cognition. Therefore, they have great possibilities to present intelligent behaviour.

Proposition 5.1: The greater the degree of cognition of the machine, the greater is its chance to present intelligent behaviour.

Proposition 5.2: The greater the degree of cognition of the machine, the greater is its autonomy.

Proposition 5.3: The greater the degree of cognition of the machine, the greater is its ability to solve complex tasks.

REFERENCES

Bäck, T., Fogel, D. B., & Michalewicz, Z. (2000). *Evolutionary Computation: Part I and II.* Institute of Physics Publishing.

Barsalou, L.W. (1999). Perceptual symbol systems. *Behavioral and Brain Science, 22,* 577-660.

Bernstein, D. A. *et al* (1997). *Psychology.* Houghton Mifflin Company.

Fogel, D. B. (2000). *Evolutionary computation: toward a new philosophy of machine intelligence.* IEEE Press.

Furukawa, K., Michie, D., & Muggleton, S. (1994). *Machine Intelligence: Machine Intelligence and Inductive Learning,* (13). Oxford University Press.

Haikonen, P. O. (2003). *The Cognitive Approach to Conscious Machines.* Imprint Academic.

Halmos, P. R. (1960). *Naive Set Theory.* D. Van Nostrand. New Jersey.

Hertz, J., Palmer, R., & Krogh, A. (1991). *Introduction to the Theory of Neural Computation*. Westview Press.

Heyes, C., & Huber, L. (2000). *The Evolution of Cognition*. The MIT Press.

Klir, G. J., & Folger, T. A. (1988). *Fuzzy Sets, Uncertainty, and Information*. Englewood Cliffs, N.J: Prentice Hall.

Klir, G. J., & Yuan, B. (1996). *Fuzzy Sets, Fuzzy Logic, and Fuzzy Systems: Selected Papers by Lotfi A. Zadeh - Advances in Fuzzy Systems - Applications and Theory*, 6. World Scientific Pub Co Inc.

Koza, J. R. (1992). *Genetic Programming: On the programming of computers by means of natural selection*. The MIT Press.

Lefrançoies, G. (1995). *Theories of Human Learning*. Brooks Cole Publishing Company.

Luger, G. F., & Stubblefield, W. A. (1998). *Artificial Intelligence: Structures and Strategies for Complex Problem Solving*. The Benjamin/Cummings Publishing Company, Inc.

Minsky, M. (1986). *The Society of Mind*. Picador.

Mitchell, T. M. (1997). *Machine Learning*. The McGraw-Hill Companies, Inc.

Newell, A. (1990). *Unified Theories of Cognition*. Harvard University.

Newell, A., & Simon, H. A. (1972). *Human Problem Solving*. Prentice-Hall.

Nobre, F. S. (2003c, January). *Fuzzy Systems*. Seminar presented for the Artificial Intelligence Research Group of the Department of Computer Sciences in the Humboldt University of Berlin. Johann von Newmann-Haus, Berlin.

Nobre, F. S. (2005). On Cognitive Machines in Organizations. *PhD Thesis*, 343 pages. University of Birmingham / Birmingham-UK. Birmingham Main Library. Control Number: M0266887BU.

Reed, S. K. (1988). *Cognition: Theory and Applications*. 2nd Ed. Brooks-Cole Publishing Company.

Reisberg, D. (1997). *Cognition: Exploring the Science of the Mind*. W.W. Norton & Company.

Simon, H. A. (1983). *Reason in Human Affairs*. Stanford University Press.

Wang, L. (1994). *Adaptive Fuzzy Systems and Control: Design and Stability Analysis*. PTR Prentice-Hall.

Zadeh, L. A. (1962). From Circuit Theory to System Theory. *Proceedings of the IRE, 50,* 856-865.

Zadeh, L. A. (1965). Fuzzy Sets. *Information and Control, 8,* 338-353.

Zadeh, L. A. (1973). Outline of a New Approach to the Analysis of Complex Systems and Decision Process. *IEEE Transactions on Systems, Man, and Cybernetics, 3*(1), 28-44.

Zadeh, L. A. (1975). The concept of a linguistic variable and its application to approximate reasoning: part I and II. In R.R. Yager *et al* (Ed.). (1987), *Fuzzy Sets and their Applications: Selected Papers by L.A. Zadeh* (pp. 219-327). John & Sons.

Zadeh, L. A. (1976). The concept of a linguistic variable and its application to approximate reasoning: part III. *Fuzzy Sets and their Applications: Selected Papers by L.A. Zadeh.* Ed. by Yager, R.R. et al. (1987): 329-366. John & Sons.

Zadeh, L. A. (1988). Fuzzy Logic. *IEEE Computer, April,* 83-92.

Zadeh, L. A. (1994). Soft Computing and Fuzzy Logic. *IEEE Software, November*: 48-56.

Zadeh, L. A. (1996a). Fuzzy Logic = Computing with Words. *IEEE Transactions on Fuzzy Systems, 4*(2), 103-111.

Zadeh, L. A. (1996b). The Evolution of Systems Analysis and Control: A Personal Perspective. *IEEE Control Systems, June,* 95-98.

Zadeh, L. A. (1997). The Roles of Fuzzy Logic and Soft Computing in the Conception, Design and Development of Intelligent Systems. In Nwana and Azarmi (Ed.), *Software Agents and Soft Computing: Towards Enhancing Machine Intelligence* (pp. 183-190). Springer.

Zadeh, L. A. (1999). From Computing with Numbers to Computing with Words – From Manipulation of Measurements to Manipulation of Perceptions. *IEEE Transactions on Circuits and Systems, 45*(1), 105-119.

Zadeh, L. A. (2001). A New Direction in AI: Toward a Computational Theory of Perceptions. *AI Magazine. Spring,* 73-84.

ENDNOTE

[1]   Memory stores are classified in sensory store (SS), short-term memory (STM) and long-term memory (LTM). SS provides a brief storage for information in its original sensory form and it extends the amount of time that a person has to recognize a pattern. STM is limited in both the amount of information it can hold (capacity) and the length of time it can hold the information (duration). LTM has neither of the two limitations of STM. STM holds a relation to LTM since it combines information that is retrieved from LTM with information that arrives from the environment (Reed, 1998).

Chapter VI
Design of
Cognitive Machines

INTRODUCTION

This chapter is concerned with the design of cognitive machines. These machines and their models were chosen in order to increase and to improve:

i. The degree of cognition of the organization,
ii. the capability of the organization for information processing and management, and
iii. the ability of the organization to make decisions.

Therefore Chapter VI introduces the design of cognitive machines with capabilities to carry out complex cognitive tasks in organizations - and in particular the task of decision-making which involves representation and organization of knowledge via concept identification and categorization along with the manipulation of perceptions (or percepts)[1], concepts[2], and mental models[3]. The ability of these machines to manipulate a percept provides them with higher levels of information-processing than other symbolic-processing machines[4]; and according to the theory of levels of processing in cognition (Reed, 1988), these machines can mimic (even through simple models) cognitive processes of humans (Nobre, 2005). Percepts and thus concepts[5] (along with mental models) are described by words, propositions and sentences of natural language (Zadeh, 2001).

A GENERAL STRUCTURE OF INFORMATION-PROCESSING MACHINES

An outline of the cognitive machine structure is sketched in the Figure 6.1. This structure is adapted from the information-processing system approach presented in (Bernstein, *et al* 1997; and Newell and Simon, 1972). In summary, such machines operate like:

1.   Stimuli from the environment are modified and transformed by the sensory system into neural activity signals. These signals are called sensations.

2.   The perceptual system maps such sensations into new structures and representations of perceptual amodal-symbols. Viewed as a process, perception organizes sensations into patterns, and furthermore, it uses knowledge stored in memory to recognize those patterns. It gives meaning to sensations through perceptions of depth, distance, motion, light, etc.

3.   The processor receives and manipulates perceptual amodal-symbols. It consists of a process of reasoning which uses the knowledge stored in memory to make decisions. Its output decisions are represented by the same structure of amodal-symbols given by the perception block.

4.   The memory stores knowledge in the form of mental models described by concepts, categories and clusters of propositions.

5.   The response block transforms amodal-symbols to a new structure compatible with the environment requirements. This block can also include task execution and actuation on the environment.

6.   The process of attention acts on the perception, decision-making and response processes. Attention provides perception with the selection of specific parts of stimuli and sensations when recognizing patterns and storing them into memory for further manipulation in decision-making and response.

A FRAMEWORK OF COGNITIVE MACHINES

This subsection introduces a framework of cognitive machines, and most importantly, it contributes by relating the functioning of such a framework with the processes of cognition.

This framework is tailored from the general structure of the information-processing system illustrated in the Figure 6.1. Its processes and functioning are designed according to the principles of fuzzy logic and fuzzy control (Lee, C.C. 1990; Mamdani, 1974; Nobre, 1997; Wang, 1994; and Zadeh, 1968 and 1973), computing with words (Zadeh, 1996a) and computation of perceptions (Zadeh, 1999 and 2001). Such

Figure 6.1. Structure of the cognitive machine as an information-processing system

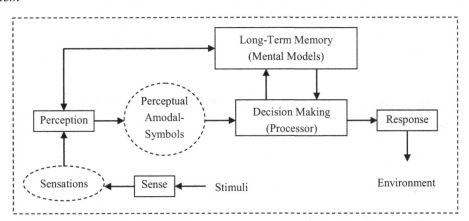

a framework involves the processes listed in the Figure 6.2 and has its architecture sketched in the Figure 6.3.

The functioning of the framework sketched in the Figure 6.3 is similar to the general structure of the information-processing system presented in the Figure 6.1. However, this framework manipulates percepts and concepts in the form of complex symbols described by words, propositions and sentences of natural language. Most importantly, such a framework is equipped with the machineries of fuzzy logic, computing with words and computation of perceptions (Zadeh, 1965, 1973, 1999 and 2001) in order to manipulate a percept and concepts, clusters of propositions and thus representations of mental models.

LEVELS OF SYMBOLIC-PROCESSING

The levels of information-processing of the cognitive machine represent layers of a simplified model of the human mind. From a bottom up perspective, the cognitive machine maps information from the levels of stimuli and sensations (neural activity signals) to the levels of percepts and thus concepts stored in memory in the form of words, propositions and sentences of natural language. At its higher level of processing, the machine manipulates percepts and thus concepts in the form of clusters of propositions which represent people's understanding on how things work. Such clusters are called metal models (Bernstein, *et al* 1997).

In such a way, fuzzy sets and fuzzy logic along with computing with words and computation of perceptions appear as appropriate tools to represent descriptions of mental models; and secondly, they also provide the necessary mechanisms to manipulate such mental representations similarly to the ability of humans to think with fuzzy concepts along with approximate reasoning (Gupta and Sanchez, 1982; Sanchez and Zadeh, 1987; and Nobre, 2005).

Table 6.1 resumes such levels of processing with the necessary tools for their engineering.

PROCESSES WITHIN THE COGNITIVE MACHINE FRAMEWORK

This section describes the functioning of the framework presented in the Figure 6.3 by associating its functional blocks to the cognitive processes of Figure 6.2.

Sensory Processing and Attention

The sensor selects stimuli, interprets them and transforms them to sensations. It involves a simplified process of attention[6].

Table 6.1. Levels of symbolic-information-processing

Information level	Processing level	Representation	Technology (Tools)
Stimuli and sensations	Sensory and neural circuit systems	Signals (electrical, optical, digital, etc)	Sensors
Sensations and percepts	Transducer and decision-making processor	Fuzzy-perceptual symbols (linguistic variables)	Fuzzy sets and fuzzy granulation
Concepts, categories and mental models	Memory and decision-making processor	Words, propositions and clusters (natural language)	Fuzzy constraints and modelling

Figure 6.2. Processes associated with the cognitive machine

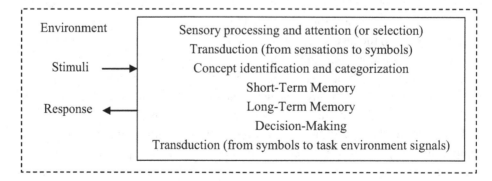

Figure 6.3. A framework of the cognitive machine as a decision-maker

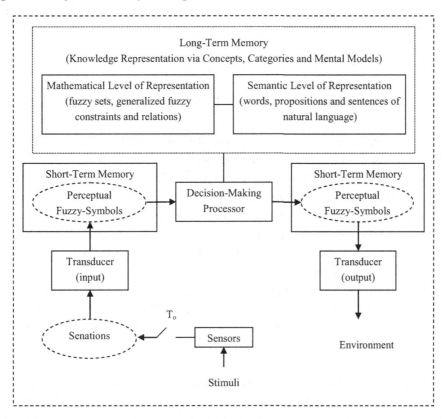

Shortly speaking, attention is a process that provides humans with the ability to focalization and concentration on specific information (Reed, 1988). It directs our sensory and perceptual systems toward certain stimuli and sensations for further processing and storage in memory (Bernstein, *et al* 1997). In organizations, attention plays the role of directing certain mental efforts of the organization participants to enhance perception, performance and mental experience during task execution.

In the Figure 6.3, a simplified process of attention is implemented by the sensory block. This block selects only part of the information which arrives from a stimulus. The selected and the rejected pieces of information by the sensor are respective synonymous with the definitions of figure and ground in perception (Bernstein *et al*, 1997). Sensors can operate with analogue or digital principles and they can be classified according to their capability to mimic vision (e.g. light and colour), hearing or audition (e.g. sound), touch (e.g. pressure, temperature and pain), olfaction (smell), gestation (taste) and even proprioception.

The key T_0 samples pieces of information which arrive from the sensory block at a discrete period of time called sampling time (KT_0). This key holds the information for a period of time represented by KT_0 whose value is specified according to the task that the cognitive machine executes and the environment where it operates. In such a way the key T_0 can be viewed as a sensory store.

Transduction: From Sensations to Fuzzy-Perceptual Symbols

The (input) transducer block is equivalent to a fuzzifier (Jager, 1995; Lee, C.C. 1990; Nobre, 1997; and Wang, 1994). It maps sensations provided by the sensory block (and sampled by the key T_0) to amodal-symbol representations. In other words, the transducer transforms signals at lower levels of meaning to more complex symbols of higher levels of meaning. An analogy can be done for instance by transforming analogue signals, digital codes or numbers like 30°C to a more complex base of symbols in the form of words like *warm* and sentences of natural language such as *warm but not too warm*.

According to the cognitive theory of levels of symbols and processing (Reed, 1998), the human brain carries information in the form of signals at low levels within neural processing circuits. In such a level of processing, neural signals and processes are beyond human power of introspection (Haikonen, 2003). However, the human brain has a remarkable ability to represent such low level neural signals by more complex symbols and thus mental models. This ability provides humans with higher levels of information-processing and hence they can manipulate information in the form of words, propositions, sentences of natural language and images. Examples of tasks which require high levels of symbolic-processing include driving in city traffic, playing football and golf, cooking a meal, summarizing a story, recruiting and managing people, etc.

For cognitive machines, sensations can be presented in the form of electrical, optical and other types of signals. Such signals are mapped by the transducer to fuzzy-perceptual symbols. These symbols are representations of words which are labels of percepts and thus concepts. This mechanism of representation of information through complex symbols provides the cognitive machine with high levels of information-processing similarly to simplified models of the human mind.

Fuzzy-Perceptual Symbols

The structure of fuzzy-perceptual symbols is constituted by mathematical representations of percepts and thus concepts. From a top-down approach, fuzzy-perceptual symbols involve three levels of processing. They are illustrated in the Figure 6.4 and described in the following through a top-down perspective.

Figure 6.4. The three levels of symbolic-processing of the cognitive machine

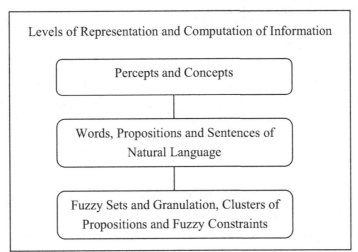

a. The first level is called perceptual and conceptual level of processing. At this level, the symbols which the cognitive machine manipulates represent percepts and concepts. Percepts and concepts are alike when a percept is recognized and classified into a category. Concepts are attributes of physical and abstract objects like colour (*blue* and *red*, etc), depth and distance (*short, long*, etc), size (*small, big*, etc), age (*young, medium age, old*), form and shape (*oval, round*, etc), motion and speed (*slow, fast*, etc), price (*expensive, cheap*, etc), truth, *justice, likelihood*, and so on. Such concepts are identified and formed from sensations extracted in one's sensory organs.

b. The second level is called natural language level of processing. At this level, concepts and thus percepts are labeled by words, propositions and sentences of a natural language such as: Mary is *young*; temperature is *hot*; Rob lives *near* to London; the car is *too fast*; Diana has *short* hair; if inflation continues to be *high* then it is *very unlikely* that there will be a *significant reduction* of taxes in the *near future*; the news is *unlikely* to be *true*; and so on, the words in italics denoting fuzzy attributes and concepts.

c. The third level is called fuzzy-perceptual level of processing. At this level, words, propositions and sentences of natural language are characterized by linguistic variables and clusters of propositions (Zadeh, 1973 and 1999) and they are mathematically represented by fuzzy sets and membership functions (Zadeh, 1965) along with fuzzy granules and generalized fuzzy constraints (Zadeh, 1996a and 1999). The machine computations at this level use the principles of fuzzy logic and fuzzy constraint propagation to manipulate such complex symbols. In such a way, the cognitive machine mimics some of the levels of processing of the human mind.

Short-Term Memory

This memory simply stores fuzzy-perceptual symbols for a period of time given by KT_o. It works as an input and output device for the decision-making process block.

Categorization

Categorization provides humans with the ability to organize knowledge via the approaches to concept identification and hierarchy of classes. One of the benefits of categorizing objects is the reduction of complexity of the environment (Reed, 1988). By classifying objects in terms of equivalence or compatibility, humans respond to them in terms of their degree of membership into a class rather than as unique items.

To categorize is to group objects into classes in order to form concepts. Furthermore, these classes can be hierarchically organized into sub-ordinate and super-ordinate relations - i.e. some categories can contain other categories such as the category furniture contains chairs and tables.

Concept Identification

Concepts are categories of physical, abstract and mental objects with common properties - like *red* and *green* are categories of colours, *short* and *tall* are categories of height, *small* and *big* are categories of size, *slow* and *fast* are categories of speed, *cheap* and *expensive* are categories of price, and so on. In fact, most of the concepts manipulated by the human mind have fuzzy boundaries (Bernstein *et al*, 1997; Lefrançois, 1995; and Zadeh, 2001) - i.e. the classification of an object into a category is a matter of degree and in this sense some objects have greater degrees of membership to a category than other objects.

In such a view, the theories of computing with words and computation of perceptions play an important part in concept identification for cognitive machines. Within such theories, concepts are described by words, propositions and sentences of natural language (Zadeh, 1996a, 1999 and 2001).

In the Figure 6.3, four blocks use concepts. They are: the long-term memory which comprises the representation of knowledge through concepts; the input transducer or fuzzifier which forms concepts (fuzzy-perceptual symbols) from input signals (sensations); the decision-making process which manipulates concepts by propagating them from premises to conclusions; and finally, the output transducer or defuzzifier which maps such concepts to signals compatible to the environment.

Similarly to the perspectives of Gestalt psychologists who proposed principles which describes how perceptual systems group sensations to form patterns (Bernstein *et al*, 1997), this book assumes that such principles are applicable to concept identification when classifying objects into categories. Some principles called "indistinguishable, similarity, proximity and functionality" have been proposed by Zadeh (2001). He asserts that objects can be drawn together by using one of these principles to form fuzzy granules. In his theory, fuzzy granules are denotations of words, and words are labels of percepts.

Concepts can be defined as artificial and natural types (Bernstein, *et al* 1997).

- **Artificial Concepts:** Artificial concepts are characterized by classes of sharp boundaries. In such a type, an object is classified as member or non-member of a given class like in the ordinary set theory (Halmos, 1960). Moreover, the discrimination of objects as members and non-members of a class is clearly defined according to a set of logical rules that comprise conjunctive, disjunctive, conditional or bi-conditional properties (Reed, 1988). Such rules are similar to the propositions and principles of ordinary logic of predicate calculus (Luger and Stubblefield, 1998) and crisp-granular computation (Zadeh, 2001).

An example of artificial concept is the class of *small* numbers which are in between 0 and 10 inclusive: $\{0 \geq X \leq 10 \mid X \in R \text{ (Real)}\}$. In such a case, the conjunctive and conditional rule given by:

if X is ≥ 0 and X is ≤ 10 then X is *small* $\qquad\qquad$ (6.1)

is the rule that constrains X within the category of *small*. However, most of the concepts humans form and manipulate - like *small* - have no sharp boundaries and they are characterized by vagueness (Black, 1937 and 1963) and fuzziness (Zadeh, 1965). Hence, the principles of ordinary sets theory and crisp computation do not provide the appropriate and necessary armament to represent and to manipulate such concepts.

Despite being used in laboratories of psychology for experimental research involving tasks such as the simulation of learning processes (Bernstein, *et al* 1997), artificial concepts of sharp boundaries fail to represent the complexity of real (natural) concepts.

- **Natural Concepts:** Natural concepts pervade our world and require complex representations which go beyond the limitations of ordinary sets theory and crisp granulation. Natural concepts have fuzzy boundaries because some of their members seem to be better examples of the category than others (Bernstein *et al*, 1997). For instance, although a large range of stimulus input may be interpreted as being *green* (i.e. belonging to the category of *greenness*) some of that input will be interpreted as being more *green* and some as less *green*. Such categories are characterized by classes whose boundaries are not clearly defined and hence the transition from membership to non-membership of their members is gradual rather than abrupt. Examples include the classes of *short* and *tall*, *young* and *old*, *black* and *white*, *poor* and *rich*, *true* and *false*, *high* and *low* performances, etc.

In such a way, fuzzy sets theory[7] (along with fuzzy logic, computing with words and computation of perceptions (Zadeh, 2001)) can provide cognitive machines with the appropriate and necessary armament for the representation of natural concepts and categories through complex symbols by using the principles of:

*   Fuzzy sets and membership functions (Zadeh, 1965; and Klir and Folger, 1988).
*   Linguistic variables and fuzzy granulation (Zadeh, 1973 and 1996a).
*   Generalized fuzzy constraints (Zadeh, 1999).

Figure 6.5 illustrates a mathematical representation of the fuzzy concept *young* via the principle of membership functions of fuzzy sets. In such an example, *young* is a linguistic value which represents the concept that constrains the variable age into such a category of *young*. Moreover, by considering that A denotes the fuzzy set *young*, $u \in U$ denotes the objects (u) in the universe of discourse (U) of age, and $\mu_A(u)$ represents the respective degree of membership of u in $A \subset U$, then the fuzzy set *young* can be symbolically equated as:

$$A = \{u, \mu_A(u) \mid \mu_A(u) \in [0,1], u \in U, A \subset U\} \qquad (6.2)$$

As much as u approaches 100 in the universe U, it assumes smaller degrees of membership within the class of *young* people. In such an example, the fuzzy set *young* is equivalent to a fuzzy-perceptual symbol.

It is important to realize that the imprecision and thus the fuzziness that is characteristic of natural concepts do not necessarily imply loss of accuracy or meaningfulness. It is for instance more meaningful and accurate to say that it is usually *warm* in the summer than to say that it is usually 25° C (Klir and Folger, 1988).

Figure 6.5. A fuzzy-perceptual symbol representing the concept of Young

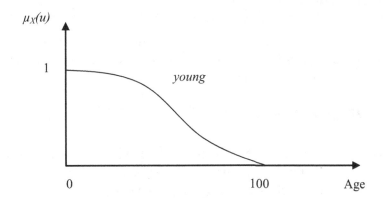

Long-Term Memory

This device stores the knowledge base of the cognitive machine and mental representations. It comprises:

a. Concepts which are denotations of words, and conversely, words which are descriptions of concepts. Words are synonymous with linguistic variables which are mathematically represented by fuzzy sets (Zadeh, 1973, 1975 and 1976).

b. Propositions P described in natural language which can be defined by fuzzy generalized constraints and represented via canonical forms. A proposition P can also be viewed as a constraint of a linguistic variable X to a particular category (e.g. $P: X$ *isr* A, where *isr* is a variable copula which defines the way that the category A constrains the linguistic variable X) (Zadeh, 1999).

c. Conditional statements (R) which describes the relations between concepts (linguistic values) in the antecedent and consequent (e.g. R: IF $X_{(i=1,...,n)}$ THEN $Y_{(j=1,...,M)} \mid i,j \in N$ *integer*). The relation between the antecedent concepts can be defined by a t-norm $\cap$ and the relation between the consequent concepts can be represented by a s-norm $\perp$ (Dubois and Prade, 1985). Moreover, the relation between the antecedent X and the consequent Y of such statements can be mathematically defined by fuzzy implications (Lee, C.C. 1990). Conditional statements of this type can also be called fuzzy conditional rules (Zadeh, 1973).

d. Clusters of propositions and conditional statements ($R_{(r=1,...,M)} \mid r \in N$ *integer*) which can be defined as a set of fuzzy rules aggregated by an s-norm (e.g. $R_1 \perp R_2 \perp ... \perp R_M$) (Dubois and Prade, 1985; and Nobre, 1997).

The design of the knowledge base of the cognitive machine can be done by (Nobre, 1997 and Wang, 1994):

- Using the experience, knowledge and heuristic rules of thumb of experts.
- Using computational programs for optimization, learning and automatic generation of conditional statements.

Decision-Making Process

This process manipulates concepts through the rules of inference in fuzzy logic (Zadeh, 1999). In other words, it propagates fuzzy constraints from premises (antecedent concepts) to conclusions (consequent concepts).

The decision-making process associates fuzzy-perceptual symbols with the knowledge base stored in memory in order to make choices through approximate reasoning mechanisms.

The concept of approximate reasoning (Gupta and Sanchez, 1982; and Sanchez and Zadeh, 1987) is used here as synonymous with economic decision-making and satisfactory outcomes as defined in bounded rationality (Simon, 1997a) rather than the high costs and unrealistic view of optimal standards and pure rationality as employed in classical economics.

One of the most popular rules of inference in fuzzy logic is the compositional rule (Zadeh, 1996a). To illustrate such a rule of inference, let us firstly define a set of fuzzy conditional statements and their aggregation given by:

$$R^{(r)}: \text{IF } x_1 \text{ isr } F_1^r \text{ AND IF } x_2 \text{ isr } F_2^r \text{ AND } \dots \text{ AND IF } x_n \text{ isr } F_n^r \text{ THEN } y \text{ isr } G^r$$

(6.3)

$$\mathbf{R} = \bigcup_{r=1}^{M} R^{(r)}$$

(6.4)

where in equation (6.3), $R^{(r)}$ denotes a fuzzy conditional statement and $r=1,...,M$ is the total number of statements, and F_1^r and G^r denotes concepts (linguistic values) of the respective fuzzy variables $x_{(i=1,...,n)}$ and y. The logical connective AND is interpreted as a t-norm $\cap$ and THEN is implemented as an implication function.

In equation (6.4), $\mathbf{R}$ denotes the aggregation of the conditional statements given by the union operator $\mathbf{U}$ which also symbolizes a s-norm $\perp$.

Equations (6.3) and (6.4) summarize mental representations of knowledge in the long-term memory. The process of decision-making comprises the manipulation of such mental representations in order to compute an output B from an input fuzzy-perceptual symbol A. Figure 6.6 illustrates such a process and equation (6.5) resumes the calculus of decisions through the compositional rule of inference.

*Figure 6.6. Decision-making process (A o **R** : B)*

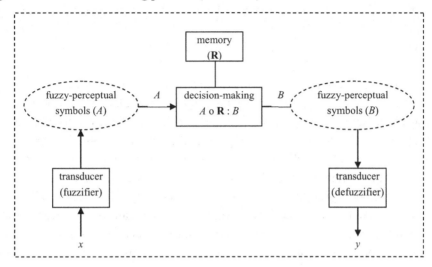

$$A \circ \mathbf{R} = \mu_B(y) = \sup_{x \in U_{(i=1,...,n)}} [\mu_A(x) \cap \mu_\mathbf{R}(x,y)] \tag{6.5}$$

where sup abbreviates supremum, $x = (x_{1,...,} x_n) \in U_{(i=1,...,n)}$ denote sensations (signals) which are mapped by the input transducer (fuzzifier) to a fuzzy-perceptual symbol A whose structure is characterized according to a fuzzy set. A denotes a word which is a description of a percept and thus a concept. B can be understood as a fuzzy-perceptual symbol calculated from equation (6.5) and $y \in V$ denotes the output signal after transduction (defuzzification).

Transduction: From Perceptual-Fuzzy Symbols to Signals

The (output) transducer is equivalent to a defuzzifier (Jager, 1995; Lee, C.C. 1990; Nobre, 1997; and Wang, 1994). It maps fuzzy-perceptual symbols inferred from the decision-making process to signals compatible with the environment.

SUMMARY

Chapter VI introduced the design of cognitive machines. These machines and their models were chosen in order to increase and to improve:

i.   The degree of cognition of the organization,
ii. The capability of the organization for information processing and management,
iii. And the ability of the organization to make decisions.

It proposed a framework of cognitive machines with capabilities to carry out complex cognitive tasks in organizations - and in particular the task of decision-making which involves representation and organization of knowledge via concept identification and categorization along with the manipulations of perceptions, concepts, and mental models. It was advocated that the ability of these machines to manipulate a percept provides them with higher levels of information-processing than other symbolic-processing machines; and according to the theory of levels of processing in cognition (Reed, 1988), these machines can mimic (even through simple models) cognitive processes of humans. Percepts and thus concepts (along with mental models) are represented by words, propositions and sentences of natural language.

REFERENCES

Bernstein, D. A. *et al* (1997). *Psychology.* Houghton Mifflin Company.

Black, M. (1937). Vagueness: An Exercise to Logical Analysis. *Philosophy of Science, 4*, 427-455.

Black, M. (1963). Reasoning with Loose Concepts. *Dialogue, 2*, 1-12.

Dubois, D., & Prade, H. (1985). A review of fuzzy set aggregation connectives. *Information Sciences, 36*, 85-121.

Gupta, M., & Sanchez, E. (1982). *Approximate Reasoning in Decision Analysis.* North-Holland.

Haikonen, P. O. (2003). *The Cognitive Approach to Conscious Machines.* Imprint Academic.

Halmos, P. R. (1960). *Naive Set Theory.* D. Van Nostrand. New Jersey.

Jager, R. (1995). Fuzzy Logic in Control. *PhD Thesis*, Delft University of Technology, Electrical Engineering Dept., Delft, The Netherlands.

Lee, C. C. (1990). Fuzzy Logic Control Systems: Fuzzy Logic Controllers – Part I and II. *IEEE Trans. on Systems, Man and Cybernetics, 20*(2), 404-435.

Lefrançoies, G. (1995). *Theories of Human Learning.* Brooks Cole Publishing Company.

Luger, G. F., & Stubblefield, W. A. (1998). *Artificial Intelligence: Structures and Strategies for Complex Problem Solving.* The Benjamin/Cummings Publishing Company, Inc.

Klir, G. J., & Folger, T. A. (1988). *Fuzzy Sets, Uncertainty, and Information.* Englewood Cliffs, N.J: Prentice Hall.

Mamdani, E. H. (1974). Application of fuzzy algorithms for control of simple dynamic plan. *Proceedings of the IEE, 121* (12), 1585-1588.

Nobre, F. S. (1997). Design and Analysis of Fuzzy Logic Controllers. *M.Sc. Thesis Dissertation,* 110 pages. Faculty of Electrical and Computer Engineering / State University of Campinas (UNICAMP), Brazil.

Nobre, F. (2005). On Cognitive Machines in Organizations. *PhD Thesis,* 343 pages. University of Birmingham / Birmingham-UK. Birmingham Main Library. Control Number: M0266887BU.

Reed, S. K. (1988). *Cognition: Theory and Applications.* 2nd Ed. Brooks-Cole Publishing Company.

Sanchez, E., & Zadeh, L. A. (1987). *Approximate Reasoning in Intelligent Systems, Decision and Control.* Pergamon Press.

Simon, H. A. (1997a). *Models of Bounded Rationality: Empirically Grounded Economic Reason, 3.* The MIT Press.

Wang, L. (1994). *Adaptive Fuzzy Systems and Control: Design and Stability Analysis.* PTR Prentice-Hall.

Wikipedia. *The Free Encyclopaedia.* From http://en.wikipedia.org

Zadeh, L. A. (1965). Fuzzy Sets. *Information and Control, 8,* 338-353.

Zadeh, L. A. (1968). Fuzzy Algorithms. *Information and Control, 12,* 94-102.

Zadeh, L. A. (1973). Outline of a New Approach to the Analysis of Complex Systems and Decision Process. *IEEE Transactions on Systems, Man, and Cybernetics, 3*(1), 28-44.

Zadeh, L. A. (1975). The concept of a linguistic variable and its application to approximate reasoning: part I and II. . In R.R. Yager *et al* (Ed.). (1987), *Fuzzy Sets and their Applications: Selected Papers by L.A. Zadeh.* (pp. 219-327). John & Sons.

Zadeh, L. A. (1976). The concept of a linguistic variable and its application to approximate reasoning: part III. In R.R. Yager *et al* (Ed.). (1987), *Fuzzy Sets and their Applications: Selected Papers by L.A. Zadeh* (pp 329-366). John & Sons.

Zadeh, L. A. (1996a). Fuzzy Logic = Computing with Words. *IEEE Transactions on Fuzzy Systems, 4*(2), 103-111.

Zadeh, L. A. (1999). From Computing with Numbers to Computing with Words – From Manipulation of Measurements to Manipulation of Perceptions. *IEEE Transactions on Circuits and Systems, 45*(1), 105-119.

Zadeh, L. A. (2001). A New Direction in AI: Toward a Computational Theory of Perceptions. *AI Magazine. Spring,* 73-84.

ENDNOTES

[1]   Perception is the process through which sensations are interpreted; using knowledge and understanding of the environment, so that they become meaningful experiences (Bernstein, *et al* 1997). In the literature, perceptions can also be found as synonymous with a percept or a set of percepts, where a percept represents a class of objects with fuzzy boundaries (Zadeh, 2001).

[2]   Concepts are categories of physical and abstract objects with common properties like the attributes of colour (*red, yellow, green*, etc), size (*small, medium, large*, etc), etc. A concept may be regarded as a percept recognized and classified into a category.

[3]   Mental models are descriptions or explanation in someone's mind for how something works in the real world. It is a kind of internal symbol or representation of external reality, hypothesized to play a major role in cognition and decision-making processes (Wikipedia's online dictionary).

[4]   Cognitive machines manipulate complex symbols in the form of words, propositions and sentences of natural language which are descriptions of percepts and concepts. Such complex symbols are codified through the principles of linguistic variables and fuzzy granulation, fuzzy sets and membership functions, and fuzzy generalized constraints; and they are manipulated through the mechanisms of fuzzy logic and fuzzy constraint propagation (Zadeh, 1973, 1975, 1976, 1988, 1996a and 1999). Therefore, such *machines* can manipulate more complex symbols than other machines whose base of computation is the classical set theory (Halmos, 1960) and crisp granulation.

[5]   Briefly, percept and concepts are alike when a percept is recognized and classified into a category. For example, by saying that Brazil is *large*, one is assuming that the size of the Brazilian land is classified as *large*, and in

fact, *large* is a concept. For simplicity, percepts and concepts are treated as synonymous throughout this book.

6   Attention encompasses bottleneck and capacity theories. The first theory views attention as a filter that selects the information (stimuli and sensations) to be perceived and recognized (as patterns) and stored in memory (as concepts). The second theory views attention as synonymous with cognitive limitation and it emphasizes the amount of mental effort that is required to a perform task (Reed, 1988).

7   Fuzzy sets theory can also be regarded as an extension of ordinary sets theory since it provides additional mathematical principles for the representation of information in the form of more complex symbols. In the approaches to computing with words and perceptions (Zadeh, 1999) these symbols denote words and percepts.

Section IV
Cognitive Machines in Organizations

Human beings, viewed as behaving systems, are quite simple. The apparent complexity of our behavior over time is largely a reflection of the complexity of the environment in which we find ourselves. (Simon, H.A. 1996, pp.53).

Section IV introduces analysis on the participation of cognitive machines in organizations. It comprises Chapter VII only.

Briefly, Chapter VII presents analyses of cognitive machines through the concepts of bounded rationality, economic decision-making, and conflict resolution. It also derives a theorem on the implications of cognitive machines for organizations and the environment. It concludes by proposing definitions and by introducing models of relationships and contracts of work between the cognitive machine, its designer and the organization.

Chapter VII
Analysis of Cognitive Machines in Organizations

INTRODUCTION

This chapter introduces analyses of cognitive machines and perspectives about their participation in organizations. Therefore, it connects cognitive machines with the discipline of organizations.

The analyses of cognitive machines comprise concepts of bounded rationality, economic decision-making and conflict resolution (Nobre, 2005). From such an analysis, this book advocates that these machines can be used to reduce or to solve intra-individual and group dysfunctional conflicts which arise from decision-making processes in organizations. Therefore, they can provide organizations with higher degrees of cognition, and consequently reduce the relative level of complexity and uncertainty of the environment. This chapter also derives a theorem on the implications of cognitive machines for organizations and the environment. It concludes by presenting perspectives about the work relationships between cognitive machines, their designer and the organization.

CAPABILITY BOUNDARIES OF COGNITIVE MACHINES

Bounded rationality and economic decision-making are characteristic processes of the human mind (Simon, 1997a). Therefore, they are discussed in this section in order to understand some capability boundaries of cognitive machines.

Bounded Rationality and Economic Decision-Making

The fundamental premises about bounded rationality are (March, 1994):

i.   Limitation of knowledge (or scarcity of information).
ii. And limitation of computational capacity (or limit of cognition).

In order to cope with such limitations, humans search for approximate and satisfactory solutions rather than optimal outcomes in their daily life (March & Simon, 1993) - where the term satisfactory is synonym for satisficing (Simon, 1997a). The process of decision used by humans which lead them to satisfactory outcomes is called economic decision-making (Nobre, 2005) and it is synonymous with approximate reasoning (Sanchez & Zadeh, 1987). Therefore, economic decision-making is concerned with economy in the processes of decision which result in satisfactory solutions rather than with processes of choice which search for optimal outcomes such as in neo-classical economics (Simon, 1997a). Economic decision-making processes play an important part in the environments where information is scarce and fuzzy, and the cost of searching and computation of information is high.

Theories of choice that do not assume the preceding premises seem to be unrealistic and they cannot provide models of human cognition (Simon, 1997a).

Extending the Boundaries of Human Cognition with Machines

With the advent of computers and communication networks, along with the disciplines of operational research and management science, new technologies sought to extend the limits of rationality established by the cognitive boundaries of individuals and organizations (March & Simon, 1993; and Simon, 1982b). A powerful combination of massive knowledge storage with high capability of symbolic-processing (and more specifically numerical and analytical computation) gave computers and thus information technology special places in organizations (Simon, 1977).

However, despite providing organizations with economic and cognitive contributions, computers and information technology have found serious limitations of applicability in those areas where problems and decisions require approximate rather than precise formulations. Such areas involve managerial roles and thus the management of decisions at the higher levels of the organization hierarchy.

The advancements of artificial intelligence in the period between the middle and the end of the 20th Century gave genesis to additional computational tools with the capability to solve classes of problems which could not be formulated before (e.g. chess and theorem proof). Nevertheless, the progress of artificial intelligence has been slow and limited in those areas where the formulation of problems falls into the category of fuzzy-granulation rather than crisp-granulation (Zadeh, 2001).

Most of the concepts that humans manipulate have fuzzy boundaries and the representation of these concepts requires new approaches to encapsulate them into more complex symbolic structures. According to the principle of a theory of levels of information-processing, humans can achieve higher levels of cognition when they reason with higher levels of symbolic representation such as words and sentences of natural language. In organizations, for instance, the higher the management level, the more complex are the concepts and mental models that humans reason with.

In such a way, further advancements in cognition and artificial intelligence research may lead researchers to engineer cognitive machines which combine the cognitive strengths of humans and computers.

On the one hand, people have a remarkable ability to reason with fuzzy concepts and to solve problems through approximate and satisfactory solutions. Types of such problems involve tasks of driving in city traffic, playing football and most of the management work at upper-levels in the organization hierarchy. Moreover, people have a large long-term memory, but a very limited short-term memory. They also have limitations to reason with numerical and analytical representations of symbols.

On the other hand, computers are still poor at solving problems which require the formulation and manipulation of natural concepts along with approximate reasoning. They have a large memory and no distinction is needed between short and long-term memories. Hence, they overcome the limits of human short-term memory. Computers also overcome the inability of humans at solving arithmetic and analytical problems (Simon, 1982b).

Figure 7.1 brings together the strengths of human cognition and computers to illustrate the abilities of a cognitive machine.

Conditions in the Design of the Cognitive Machine

The design of the cognitive machine framework presented in Part III assumes similar conditions to bounded rationality and human decision-making processes (March & Simon, 1993; and Simon, 1997a):

- Alternatives of choice are not simply given but they must be generated through a process of search.
- The probability distributions of outcomes are unknown and may be only estimated through high computational costs.
- Humans manipulate natural concepts (Bernstein, *et al* 1997). Therefore, most of the uncertainty that pervades the alternatives and their consequences are classified into fuzziness rather than probabilistic uncertainty.

Figure 7.1. Abilities of the cognitive machine

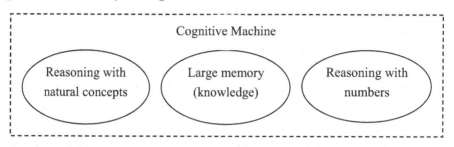

- Satisfactory strategies of choice and outcomes are preferable to maximization (the search for optimal solutions). The latter requires a higher cost of computation and may not represent a robust procedure (Zadeh, 1994 and 2001).

Therefore, in order to satisfy such conditions, the design of the cognitive machines assumes that:

- Alternatives (conditional statements or rules) which form the knowledge base of the machine are searched and generated by human experts or with the support of computational tools of adaptive and learning capabilities (Nobre, 1997; and Wang, 1994). The process of search and generation of conditional statements is better described by a combination of the logic of appropriateness and the logic of consequences[1] (March, 1994; and Simon, 1982b). Therefore, it involves experience, intuition, expertise along with calculation.
- The higher the number of alternatives, the higher is the number of rules; the higher the number of rules, the higher is the completeness of the knowledge base (Nobre, 1997); the higher the completeness of the knowledge base, the higher is the design complexity.
- Fuzziness is the type of uncertainty that pervades the alternatives (antecedents) and their consequences (conclusions). The knowledge base of the cognitive machine comprises antecedents and conclusions which describe relations between natural concepts. Such concepts have fuzzy boundaries. Therefore, fuzzy sets theory is a necessary tool for the representation of such concepts.
- A satisfactory and more robust strategy for decision-making is implemented through the principles of fuzzy logic, computing with words and computation of perceptions (Sanchez and Zadeh, 1987; and Zadeh, 1996a and 1999).

THE ROLE OF COGNITIVE MACHINES IN CONFLICT RESOLUTION

This section regards cognitive machines as decision-makers in organizations. It describes how such machines can contribute to improve processes of choice in the organization by reducing decision conflicts.

Decision Processes in Organizations

Organizations comprise several kinds of decisions (March & Simon, 1993). However, this book is mainly concerned with decisions that influence and control the organization business and management. Such decisions are made by the participants within the organization and they involve conflicts (frictions).

Conflicts in Organizations

*   **Constructive and Dysfunctional Conflicts:** Conflicts shape and affect the behaviour of individuals, groups and organizations (Daft and Noe, 2001). They can be classified into constructive and dysfunctional conflicts.

On the one hand, constructive conflicts are classes of conflicts which contribute to improve the behaviour and performance of individuals, groups and organizations. On the other hand, dysfunctional conflicts are synonymous with obstacles which limit the action and performance of individuals, groups and organizations.

This book is concerned with dysfunctional conflicts which arise from decision-making processes in organizations.

*   **Intra-Individual Conflict:** Processes of decision-making involve trade-offs among alternatives which are characterized by uncertainty, incomparability and unacceptability and hence they can lead organization participants to intra-individual conflict (March & Simon, 1993). Such a kind of conflict arises in an individual mind and it also can emerge from the influence of others.

The Problem of Uncertainty: When considering models of rational choice and calculation which follow a logic of consequences, uncertainty means that the probability distributions of outcomes are unknown (March, 1994; and Simon, 1982b). This book assumes either: that such probabilities cannot be estimated or they can be calculated only with unrealistic costs of computation.

The Problem of Incomparability: It means that the individual (participant in the organization) cannot recognize a most preferred alternative. It can happen for instance when the individual has to decide between two alternatives with the same label such as *good*.

The Problem of Unacceptability: It means that the most preferred alternative as identified by the individual does not satisfy standard criteria.

- **Group Conflict:** In addition to the factors that lead participants to intra-individual conflict, members of groups in organizations can differ in their perceptions, values and culture, needs and goals (Daft and Noe, 2001). Hence, they can disagree in their decisions causing group conflict (March & Simon, 1993). This kind of conflict arises from differences between the choices made by distinct participants within the organization.

- **Relations between Conflicts and Bounded Rationality:** The intra-individual and group conflicts which arise in organizations are mainly influenced by lack of information and uncertainties, and most importantly by cognitive limitations. In such a way, these conflicts cannot be solved by incentive and reward systems. Such cognitive and information constraints are synonymous with bounded rationality (March, 1994; March & Simon, 1993; Simon 1997a and 1997b). However, this book asserts that cognitive machines can be used to reduce or to solve such conflicts.

Cognitive Machines in Conflict Resolution of Decisions

This subsection proposes principles to support the assertion that cognitive machines can reduce or solve intra-individual and group dysfunctional conflicts in organizations.

- **Resolution of Intra-Individual Conflict:** The reduction of the frictions in intra-individual conflicts can be achieved by providing the organization with means to cope with uncertainty, incomparability and unacceptability factors.

A Solution to Uncertainty: According to the theory of natural concepts proposed in the literature of cognition (Bernstein *et al*, 1997), most of the concepts which humans manipulate have fuzzy boundaries. Hence, fuzziness is the principal kind of uncertainty that the cognitive machine must deal with and manage during task execution and decision-making. Fuzzy concepts can be represented through complex symbols whose structure is properly defined via fuzzy sets along with the principles of fuzzy logic, computing with words and computation of perceptions (Zadeh, 1999 and 2001).

A Solution to Incomparability: Instead of identifying a most preferred conditional rule (or an alternative) the cognitive machine fires (or selects) a set of rules according to a criterion - for instance, the rules whose value is greater than 0 - and then it unifies (or aggregates) the fired set of rules through the application of one of the operators in fuzzy logic. Such operators comprise s-norm and union (Jager, 1995). Therefore, aggregation of preferences and rules is applied rather than the selection of only one alternative.

A Solution to Unacceptability: This is avoided by using criteria of design during the specification of the cognitive machine's knowledge base. For such a purpose, the criteria of completeness must be applied in order to guarantee that for each state there is an associated output (Jager, 1995; and Nobre, 1997).

- **Resolution of Group Conflict:** The absence of intra-individual conflict reduces group conflict, but it does not extinguish the problem since it is not a sufficient condition. By assuming such an absence, this subsection discusses the additional agents of group conflict and it proposes solutions to solve it.

Group conflict also arises from divergences of opinions of the participants in a group which can be a consequence of the differences in their needs, goals, values and perceptions. On the one hand, such a type of conflict could be reduced by equalizing the participants' perceptions, opinions and knowledge. On the other hand, it could be solved through a methodology which supports the integration of the participants' perceptions, opinion and knowledge. The latter is the selected approach used in this research to justify the way in which cognitive machines reduce (or solve) group conflicts. It consists of the integration and storage of the participants' perceptions, opinion and knowledge in a common knowledge base (device storage or memory).

The design of the cognitive machines introduced in Part III comprises the specification of a knowledge base through commonsensical expertise – i.e. different experts express their perceptions, opinions and knowledge in the form of words and sentences of natural language which take the form of linguistic rules or conditional statements (Zadeh, 1973 and 1996a). Such rules may also be generated automatically, modified and improved through the principles of adaptive and learning systems (Wang, 1994). During the functioning of the cognitive machine, the activation of rules and their aggregation represent an integrated and common sense process which takes into account the perceptions, opinion and knowledge of different experts.

Therefore, decision-making processes are automated through the rules of inference of fuzzy logic (Zadeh, 1996a, 1999 and 2001). Moreover, intra-individual and group mental models are represented through a set of fuzzy propositions and fuzzy conditional statements (rules) - which can be mathematically defined through fuzzy generalized constraints (Zadeh, 1999).

- **Networks of Cognitive Machines in Conflict:** When operating in networks, similarly to multi-agent systems (Weiss, 1999), cognitive machines can get in conflict during negotiation. This topic will be investigated in further work.

THEOREM FOR COGNITIVE MACHINES, ORGANIZATIONS AND THE ENVIRONMENT

The statements proposed in this section are derived from the propositions on organizational cognition (introduced in Part II) and cognitive machines (introduced in Part III). These statements put forward cognitive machines as a fundamental and necessary element if we aim to improve the degree of organizational cognition.

Premise 7.1: Technology of cognitive machines can provide the organization with higher degrees of cognition.

Proposition 7.1: Cognitive machines increase the level of complexity of the organization, and thus it improve the degree of cognition of the organization.

By concluding, we state that:

Theorem 7.1: The technology of cognitive machines increases the degree of organizational cognition, and it relatively reduces the level of environmental complexity and uncertainty that the organization needs to manage.

Theorem 7.1 does not mean that the levels of environmental complexity and uncertainty reduce, but that such levels are relatively reduced when compared to the growth in the level of organizational cognition.

COGNITIVE MACHINES, DESIGNERS AND ORGANIZATIONS: RELATIONSHIPS

This section describes relationships between the cognitive machine, its designer and the organization within which the machine participates. It proposes definitions of designers of cognitive machines and their duties; consciousness of the cognitive machine in the organization; and work responsibilities of the cognitive machine, its designer and the organization.

On Designers of Cognitive Machines

Definition 7.1: The designer (which involves the manufacturer) of a cognitive machine is the person (or entity - organization) responsible for the cognitive abilities and the behaviour of the machine. Such a kind of designers can have independent legal identity which enables them to make contracts and to seek court enforcement of those contracts if necessary.

Definition 7.2: Designers can use technologies for automatic design and generation of cognitive machines. Genetic programming for instance is a paradigm which has provided a profound impact on the design of software programs capable of generating tangible replicas and with enough ability to perform at least similar functions (Koza, 1992). Such technologies are classified as artificial designers and they cannot ask for, nor answer, a formal contract. Therefore, their first designer (a person or an organization) is the agent who is able to make it.

On Consciousness of Cognitive Machines in Organizations

This book does not intend to investigate whether cognitive machines are able to be conscious[2] or whether they can be self-aware of their roles and tasks in organizations. It would require a profound analysis of the subject of consciousness in cognitive science and artificial intelligence research (Haikonen, 2003). Nevertheless, this book puts forward a definition of what machine consciousness means to organizations.

Definition 7.3: Machine consciousness represents the awareness of its designer in relation to the cognitive processes and abilities that the machine carries on during task execution.

On Responsibility: The Designer, the Machine and the Organization

What is the relationship between a cognitive machine, its tasks and its roles in the organization? And what is the work relationship between the cognitive machine, the machine designer and the organization?

Definition 7.4: The work relationship between the machine designer and the organization can be regularized by a contract which makes explicit the cognitive abilities of the machine; the tasks that the machine can perform within the organization; the roles that the machine fulfils in the organization; and also the designer and the organization attestation (or signatures).

Definition 7.5: The organization is responsible for the assignment of roles to the cognitive machine, and the machine is responsible for the roles it fulfils in the organization. However, the machine designer and the organization are the main parts responsible for the machine results and performance. If the machine exhibits deviant behaviour during task execution or performance below specified criteria, then the contract between the organization and the machine designer is the object of analysis and judgement.

SUMMARY

Chapter VII introduced analyses of cognitive machines and perspectives about their participation in organizations. It contributed by connecting cognitive machines with the discipline of organizations.

The analyses of cognitive machine comprised concepts of bounded rationality, economic decision-making and conflict resolution. Such analyses indicate that these machines can be used to reduce or to solve intra-individual and group dysfunctional conflicts which arise from decision-making processes in organizations. Therefore, they can provide organizations with higher degrees of cognition – and thus they can improve the capabilities of the organization for information processing and uncertainty management.

Chapter VII also derived a theorem on the implications of cognitive machines for organizations and the environment. It was proposed that:

For **cognitive machines**, **organizations** and the **environment**:

Theorem 7.1: The technology of cognitive machines increases the degree of organizational cognition, and it relatively reduces the level of environmental complexity and uncertainty that the organization needs to manage.

Chapter VII concluded by presenting definitions and models of work relationships and contracts between the cognitive machine, its designer and the organization. As a participant within the organization, the cognitive machine must fulfil roles as designated by the organization. Additionally, a contract can form the relationship between the designer of the cognitive machine and the organization in order to ensure responsibility.

REFERENCES

Bernstein, D. A. *et al* (1997). *Psychology.* Houghton Mifflin Company.

Daft, R. L., & Noe, R. A. (2001). *Organizational Behavior.* Harcourt, Inc.

Haikonen, P. O. (2003). *The Cognitive Approach to Conscious Machines.* Imprint Academic.

Jager, R. (1995). Fuzzy Logic in Control. *PhD Thesis*, Delft University of Technology, Electrical Engineering Dept., Delft, The Netherlands.

Koza, J. R. (1992). *Genetic Programming: On the programming of computers by means of natural selection.* The MIT Press.

March, J. G. (1994). *A Primer on Decision Making: How Decisions Happen.* The Free Press.

March, J. G., & Simon, H. A. (1993). *Organizations.* 2nd Ed. John Wiley & Sons, Inc.

Nobre, F. S. (1997). Design and Analysis of Fuzzy Logic Controllers. *M.Sc. Thesis Dissertation*, 110 pages. Faculty of Electrical and Computer Engineering / State University of Campinas (UNICAMP), Brazil.

Nobre, F. (2005). On Cognitive Machines in Organizations. *PhD Thesis*, 343 pages. University of Birmingham / Birmingham-UK. Birmingham Main Library. Control Number: M0266887BU.

Reed, S. K. (1988). *Cognition: Theory and Applications.* 2nd Ed. Brooks-Cole Publishing Company.

Sanchez, E., & Zadeh, L.A. (1987). *Approximate Reasoning in Intelligent Systems, Decision and Control.* Pergamon Press.

Simon, H. A. (1977). *The New Science of Management Decision.* Prentice-Hall, Inc.

Simon, H. A. (1982b). *Models of Bounded Rationality: Behavioral Economics and Business Organization, 2.* The MIT Press.

Simon, H. A. (1997a). *Models of Bounded Rationality: Empirically Grounded Economic Reason, 3.* The MIT Press.

Simon, H. A. (1997b). *Administrative Behavior: A Study of Decision-Making Processes in Administrative Organizations.* The Free Press.

Wang, L. (1994). *Adaptive Fuzzy Systems and Control: Design and Stability Analysis*. PTR Prentice-Hall.

Weiss, G. (1999). *Multiagent Systems – A Modern Approach to Distributed Artificial Intelligence*. The MIT Press.

Zadeh, L. A. (1973). Outline of a New Approach to the Analysis of Complex Systems and Decision Process. *IEEE Transactions on Systems, Man, and Cybernetics*, *3*(1), 28-44.

Zadeh, L. A. (1994) Soft Computing and Fuzzy Logic. *IEEE Software, November*, 48-56.

Zadeh, L. A. (1996a). Fuzzy Logic = Computing with Words. *IEEE Transactions on Fuzzy Systems*, *4*(2), 103-111.

Zadeh, L. A. (1999) From Computing with Numbers to Computing with Words – From Manipulation of Measurements to Manipulation of Perceptions. *IEEE Transactions on Circuits and Systems, 45*(1), 105-119.

Zadeh, L. A. (2001) A New Direction in AI: Toward a Computational Theory of Perceptions. *AI Magazine. Spring*, 73-84.

ENDNOTES

[1] In the logic of consequences, actions are selected by evaluating their expected consequences for the preferences of the actor. It is related to the conception of calculation and analysis. In the logic of appropriateness, actions are matched to situations by means of rules. It involves conceptions of experience, roles, intuition and expertise (March, 1994; and March & Simon, 1993).

[2] Consciousness concerns mental states of being aware of ourselves and our environment. It assumes the awareness of our own mental processes, thoughts, feelings and perceptions. Consciousness states can vary from deep sleep to alert wakefulness (Bernstein, D.A. *et al* 1997).

Section V
Industrial Case Study

...as the complexity of a system increases, our ability to make precise and yet significant statements about its behaviour diminish until a threshold is reached beyond which precision and significance (or relevance) become almost exclusive characteristics. It is in this sense that precise quantitative analyses of the behaviour of humanistic systems are not likely to have much relevance to the real-world societal, political, economic, and other types of problems which involve humans either as individual or in groups.

Principle of Incompatibility stated by Lotfi A. Zadeh (1973, p.28)

This book supports the statement of Zadeh with the perspective of humanistic systems being defined by social and organizational systems – that is systems whose behaviour is preponderantly influenced by emotions, cognition, and social networks. Therefore, besides quantitative analysis, the book uses qualitative and computational approaches to the study of organizations and machines which involve the representation of percepts, concepts, and mental models through words, sentences, and propositions (linguistic conditional statements) of natural language.

Section V provides additional contributions to organizational cognition and cognitive machines. It presents evidence of this book and it indicates the alignment of its premises and propositions with results of an industrial case study. Its central point of contribution is concerned with the development of approaches and measures to evaluate the degree of organizational cognition.

Section V consists of Chapters VIII to XI which are complemented with the definitions, models, data, theorem proof, and concepts presented in the Appendixes F, G, H and I.

Chapter VIII introduces the organization of study and the approaches selected for its investigation. It explains the scope, the purpose, and the motivations for this industrial case study. With its content, it outlines problems to be analyzed, solutions to be designed and expected findings.

Chapter IX is concerned with the implementation of The Capability Maturity Model - which is a continuous and evolutionary process improvement model - in the organization of study. From this investigation, we define measures of organization process improvement and we propose correlations between them and organizational cognition. Among these measures are included organization process maturity, capability, and performance. From such correlations, we also define an association between organizational cognition and organizational learning.

Chapter X is concerned with the design of a management control system whose functional elements execute cognitive tasks of analysis, decision, and control of the organization process performance. The management control system works in the form of an Adaptive Learning Cycle (ALC) whose principles of operation are based on single-loop and double-loop learning. Among its elements, it includes the participation of a cognitive machine whose responsibility involves the evaluation of the organization process performance through the tasks of analysis and decision. The design of the cognitive machine is reinforced with a set of criteria along with qualitative and quantitative analysis.

Chapter XI presents data analysis, results and conclusions about the industrial case study. Findings indicate that improvements in the level of organization process performance are associated with improvements in the level of organization process maturity, and thus with improvements in the degree of organizational cognition. It also outlines the main contributions and limitations found with the implementation of The Capability Maturity Model in the organization of study.

Chapter VIII
The Organization
of Study

INTRODUCTION

This chapter presents the organization[1] of study and the research methods selected for its investigation. It explains the scope, the purpose, and the motivations for this industrial case study. With its content, it outlines problems to be analyzed, solutions to be designed, and expected findings.

APPROACHES TO THE STUDY OF THE ORGANIZATION

The approaches to the study of the organization were selected according to the criteria introduced in Appendix A and their definitions are briefly reviewed in the following.

Participant Observation

The participant observation approach regards the practical employee experience and thus the participation of the first author of this book in the organization of study during the period between 1997 and 2000. During that period, the organization was investing in new process improvement models and the first author was employed as a full-time electronics engineer in the organization - where he was fulfilling the role of an expert in software project engineering and management, quality control and as well as in organizational policies design for software process improvement.

Computational Modeling

The computational modelling approach involves the design, analysis and the simulation of a cognitive machine through computational tools. This machine was designed and implemented in the organization of study in 1998 by the first author. This adventure yielded him in 1998 the Industrial Director Award in the category of Process Improvement and Quality Management.

Qualitative and Quantitative Research

Qualitative and quantitative studies are used in this investigation to support the design and analysis of the cognitive machine, and also to explain data results and findings on measures of organization process improvement and its association with degree of organizational cognition.

THE ORGANIZATION: NEC / NOB

Characteristics

The industrial plant of NEC of Brazil is the organization of study. NEC of Brazil is a subsidiary of NEC[2] Corporation which is a Japanese enterprise, with multinational actions, and thus playing worldwide business and activities in the global market of communications, multimedia, information technology, semiconductors, computers, along with other technological fields. NEC of Brazil (hereafter sometimes abbreviated by NOB) is a telecommunications company which acts in the Brazilian along with the Latin American market by providing solutions, services and products to its customers of governmental and private sectors. Its main industrial plant in Brazil has been settled in the city of Sao Paulo. Table 8.1 presents some of the data about NOB such as its size, wealth and age which were collected in 1998 and published in (Volpe & Nobre, 2000).

NOB provides customers with telecommunications solutions, services and products whose performance and quality criteria are highly dependent on complex and large-scale software systems which involve real time and embedded applications, and also Graphical User Interface [3] systems.

Structure of the Organization

A simplified model of the structure of the industrial plant of NEC of Brazil (NOB) is illustrated in Figure 8.1. This structure was the working model of NOB in the period

Table 8.1. NEC of Brazil (NOB) – data of 1998

Foundation	26th/11/1968
Liquid Wealth	US$ 1,154.00 (millions) / in 1998
Market products	Telecommunications systems (TMN – Telecommunications Management Networks, Wireless, Radio, Transmission and Switching systems)
Number of employees	2,932 (in December 1998)
Address	Rod. Presidente Dutra, km 214, Guarulhos-Sao Paulo, 07210-902, Brazil
Competitors	Ericsson, Siemens, Motorola, Nortel-Lucent

between 1997 and 2000 (Volpe & Nobre, 2000). It was organized by four divisions: Radio, Transmission, Switching and Wireless Communications Systems.

During that period, these four divisions were managed by an Industrial Director Board who had the responsibility to communicate and respond their results to the President of NOB. Each division comprised several departments among those of accounting, planning, engineering, manufacturing, production, quality assurance, test and maintenance.

The Core Unit of Study in the Organization

The Telecommunications Management Networks (TMN) Section is the core unit of study in the organization (NOB). Therefore, most of the data investigated in this industrial case study was collected in this unit. Therefore, it is briefly described in this subsection.

The TMN Section was part of the Engineering Department of the Radio Systems Division of NOB. It was the principal actor in NOB responsible for the development of complex and large-scale software systems, and thus it played core roles of engineering and management of software projects, software processes and software products. The main class of software projects of the TMN Section was concerned with Telecommunications Management Networks[4] of International Telecommunication Union (ITU) standards – where ITU is the United Nations Specialized Agency in the field of Telecommunications (ITU-T, 2000).

Figure 8.2 illustrates the structure of NEC of Brazil (NOB) with emphasis on the Radio Systems Division and it highlights the TMN Section with a circle.

Period and Data of Study

During the period between 1997 and 2000, the first author was employed as a full-time electronics engineer in the organization, and more specifically in the TMN

Figure 8.1. Structure and divisions of the industrial plant of NEC of Brazil (NOB)

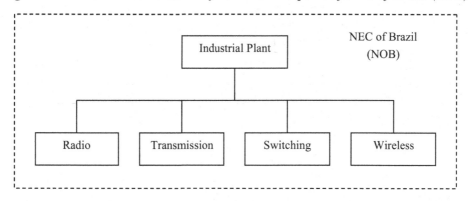

Figure 8.2. Top-down structure and the TMN Section of NEC of Brazil (NOB)

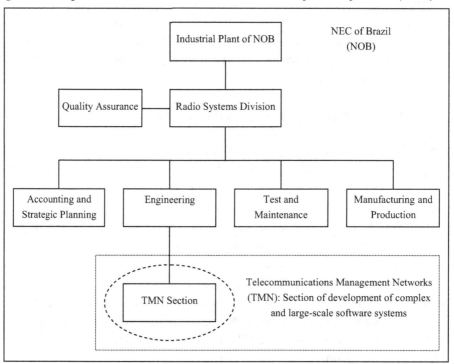

Section - where he was fulfilling the role of an expert in software project engineering and management, quality control and as well as in organizational policies design for software process improvement. Therefore, most of the data about this investigation were collected in the organization of study in the period between 1997 and 2000, and they were also selected from international publications of the first author with co-authoring of other employees with NOB (Nobre, 2005; Nobre *et al*, 2000; Nobre & Volpe, 1999; Nobre & Nakasone, 1999; and Volpe & Nobre, 2000).

THE PURSUIT OF EXCELLENCE IN THE ORGANIZATION

NEC of Brazil (NOB) has been a well-known and recognized organization for his excellence in quality management programs which lead itself to successful achievements with international certifications in areas of ISO 9000 and ISO 14000[5] during the 1990's.

Nevertheless, in 1996 NOB had the initiative to invest in additional organization process improvement models in order to support its business and to enhance competitive advantage through new engineering, management and organizational processes in the sector of software systems. This initiative complemented its efforts in the pursuit of excellence in Total Quality Management (TQM) and customer satisfaction.

After researching the market and consulting experts in partnership with the University of Sao Paulo[6], NOB chose The Capability Maturity Model of the Software Engineering Institute of Carnegie Mellon University (Paulk, *et al* 1994) to be its new process of organizing for its software business areas. Therefore, from 1997 to 2000, the CMM (the abbreviation of The Capability Maturity Model) was carefully examined and tailored in the organization, resulting in new policies and guidelines for software process improvement in the NOB.

SCOPE, PURPOSE, AND MOTIVATIONS FOR THE STUDY

The central point of contribution of this industrial case study, as compiled in the chapters of Part V, is concerned with the development of approaches and measures to evaluate the degree of organizational cognition. For this purpose it looks carefully at three complementary activities.

The first activity, which is most introduced in Chapter IX, is about processes of organizing and it presents a continuous and evolutionary process improvement model which was implemented in the organization of study. In this part, we contribute by defining correlations between measures of organization process improvement and degree of organizational cognition. Among the measures of process improvement are included organization process maturity, capability and performance. From the correlations, we also derive conclusions about the association between organizational cognition and organizational learning.

The second activity, which is most introduced in Chapter X, is about the development of an approach to evaluate the process of organizing and it proposes the design of a management control system which performs the tasks of analysis, decision and control of the organization process performance. The computation of performance indexes of the organization process is executed by a cognitive machine which is engineered through a set of criteria of design along with qualitative and quantitative analysis.

The third activity, which is most discussed in Chapter XI, is concerned with data analysis, results and conclusions about the industrial case study. From the findings we associate improvements in the level of organization process performance with improvements in the level of organization process maturity. Proceeding further, we associate these results with improvements in the degree of organizational cognition, and thus we open new directions to assess, to evaluate and to measure the degree of organizational cognition from appraisal methods such as those of organization process improvement models. We also outline the main contributions and limitations found with the implementation of The Capability Maturity Model in the organization of study.

STRATEGY AND EXPECTED FINDINGS

Organizational cognition involves a set of processes that provide the organization with the capability to learn, to solve problems and to make decisions. Consequently, we also believe that organizational cognition provides organizations with improvements in their technical, managerial, institutional and business processes. Therefore, in this industrial case study, our developments of approaches and measures to evaluate the degree of organizational cognition is done by associating concepts, practices and results of organization process improvement with organizational cognition. Such developments have two major complementary proposals.

In the first proposal, we associate organization process maturity with organizational cognition. Shortly speaking, organization process maturity is concerned with the level of specification of a process and it provides organizations with the potential for capability and performance growth. The concept of organization process maturity, capability and performance are proposed within the Capability Maturity Model - CMM - (Paulk *et al*, 1994) and they are introduced in Chapter IX. Moreover, the CMM proposes a set of appraisal frameworks in order to asses and to evaluate the process maturity level of organizations. In this particular investigation of the industrial case study, we give special attention to the CMM version of staged representations of five maturity levels of the organization. Therefore, we associate the five maturity levels of the CMM with degrees of organizational cognition.

Nevertheless, despite providing appraisal frameworks for evaluation and assessment of the level of organization process maturity, the CMM does not provide prescriptions for an approach to measure the level of organization process performance. Hence, we develop a method for this task as described in the next paragraph.

In the second proposal, we associate improvements in organization process performance with organizational cognition. With this purpose, we propose a management control system of the organization process performance. Among its elements, the management control system includes the participation of a cognitive machine whose responsibility involves the evaluation of the organization process performance through the tasks of analysis and decision. In this application, we select data of a set of five successive large-scale software projects which were engineered and managed in the Telecommunications Management Networks (TMN) Section of NEC of Brazil (NOB). These data include project cost (C) and project requirements completeness (R) and they represent the state variables of the software process of the TMN Section. C and R are fed into the cognitive machine which performs the computation of performance indexes of the software process of the TMN Section. The performance indexes include Customer Satisfaction (CS) and Project Management Quality (PMQ). Therefore, the cognitive machine executes the mapping of the inputs (C and R) to the outputs (CS and PMQ). In this perspective, organization process performance is synonymous with the TMN Section's process performance.

SUMMARY

Chapter VIII introduced the organization of study and the research methods selected for its investigation. It explained the scope, the purpose and the motivations for this industrial case study. With its content, it outlines problems to be analyzed, solutions to be designed and expected findings.

It emphasized that the central point of contribution of this industrial case study is concerned with the development of approaches and measures to evaluate the degree of organizational cognition. For this purpose it presented a summary of the three complementary activities which form the path for the achievement of this important contribution.

The first activity is about processes of organizing and it is introduced in Chapter IX. It involves the implementation of a continuous and evolutionary process improvement model in the organization of study.

The second activity is about the evaluation of the process of organizing and it is introduced in Chapter X. It involves the design of a management control system that performs the tasks of analysis, decision and control of the organization process performance. The computation of the indexes of organization process performance is executed by a cognitive machine.

The third activity is concerned with data analysis, results and conclusions about the industrial case study and it is presented in Chapter XI. From the findings, we open new directions to assess, to evaluate and to measure the degree of organizational cognition from appraisal methods of organization process improvement models.

REFERENCES

ITU-T (2000). Principles for a telecommunications management network. *Recommendation M.3010*. International Telecommunication Union.

Nobre, F. S., & Nakasone, J. (1999). A Fuzzy Computational Approach for Evaluating Process Control Quality. *IEEE International Conference on Fuzzy Systems.* Proceedings: 1701-1706. Seoul, Korea.

Nobre, F. S., & Volpe, R. (1999). SEI-CMM Implementation at the NEC Brasil S.A. *Proceedings of the International Conference on Software Technology: Industrial Track* (pp. 45-72). Curitiba, Brazil.

Nobre, F. S. *et al* (2000). Fuzzy Logic in Management Control: A Case Study. *IEEE Proceedings of the International Engineering Management Conference* (pp. 414-419). Albuquerque-NM, USA.

Nobre, F. S. (2005). On Cognitive Machines in Organizations. *PhD Thesis*, 343 pages. University of Birmingham / Birmingham-UK. Birmingham Main Library. Control Number: M0266887BU.

Paulk, M. C. *et al* (1994). *The Capability Maturity Model: Guidelines for Improving the Software Process*. Addison Wesley Longman, Inc.

Volpe, R., Nobre, F. S., *et al* (2000). The Role of Software Process Improvement into TQM: An Industrial Experience. *IEEE Proceedings of the International Engineering Management Conference* (pp. 29-34). Albuquerque-NM, USA.

ENDNOTES

[1]   The organization is defined according to Part II. Additionally, in Part V we consider that the organization can be regarded as a unit (such as a division or department) within a company or other entity which manages a set of projects.

These projects within the organization share common management and policies (Paulk *et al*, 1994).

2   NEC (http://www.nec.com)

3   Graphical User Interface (GUI) is a kind of software user interface which allows people to interact with a computer, its program and other devices in a more friendly way.

4   The concept of Telecommunications Management Networks is presented in (ITU-T, 2000).

5   ISO is the abbreviation for International Organization for Standardization (http://www.iso.org). In summary, ISO 9000 is a family of standards for quality management systems, and ISO 14000 is a family of standards for environmental management systems.

6   University of Sao Paulo - USP (http://www.usp.br)

Chapter IX
Organizational Cognition in the Industrial Case Study

INTRODUCTION

This chapter is concerned with the implementation of The Capability Maturity Model in the organization of study. In this application, we define measures of organization process improvement and we propose correlations between them and organizational cognition. Among these measures are included organization process maturity, capability, and performance. Therefore, we define correlations between organizational cognition and organization process maturity, and also between organizational cognition and organization process capability and performance. From such correlations, we also define an association between organizational cognition and organizational learning. Hence, we outline new directions to the development of approaches to assess, to evaluate and to measure the degree of organizational cognition from appraisal methods of The Capability Maturity Model and of other organization process improvement models.

Moreover, Chapter IX is complemented by Appendix I which summarizes concepts and characteristics about the five maturity levels of The Capability Maturity Model.

THE CAPABILITY MATURITY MODEL: OVERVIEW

This section overviews the main purpose and concepts of The Capability Maturity Model (hereafter sometimes abbreviated by CMM) which play an important part in this industrial case study. A summary with additional information about definitions and characteristics of the five maturity levels of the CMM framework is presented in Appendix I.

The CMM comprises a family of maturity frameworks proposed by the Software Engineering Institute of the Carnegie Mellon University (Paulk, *et al* 1994). It provides organizations with process improvement guidelines of staged and continuous representations for systems engineering, software engineering, integrated product and process development, supplier sourcing, personnel and talent management, among other areas. The CMM has received increasing attention since the 1990's with applications in worldwide organizations that pursue high levels of process maturity mainly in software business (Herbsleb, J., *et al* 1994; and CMU-SEI, 2002, 2004 and 2007). It has its pillars based on concepts of Total Quality Management (TQM), process and technology change management, systems engineering, organizational learning, among other disciplines.

The Capability Maturity Model for Software Process Improvement with staged representations of process maturity levels (hereafter abbreviated as CMM) is the earliest model among the different versions and frameworks of the CMM family. Therefore, the CMM is also the most well-known and tested software process improvement model in worldwide organizations. This earliest model was the one selected and applied in the industrial case study of this book.

The CMM provides recommendations and guidelines for improving software engineering, management and organizational processes. These processes develop gradually in details, complexity and maturity according to an evolutionary path of five levels of maturity. By following this path from level 1 to 5 the organization improves its process maturity, capability and performance. The CMM is also equipped with appraisal methods to evaluate and to assess the maturity level of the software processes of the organization (Masters & Bothwell, 2005; and Paulk *et al*, 1994).

Recent research reported by the Software Engineering Institute of the Carnegie Mellon University has shown that the number of organizations using the CMM has reached more than 1,500 organizations worldwide (CMU-SEI, 2004). A summary of important benefits of the CMM to organizations can be found in (Herbsleb *et al*, 1994; and Paulk & Chrissis, 2000). Among the measurements and improvements found in the assessments include return on investment (ROI), gain per year in productivity, reduction of schedule to develop software systems, product quality and defect reduction.

ORGANIZATION PROCESS CAPABILITY, MATURITY AND PERFORMANCE

Process capability, maturity and performance are distinct but complementary definitions within the CMM (Paulk *et al*, 1994). These terms are defined in the following because they are often used throughout Part V.

Organization Process Capability

This is concerned with the expectation of results and thus predictability - i.e. with the amount of expected results that can be achieved by following a process. Therefore, the higher the process capability, the higher is the predictability of outcomes of the organization.

Organization Process Maturity

This is concerned with the level of specification of a process and it comprises the extent to which a particular process is explicitly designed, defined, institutionalized, managed, controlled and effective. Process maturity provides organizations with the potential for capability and performance growth.

Organization Process Performance

This is concerned with actual results achieved by following a process – i.e. the results of a process.

MATURE *VS.* IMMATURE ORGANIZATIONS

This subsection differentiates immature from mature software organizations.

Immature Organizations

Immature organizations are characterized by low levels of predictability[1], control[2] and effectiveness[3] (Paulk *et al*, 1994). Their process is poorly understood and their ability to solve problems depends on the particular skills of an expert during crisis. Such organizations routinely exceed schedules and budgets because they are not based on realistic planning. Consequently, it is highly probable that immature organizations cannot satisfy their goals, targets and strict criteria of customer satisfaction, quality, time, cost, etc. Nevertheless, immature organizations can achieve successful results when they pay a high price for heroic experts.

Mature Organizations

In contrast, mature organizations are characterized by high levels of predictability, control and effectiveness. Their process is clearly defined and their projects are based on realistic planning. In such a type of organizations, activities are carried out according to a planned process and hence it is most probable that they can satisfy their goals, targets and criteria. Additionally, mature organizations comprise continuous process improvement practices which provide them with the abilities to learn by creating and managing knowledge (Argote, 1999).

Therefore, we can state that:

Proposition 9.1: The higher the level of process maturity of the organization, the higher is its level of predictability, control and effectiveness.

ORGANIZATIONAL COGNITION *VS.* ORGANIZATION PROCESS MATURITY

As defined in Part II, organizational cognition comprises a set of processes which together provide the organization with the ability to learn, to make decisions and to solve problems. It was also defined in Part II that the degree of organizational cognition is associated with, and contingent upon, the level of details, elaboration and integration of the cognitive processes of the organization.

Therefore, it can be assumed that the degree of cognition of the organization can be associated with and thus defined as contingent upon the level of process maturity of the organization. Hence, by considering this perspective and by assuming Proposition 9.1, it can be derived that:

Proposition 9.2: The higher the degree of organizational cognition, the higher is the level of predictability, control and effectiveness of the organization.

Proposition 9.3: The higher the degree of organizational cognition, the higher is the level of process maturity of the organization.

Proposition 9.3 plays an important part in this book since it associates degree of organizational cognition with measures of process maturity. In such a way, the degree of organizational cognition can be associated with one of the five maturity levels of the CMM. Therefore, the degree of organizational cognition can be measured in the integer interval [1,5], where 1,…,5 represent the levels of process maturity of the CMM.

An important implication and contribution of this correlation is that it opens new directions in the development of research approaches to assess and to measure the degree of organizational cognition from the appraisal methods of The Capability Maturity Model and thus from other continuous process improvement models. Therefore, we can state that we have pointed out an approach to evaluate and to measure the degree of organizational cognition.

Figure 9.1 illustrates the direct relation between levels of organization process maturity and degrees of organizational cognition. The dotted arrow indicates a direct relation between these variables.

ORGANIZATIONAL COGNITION *VS*. ORGANIZATION PROCESS CAPABILITY AND PERFORMANCE

It was defined that process maturity provides organizations with the potential for capability and performance growth. Therefore, this section assumes that organiza-

Figure 9.1. Level of process maturity vs. degree of organizational cognition

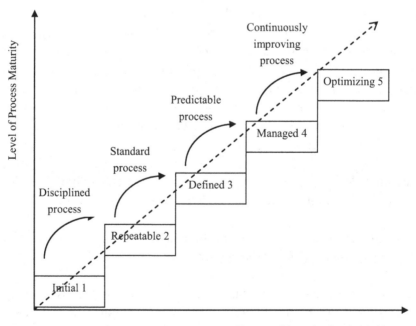

tion process capability and performance can be associated with, and thus defined as contingent upon, the level of process maturity of the organization. Hence, it proposes that:

Proposition 9.4: The higher the level of process maturity of the organization, the greater is the chance of the organization to achieve high levels of process capability and performance.

Proposition 9.4 plays an important part in this chapter since it associates levels of organization capability and performance with measures of process maturity and thus organizational cognition. Therefore, we can derive that:

Proposition 9.5: The higher the degree of organizational cognition, the greater is the chance of the organization to achieve high levels of process capability and performance.

ORGANIZATIONAL COGNITION *VS.* ORGANIZATIONAL LEARNING

At this stage of conclusions, after having derived that degrees of organizational cognition can be associated with levels of organization process maturity, capability and performance respectively, we also assert that improvements in organizational cognition can be associated improvement in organizational learning. This assertion is reinforced when we observe that improvements in organization performance and productivity have been associated with practices and concepts of organizational learning in the literature (Argote, 1999; and Brynjolfsson & Hitt, 2000).

Therefore, we also define an association of organizational cognition with organization learning by stating that:

Proposition 9.6: The higher the degree of organizational cognition, the higher is the level of organizational learning.

Where, the higher the level of organizational learning, the higher is the capability of the organization to learn.

THE CMM IN NEC / NOB

Motivations

A simplified structure of the industrial plant of NEC of Brazil (NOB) was illustrated in Figure 8.1. This structure was the working model for NOB in the period between 1997 and 2000 (Volpe & Nobre, 2000). It was structured with four divisions: Radio, Transmission, Switching and Wireless Communications Systems.

These divisions shared common organization processes whose policies, procedures and practices were defined according to ISO 9000, ISO 14000 and Just in Time (JIT) systems, among other norms and concepts of Total Quality Management (TQM) and continuous process improvement (Nobre & Volpe, 1999). Additionally, each division of NOB used to develop its own software process until 1996. However, from the end of 1996 and beginning of 1997 the organization (NOB) started to invest in the research and implementation of the Capability Maturity Model (CMM) for standardization of common guidelines and policies for software process improvement in all departments responsible for software projects and software business in the whole enterprise.

Strategy

The strategy, process and structure of implementation of the CMM in NOB are illustrated in Figure 9.2 and described in the next paragraph.

In this implementation and institutionalization of the CMM into NEC of Brazil (NOB), the CMM Guidelines were understood by a Software Engineering Process Group (SEPG) of NOB who followed a tailoring process to write the Organization's Standard Software Process (OSSP). The OSSP represented the common general policies and procedures of NOB for software process improvement. It was written by the SEPG in the form of a manual which was used by them for training engineers and managers of software projects among other participants in the whole organization (NOB). Proceeding further, the OSSP was understood by local Software Engineering Process Groups in the four divisions of NOB and thus adapted to Project's Defined Software Process (PDSP). PDSP is a tailored version of the OSSP which is developed to fit the specific characteristics of a project. Results, measurements, data and best practices were selected by Software Engineering Process Groups and stored in the Organization Data Base for Software Process Improvement with the purpose of exchange information and experience across the divisions and units of the organization.

Figure 9.2. CMM process in the organization

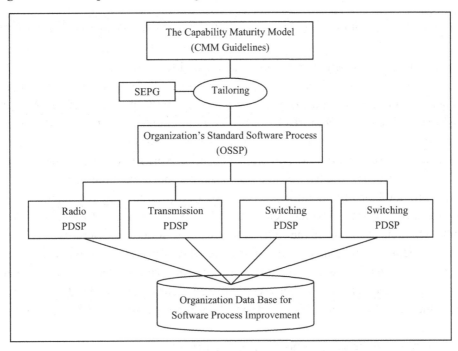

Assessment

In the period between 1997 and 1998, the four divisions of NOB were assessed by a lead evaluator who was authorized and certified by the Software Engineering Institute of the Carnegie Mellon University to perform the assessment process. The four divisions were officially recognized for completely satisfying and filling the main goals and requirements of the key process areas of the CMM Level 2. Therefore, motivated by its preliminary results, NOB preceded with new investments towards the pursuit and achievement of the CMM Level 3. Nevertheless, the achievement of level 3 was unsuccessful until the end of 2000 due to budget constraints in the organization and also because of some disruptive and normative changes that occurred in the Brazilian market of telecommunications in the late 1990's. Changes were caused by national privatizations of governmental telecommunications companies as well as by the entrance of new multinational competitors in Brazil (Volpe & Nobre, 2000).

SUMMARY

Chapter IX outlined the implementation of The Capability Maturity Model in the organization of study, and more specifically, in the industrial plant of NEC located in Sao Paulo, Brazil, which was abbreviated as NEC of Brazil (NOB).

The CMM was introduced as a continuous and evolutionary process improvement model proposed by the Software Engineering Institute of the Carnegie Mellon University. The CMM comprises guidelines and policies for improving the levels of process maturity, capability and performance of the organization and it also contributes by proving people with appraisal frameworks in order to assess and to measure the process maturity level of the organization. The implementation of the CMM provided the organization with new software engineering, management and organizational processes which were standardized and institutionalized in the whole NOB. This action enhanced the NOB's culture and practices for continuous process improvement, Total Quality Management (TQM) and customer satisfaction.

In this application, we defined measures of organization process improvement and we proposed correlations between them and organizational cognition. Among these measures were included organization process maturity, capability and performance.

Therefore, we derived propositions that correlate:

Organizational cognition with organization process maturity:

Proposition 9.3: The higher the degree of organizational cognition, the higher is the level of process maturity of the organization.

Organizational cognition with organization process capability and performance:

Proposition 9.5: The higher the degree of organizational cognition, the greater is the chance of the organization to achieve high levels of process capability and performance.

And organizational cognition with organizational learning:

Proposition 9.6: The higher the degree of organizational cognition, the higher is the level of organizational learning.

Where, the higher the level of organizational learning, the higher is the capability of the organization to learn.

An important implication and contribution found with these definitions of correlations is that they open new directions to the development of approaches to assess and to measure the degree of organizational cognition from the appraisal frameworks of The Capability Maturity Model and thus also from other continuous process improvement models. Therefore, we can state that we have pointed out an approach to evaluate and to measure the degree of organizational cognition.

Chapter IX was complemented with Appendix I which summarizes concepts of the five maturity levels of the Capability Maturity Model.

REFERENCES

Argote, L. (1999). *Organizational Learning: Creating, Retaining and Transferring Knowledge*. Kluwer Academic Publishers.

CMU-SEI (2002). CMMI for Systems Engineering, Software Engineering, Integrated Product and Process Development, and Supplier Sourcing: Staged Representation. Version 1.1. CMMI/SE/SW/IPPD/SS. *Report CMU/SEI-TR-012*. Carnegie Mellon University. http://www.sei.cmu.edu.

CMU-SEI (2004). *Process Maturity Profile: Software CMM*. August 2004. Carnegie Mellon University. http://www.sei.cmu.edu.

CMU-SEI (2007). *Process Maturity Profile: CMMI v1.1, SCAMPI v1.1, Class A - Appraisal Results*. March 2007. Carnegie Mellon University. http://www.sei.cmu. edu.

Herbsleb, J., *et al* (1994). Benefits of CMM-Based Software Process Improvement: Executive Summary of Initial Results. *Special Report CMU/SEI-94-SR-013. September*.

Masters, S., & Bothwell, C. (2005). CMM Appraisal Framework version 1.0. *Technical Report CMU/SEI-95-TR-001*. Carnegie Mellon University. http://www. sei.cmu.edu.

Nobre, F. S., & Volpe, R. (1999). SEI-CMM Implementation at the NEC Brasil S.A. *Proceedings of the International Conference on Software Technology: Industrial Track* (pp. 45-72). Curitiba, Brazil.

Paulk, M. C. *et al* (1994). *The Capability Maturity Model: Guidelines for Improving the Software Process*. Addison Wesley Longman, Inc.

Paulk, M. C., & Chrissis, M. B. (2000). The November 1999 High Maturity Workshop. *Special Report CMU/SEI-2000-SR-003, March*.

Volpe, R., & Nobre, F. S., *et al* (2000). The Role of Software Process Improvement into TQM: An Industrial Experience. *IEEE Proceedings of the International Engineering Management Conference* (pp. 29-34). Albuquerque-NM, USA.

ENDNOTES

[1]   Improvements in predictability reduce the difference between target and actual results across projects.

[2]   Improvements in control reduce the variability of actual outcomes around target results.

[3]   Improvements in effectiveness improve target results and thus provide the organization with the ability to satisfy stricter criteria - such as lower cost, shorter schedule (time), and higher productivity and quality.

Chapter X
A Cognitive Machine in the Organization of Study

INTRODUCTION

Chapter X is concerned with the design of a management control system whose functional elements execute cognitive tasks of analysis, decision and control of the organization process performance. The management control system works in the form of an Adaptive Learning Cycle (ALC) whose principles of operation are based on single-loop and double-loop learning. Among its elements, it includes the participation of a cognitive machine whose responsibility involves the evaluation of the organization process performance through the tasks of analysis and decision. The design of the cognitive machine is reinforced with a set of criteria along with qualitative and quantitative analysis. Chapter X is complemented with Appendixes F, G and H. Appendix F defines the state variables (X) which are used in the management control of the organization process performance. Appendix G presents linguistic descriptions of the mental models which were designed and written for the cognitive machine. Appendix H demonstrates theorem proof as part of the quantitative analysis of the cognitive machine.

OBJECTIVES

The proposal of the management control system in this chapter is motivated in order to:

a. Provide managers and stakeholders with data about the organization process performance, including information about quality and customer satisfaction.
b. Support managers in the analysis, decision and control of the organization process performance.
c. Reduce intra-individual and group dysfunctional conflicts which arise from managerial decision-making.
d. Enhance actions for continuous process improvement.
e. Improve the cognitive processes and thus the degree of cognition of the organization of study.

SCOPE OF THE APPLICATION

As a participant of NEC of Brazil (NOB) in the period between 1997 and 2000, the first author designed a management control system for the organization of study, and in particular, for the Telecommunications Management Networks (TMN) Section of the Engineering Department of the Radio Systems Division of NOB. Among the elements of the management control system, he introduced a cognitive machine which was responsible to evaluate the software process performance of the TMN Section through the tasks of analysis and decision. Therefore, in this particular application, the organization process performance was reduced to, and synonymous with, the TMN Section's process performance.

The engineering of the cognitive machine, as demonstrated later in this chapter, was supported with criteria of design and analysis, and it was implemented in a personal computer through MATLAB software programs (Gilat, 2008). Through this approach, the first author simulated the participation of the cognitive machine in the management control system of the TMN Section of the Engineering Department of the Radio Systems Division of the NEC of Brazil (NOB).

THE PURSUIT OF INNOVATION IN THE ORGANIZATION

During the 1990's, NEC of Brazil (NOB) was living in a climate for technological and organizational innovations in the sector of telecommunications and software business. Late in 1998, NOB was benefiting from its apogee in software and organization process improvement. It was at that period that NOB was promoting incentives to its employees through reward systems and awards such as The Industrial Director Honour Prize for innovators and contributors in the areas of organization process improvement, quality management, productivity growth, technology innovation, among other fields. It was in 1998 that the first author was awarded by NOB with this competitive prize for his development of an initial version of the management control system - which includes the participation of the cognitive machine - as presented in this chapter. It was later that a more detailed version of this work was published in (Nobre *et al*, 2000; and Nobre & Steiner, 2001a).

MANAGEMENT CONTROL IN THE ORGANIZATION

NEC of Brazil (NOB), like other business organizations, comprises processes and structure which are closer to the characteristics of open-rational systems[1]. This kind of organization needs an effective and efficient management control system to drive and to govern its state variables towards its goals and targets.

Management control is a continuous process used to improve the capability of the organization to carry out its activities towards the achievement of its goals (Anthony *et al*, 1984). The implementation of the process of management control requires the:

i.   Design of a structure or framework of a management control system.
ii. Definition of the state variables[2] of the organization.
iii. Gathering measurements of the state variables in the form of quantitative and qualitative information.
iv. Storage of this information in the organization database (memory);
v.   Analysis of this information which involves decisions in order to derive conclusions about the organization process performance.
vi. Control and governance of the organization process in order to improve performance.

This book is concerned with such a perspective of management control. Steps (iii) to (vi) repeat continuously and thus the management control system constitutes an Adaptive Learning Cycle (ALC). In this cycle, the element of control and governance (vi) determine the type of learning of the ALC which can be either single-loop or double-loop learning. On the one hand, with single-loop learning the organization identifies problems and makes corrections by using previous solutions and present procedures. On the other hand, with double-loop learning the organization identifies problems and makes corrections by changing present procedures, policies and processes (Daft & Noe, 2001). Both learning strategies are used in this industrial case study.

COGNITIVE MACHINES IN MANAGEMENT CONTROL

Motivations

The development of fuzzy sets theory and fuzzy logic (Zadeh, 1965 and 1973) was widely motivated by the need for an alternative and complementary approach, of mathematical and computational background, to the analysis of complex systems – like the systems found within the category of organizational and social sciences – i.e. systems whose behaviour is determined by human emotion, cognition and social networks (Nobre, 2005; and Karwowski & Mital, 1986). Most recently, theories of computing with words (Zadeh, 1996a) and computation of perceptions (Zadeh, 1999 and 2001) were proposed to provide the literature with new approaches to the representation and manipulation of mental models. From this perspective, this section takes advantage of the elements of these disciplines in order to design a cognitive machine whose normative and behavioural processes are based on quantitative analysis along with mental models of managers and engineers of the Telecommunications Management Networks (TMN) Section of the Engineering Department of NOB.

Challenges

To supply stakeholders and managers with feedback information about the organization process performance encompasses three key problems (Nobre, 2005; Nobre & Steiner, 2001a; and Nobre & Nakasone, 1999):

i.   The first problem is concerned with the concept of performance as well as with the identification of the state variables which influence the organization process performance.

ii. The second problem is concerned with the vagueness (Black, 1937 and 1963) and fuzziness (Klir & Folger, 1988; and Zadeh, 1965) inherent in the concept of performance. Hence, the representation of the qualitative aspects of this concept through a precise quantitative symbol becomes a difficult task.

iii. The third problem is concerned with intra-individual and group dysfunctional conflicts which arise from decision-making processes involving definitions of the concept of performance. Such decisions comprise subjective judgments and also alternatives which are characterized by uncertainty, incomparability and unacceptability as explained in Chapter VII. These alternatives include propositions with state variables in their premises and in their conclusions; such state variables influence the organization process performance and they are most represented by natural concepts which are inherently characterized with fuzzy boundaries (Bernstein *et al*, 1997).

Solution

To contribute to the solution of the previous problems, this book proposes the definitions whose features are presented in the following.

i.   Organization process performance is defined as contingent upon indexes of Customer Satisfaction (CS) and Project Management Quality (PMQ).

ii. These performance indexes (CS and PMQ) are defined as contingent upon project cost (C), project schedule (T) and project requirements completeness (R). C, T and R are performance factors of the organization projects; they represent state variables and their relations form the premises to the conclusion about CS and PMQ. Definitions of C, T and R are presented in Appendix F.

iii. The concepts of the factors (C, T and R) and indexes (CS and PMQ) of the organization process performance are mathematically represented through membership functions of fuzzy sets theory (Zadeh, 1965). Therefore, the fuzzy boundaries inherent in these concepts take the form of complex symbols whose structures are represented by fuzzy sets.

iv. Intra-individual and group's mental models are represented through a set of fuzzy propositions and fuzzy conditional statements - which can be mathematically defined by fuzzy generalized constraints (Zadeh, 1999). Fuzzy conditional statements also play an important part in this application by providing measures (f) in order to map the factors X=(C, T, R) to the indexes Y=(CS, PMQ):

$$f: X \rightarrow Y \tag{10.1}$$

v.   Decision-making processes about the organization process performance are automated through the rules of inference of fuzzy logic which are also extended to applications in computing with words and computation of perceptions (Zadeh, 1996a, 1999 and 2001).

In such a way, the organization process performance's indexes - as defined by Customer Satisfaction (CS) and Project Management Quality (PMQ) - can be used as additional indicators to measure the progress of the Capability Maturity Model (CMM) in the organization of study.

Before introducing the design of the cognitive machine and its analysis, the next section introduces a framework of a management control system which is used in the analysis, decision and control tasks of the organization process performance. Moreover, it describes the role of the cognitive machine into such a framework.

THE MANAGEMENT CONTROL SYSTEM

The framework of the management control system is illustrated in Figure 10.1. It is composed by a managerial cycle with principles of feedback control systems and continuous process improvement (Nobre, 2005). Additionally, it can be regarded as an Adaptive Learning Cycle (ALC) whose principles of operation are based on single-loop and double-loop learning.

The organization process comprises a normative structure composed by a set of procedures, norms and policies for software process improvement which are mostly based on the guidelines of the Capability Maturity Model (CMM). These procedures, norms and policies are applied to govern processes of engineering, development and management of complex software projects in the Telecommunications Management Network (TMN) Section of the Engineering Department of NOB. Therefore, in this application, organization process performance is synonymous with the software process performance in the TMN Section.

In summary, this framework involves the activities of:

i. Planning: This is concerned with strategic planning. It involves the design of the organization goals and it includes the specification of the organization process performance's criteria, indexes and factors along with measures. A performance criterion represents the boundaries of a target to be achieved. Indexes (Y) are representations of the organization process performance and in

Figure 10.1. Management control system of the organization process performance

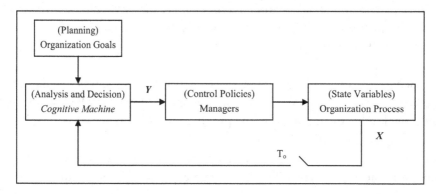

this investigation they include Customer Satisfaction (CS) and Project Management Quality (PMQ): $Y = (CS, PMQ)$; indexes are contingent upon performance factors. Factors (X) are represented by the state variables of the organization process and they comprise project cost (C), project schedule (T) and project requirements completeness (R): $X = (C, T, R)$; during the stage of planning their values are estimated through statistical tools and also by experience. The factors C, T and R are defined according to Appendix F. Measures are functions (f) used to map factors (state variables X) to performance indexes (Y) according to equation (10.1).

ii. Sampling T_o: This is concerned with the collection of qualitative and quantitative information about the state variables (X) of the organization process. The vector X includes C, T and R which represent the performance factors of the organization process. The sampling time (T_o) represents the period of time for the collection of new information about X. In this investigation T_o is defined as equal to the period of planning schedule. Therefore, information about the actual cost (C_A) and actual requirements completeness (R_A) of a project is collected from the organization process when T_o is equal to the planning schedule.

iii. Analysis and Decision: This is concerned with the evaluation and computation of the organization process performance's factors and indexes. This block maps the factors C, T and R to the performance indexes CS and PMQ. The task of analysis and decision is performed by a cognitive machine. It computes the CS and PMQ indexes from the actual cost (C_A) and the actual requirements completeness (R_A) information which are sampled at time T_o from the organization process. The planning stage provides the cognitive machine with information about C_o and R_o (which represent the planning cost and the planning requirements completeness respectively, as defined in Appendix F). Figure 10.2 illustrates the input-output information with the cognitive machine. The actual schedule (T_A) is assumed as equal to the sampling time T_o and thus it is not considered as a state variable of computation.

iv. Control Policies: They govern the behaviour of the organization. They are concerned with the norms and procedures that guide managers to act in order to improve the indexes of organization process performance. It comprises organizational learning practices of single-loop or double-loop types. The control policies are based on normative processes of the organization, and in this particular application, they are mostly based on the Capability Maturity Model guidelines. Hence, they contribute to improve software processes in the organization, and specifically in the TMN Section where complex and large-scale software projects are developed and managed.

Figure 10.2. Input-output information with the cognitive machine

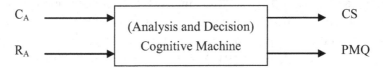

DESIGN OF THE COGNITIVE MACHINE

Structure

The structure of the cognitive machine along with its functional blocks is presented in Figure 10.3. This structure was tailored from the general framework presented in Figure 9.3 and its decision-making process works according to the Figure 9.6. Additionally, this structure is based on the classic configuration of fuzzy logic controllers (Lee, C.C. 1990; Nobre, 1997; and Wang, 1994).

Criteria of Design

The cognitive machine was designed to satisfy the set of criteria as presented in the following (Nobre, 2005 and 1997). These criteria involve terminologies and concepts which are defined throughput the literature of fuzzy systems (Klir and Folger, 1988; Pedrycz and Gomide, 1998 and 2007; and Wang 1994).

Criteria C1: The fuzzy sets of the input variables satisfy the definition of fuzzy numbers and fuzzy partitions.
Criteria C2: The fuzzy sets of the output variables satisfy the definition of fuzzy numbers and their centre contains only one element.

Figure 10.3. Structure of the cognitive machine

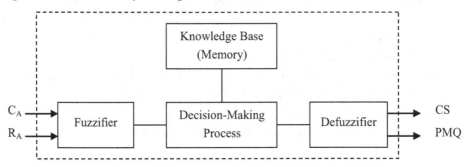

Criteria C3: The rule base (or the set of fuzzy conditional statements) satisfies the definition of strict completeness.

Criteria C4: The AND logical operator is implemented as the algebraic product.

Criteria C5: The OR logical operator is implemented as the bounded sum.

Criteria C6: The implication function satisfies the criteria of fuzzy conjunction and it is implemented as the algebraic product.

Criteria C7: The singleton fuzzifier is the operator defined to the fuzzification of input variables.

Criteria C8: The centre average defuzzifier is the operator defined to the defuzzification of output variables.

The definitions of criteria C1 to C8 were motivated because they provide the designer with a cognitive machine whose structure and algorithm can be normally implemented in computers, and most important, investigated through mathematical approaches to convergence and stability analysis (Nobre, 1997 and 2005; and Wang, 1994). Moreover, criterion C3 guarantees that for all states assumed by the input variables $X = (C, R)$, there exists an output state $Y = (CS, PMQ)$ which can be computed by the machine (Jager, 1995; and Nobre, 1997).

The specification of the functional blocks and parameters of the cognitive machine are presented in the following.

Description of Percepts via Words and Linguistic Variables

Linguistic variables involve descriptions of percepts via words and fuzzy granules which are synonymous with linguistic values of a variable. The input C and R and the output variables CS and PMQ have their linguistic values presented in the following. Their granularity and concepts were defined according to the experience and knowledge of the cognitive machine designer (i.e. the first author) along with the expertise of the manager and skills of the engineers in the TMN Section of NOB.

- Input Variables

C = (cheap, not so cheap, expensive)
R = (empty, almost empty, partial, almost full, full)

- Output Variables

CS = (very low, low, medium, high, very high)
PMQ = (really bad, very bad, bad, moderate, good, very good, really good)

Representation of Concepts via Membership Functions of Fuzzy Sets

Membership functions of fuzzy sets are used to represent linguistic variables and words (and thus percepts and natural concepts) through complex symbols of mathematical background[3]. The representations of the input (C and R) as well as the output variables (CS and PMQ) via fuzzy sets are depicted in Figures 10.4 and 10.5. They were defined according to criteria C1 and C2. Their triangular shape and universe of discourse were specified according to the experience and knowledge of the cognitive machine designer along with the expertise of the manager and skills of the engineers in the TMN Section of NOB.

In Figure 10.4, μ_{CA} and μ_{RA} denote the degrees of membership of C_A and R_A in their respective fuzzy sets, where: μ_{CA} and $\mu_{RA} \in [0,1]$; the words *cheap, not so cheap* and *expensive* are labels of the fuzzy sets which characterize the concept of cost (C) defined on the universe of discourse C_A; and the words *empty, almost empty, partial, almost full* and *full* are labels of the fuzzy sets which characterize the concept of requirements completeness (R) defined in the universe of discourse R_A.

In Figure 10.5, μ_{CS} and μ_{PMQ} denote the degrees of membership of CS and PMQ in their respective fuzzy sets, where: μ_{CS} and $\mu_{PMQ} \in [0,1]$; the words *very low, low, medium, high* and *very high* are labels of the fuzzy sets which characterize the concept of Customer Satisfaction (CS) defined in the universe of discourse CS; and the words *really bad, very bad, bad, moderate* and *good, very good* and *really good* are labels of the fuzzy sets which characterize the concept of Project Management Quality (PMQ) defined in the universe of discourse PMQ.

Representation of Mental Models via Fuzzy Conditional Statements

Fuzzy conditional statements describe relations between two or more fuzzy variables in the form of:

IF A THEN B: (A→B)   (10.2.)

where A and B denote fuzzy variables; the operator THEN can be defined as a fuzzy implication (A→B); and the symbol → denotes an implication function (Zadeh, 1973).

Fuzzy conditional statements can be classified as a particular approach to perception-based system modelling (Zadeh, 2001). In this chapter, this approach is used to design and to represent propositions and mental models which describe the

Figure 10.4. Fuzzy sets of the organization process performance's factors: (X)

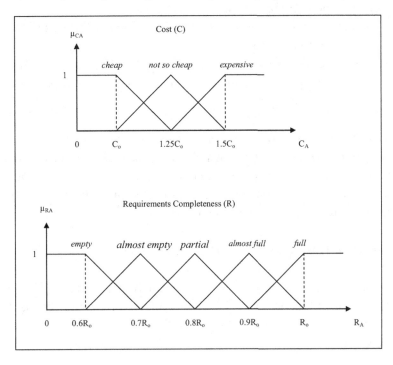

Figure 10.5. Fuzzy sets of the organization process performance's indexes: (Y)

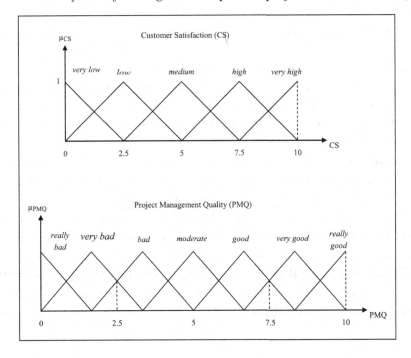

relations between input (factors) and output (indexes) variables for the management control system of the organization process performance.

In this case, mental models are representations of the normative and behavioural processes of the cognitive machine. They were written according to the experience, knowledge and perception of the participants in the TMN Section of NOB (designer, engineers and manager) to the pursuit of excellence in customer satisfaction as well as in software project management.

- **Design of the Fuzzy Rule Bases:** The set of fuzzy conditional statements comprises two fuzzy rule bases which satisfy the criterion C3. The first one is concerned with the analysis and conclusion about the Customer Satisfaction (CS) which is inferred from project requirements completeness (R). Therefore, it describes relations between R and CS:

Fuzzy Rule Base 1: IF R THEN CS: (R → CS)   (10.3)

The second rule base is concerned with the analysis and conclusion about the Project Management Quality (PMQ) which is inferred from project cost (C) and project requirements completeness (R). Therefore, it describes relations between C, R and PMQ:

Fuzzy Rule Base 2: IF C AND IF R THEN PMQ: (C AND R → PMQ) (10.4)

where AND satisfies the criterion of design C4 and the implication function → satisfies C6.

The fuzzy rule base 1, given by equation (10.3), does not include project cost (C) because this variable is not a matter of interest for the customer. On the other hand, project cost (C) is a control variable to project managers and organization stakeholders. Hence, C is included in the fuzzy rule base 2, given by equation (10.4).

The set of fuzzy conditional statements of the fuzzy rule bases 1 and 2 are represented in Figures 10.6 and 10.7 respectively. The aggregation of the statements of each fuzzy rule base satisfies the criterion of design C5.

In Figure 10.6, the cells above the horizontal axis (arrow) contain the linguistic values of R and those cells below it contain the linguistic values of CS. The fuzzy conditional statements are symbolically represented by the pairs of cells constituted by the linguistic values of R and CS which are opposite to each other and separated by the axis. This rule base comprises a set of five fuzzy conditional statements and they are described according to Appendix G. As an example, the first pair of cells

Figure 10.6. Fuzzy rule base on customer satisfaction: R → CS

Customer Satisfaction (CS)'s Mental Models					
R	*empty*	*almost empty*	*partial*	*almost full*	*full*
CS	*very low*	*low*	*medium*	*high*	*very high*

whose linguistic values are in the front of R and CS forms one fuzzy conditional statement defined as:

IF R is empty THEN CS is very low   (10.5)

In Figure 10.7, the cells on the left side of the vertical axis contain the linguistic values of C and those cells below the horizontal axis contain the linguistic values of R. The other cells, located in between the C and R axes (in the first quadrant) contain the linguistic values of PMQ which represent the conclusions of the fuzzy conditional statements. Such a rule base comprises a set of fifteen fuzzy conditional statements and they are described according to Appendix G. As an example, when the variables C and R assume the respective linguistic values of *not so cheap* and *full*, then PMQ assumes the linguistic value of *very good*. This fuzzy conditional statement is described as:

Figure 10.7. Fuzzy rule base on project management quality: (C AND R) → PMQ

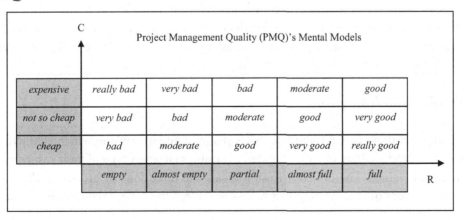

C						
	Project Management Quality (PMQ)'s Mental Models					
expensive	*really bad*	*very bad*	*bad*	*moderate*	*good*	
not so cheap	*very bad*	*bad*	*moderate*	*good*	*very good*	
cheap	*bad*	*moderate*	*good*	*very good*	*really good*	
	empty	*almost empty*	*partial*	*almost full*	*full*	R

IF C is not so cheap AND R is full THEN PMQ is very good   (10.6)

Decision-Making via the Compositional Rule of Inference

The compositional rule of inference of fuzzy logic (Zadeh, 1973 and 1999) was the mechanism used to implement the decision-making process of the cognitive machine. This mechanism is described in Chapter VI. Shortly speaking, it manipulates concepts (and thus percepts) by propagating them from premises (antecedents of fuzzy conditional statements) to conclusions. It can also be defined as a mechanism to reason with linguistic representations of mental models.

ANALYSIS OF THE COGNITIVE MACHINE

In this section we introduce an approach to the analysis of the cognitive machine which involves qualitative and quantitative studies. This approach represents a tailored version of the broader methodology proposed in (Nobre, 1997) and whose base was most derived from (King & Mamdani, 1977; MacVicar, 1976; Braae & Rutherford, 1979; and Li & Gatland, 1995).

The qualitative analysis is concerned with the design of the set of linguistic rules which form the mental models of the cognitive machine. This approach is based on the concept of linguistic phase plane - which is a phase plane whose state space is represented with linguistic values, similarly to the representations in Figures 10.6 and 10.7. It contributes by providing the designer with a methodology to:

a)   Specify an initial set of linguistic rules for the cognitive machine.
b)   Modify the linguistic rules in order to enhance improvements in the perfor-
     mance of the cognitive machine.

The quantitative analysis is concerned with the description of the set of linguistic rules of the cognitive machine through analytical equations. It provides the designer with a methodology to study mathematically some functional properties of the cognitive machine such as stability analysis.

Qualitative Analysis

Figure 10.8 illustrates a linguistic phase plane of one dimension which characterizes the relations between the linguistic variables (R and CS) and their respective linguistic values. The dotted arrows indicate the directions of growth in the linguistic values of R and CS. It can be observed that the higher the linguistic value

Figure 10.8. Analysis of customer satisfaction: R vs. CS

Customet Satisfaction (CS)'s Mental Models					
R	*empty*	*almost empty*	*partial*	*almost full*	*full*
CS	*very low*	*low*	*medium*	*high*	*very high*

of R, the higher is the linguistic value of CS, because the higher the completion of the project requirements (R) at time T_o, the higher is the Customer Satisfaction (CS) (Nobre, 2005; and Nobre *et al*, 2000).

Figure 10.9 illustrates a linguistic phase plane of two dimensions that characterizes the relations between the linguistic variables (C, R and CS) and their respective linguistic values. The dotted arrows indicate the directions of growth in the linguistic values of Project Management Quality (PMQ). It can be observed that the higher the linguistic value of R, the higher is the linguistic value of PMQ, because the higher the completion of the project requirements (R) at time T_o, the higher is PMQ. Moreover, Figure 10.9 shows that the higher the linguistic value of C, the lower is the linguistic value of PMQ, because the higher the project cost (C) at time T_o, the lower is the Project Management Quality (PMQ) (Nobre, 2005; and Nobre *et al*, 2000).

Figure 10.9. Analysis of project management quality: (C AND R) vs. CS

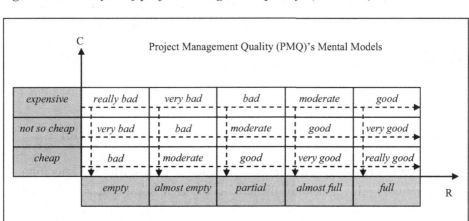

Quantitative Analysis

This subsection investigates the boundaries and convergence of the output variables of the cognitive machine for the state space defined to its input variables. Most of its results are derived from (Nobre, 2005; and Nobre *et al*, 2000). It starts by proposing the following:

Theorem 10.1: The application of criteria C1 to C8 gives the cognitive machine an output variable (or response) defined by:

$$y(t) = \sum_{r=1}^{M} \alpha_r . u_r \tag{10.7}$$

where

$$\alpha_r = \prod_{i=1}^{N} \mu(x_i(t)) \tag{10.8}$$

y(t) denotes an output variable calculated at time *t* after the operation of defuzzification; *M* denotes the number of fuzzy rules; u_r denotes the centre of the fuzzy sets of the output variable; *i=1,...,N* is the number of input variables $x_i(t)$; and $\mu(x_i(t))$ denotes membership functions of $x_i(t)$.

Proof 10.1: The proof is found in (Nobre, 1997; and Jager, 1995).

Therefore, the output variables of the cognitive machine - i.e. Customer Satisfaction (CS) and Project Management Quality (PMQ) - can be derived from Theorem 10.1.

- Analytical Calculus of Customer Satisfaction: **Theorem 10.2:** According to Theorem 10.1, Customer Satisfaction (CS) can be defined as:

$$CS(t) = \sum_{r=1}^{5} \alpha_r . c_r \tag{10.9}$$

where

$$\alpha_r = \mu_{R(t)} \tag{10.10}$$

CS(t) denotes customer satisfaction calculated at time *t* after the operation of defuzzification; *r* =1,…,5 denotes the number of fuzzy rules; c_r denotes the centre of the fuzzy sets of CS; *R(t)* denotes the value of project requirements completeness (R) at time *t*; and $\mu_{R(t)}$ represents the membership function of *R(t)*.

Proof 10.2: Theorem 10.2 is a particular application of Theorem 10.1. Therefore, the proof of Theorem 10.2 is derived from Theorem 10.1.

* **Analytical Calculus of Project Management Quality:** Theorem 10.3: According to Theorem 10.1, Project Management Quality (PMQ) can be defined as:

$$PPQ(t) = \sum_{r=1}^{15} \alpha_r \cdot p_r \tag{10.11}$$

where

$$\alpha_r = \mu_{C(t)} (\mu_{R\ t}) \tag{10.12}$$

PMQ(t) denotes project management quality calculated at time *t* after the operation of defuzzification; *r*=1,…,15 denotes the number of fuzzy rules; p_r denotes the centre of the fuzzy sets of PMQ; *C(t)* and *R(t)* denotes the values of project cost (C) and project requirements completeness (R) at time *t*; and $\mu_{C(t)}$ and $\mu_{R(t)}$ represent the membership functions of *C(t)* and *R(t)*.

Proof 10.3: Theorem 10.3 is a particular application of Theorem 10.1. Therefore, the proof of Theorem 10.3 is derived from Theorem 10.1.

* **Boundaries and Convergence Analysis: Theorem 10.4:** Given that the input variables (C and R) assume any real value in their respective universes of discourse, Theorems 10.2 and 10.3 guarantee that the output variables (CS and PMQ) of the cognitive machine converge to real values which are bounded to the interval [0,10] defined to their respective universes of discourse.

Proof 10.4: The proof of Theorem 10.4 is demonstrated in Appendix H.

SUMMARY

Chapter X introduced the design of a management control system whose functional elements execute cognitive tasks of analysis, decision and control of the organization process performance. The management control system works in the form of an Adaptive Learning Cycle (ALC) whose principles of operation are based on single-loop and double-loop learning. Among its elements, it included the participation of a cognitive machine whose responsibility involves the evaluation of the organization process performance through the tasks of analysis and decision. The design of the cognitive machine was reinforced with a set of criteria along with qualitative and quantitative analysis.

The proposal of the management control system was motivated in order to:

a.   Provide managers and stakeholders with data about the organization process performance, including information about quality and customer satisfaction.
b.   Support managers in the analysis, decision and control of the organization process performance.
c.   Reduce intra-individual and group dysfunctional conflicts which arise from managerial decision-making.
d.   Enhance actions for continuous process improvement.
e.   Improve the cognitive processes and thus the degree of cognition of the organization of study.

Chapter X was complemented with Appendixes F, G and H. Appendix F defined the state variables (X) which are used in the management control of the organization process performance. Appendix G presented linguistic descriptions of the mental models which were designed for the cognitive machine. Appendix H demonstrated a theorem proof as part of the quantitative analysis of the cognitive machine.

REFERENCES

Anthony, R.N., Dearden, J. & Bedford, N.M. (1984) *Management Control Systems.* Richard D. Irwin, Inc.

Bernstein, D.A. *et al* (1997) *Psychology.* Houghton Mifflin Company.

Black, M. (1937) Vagueness: An Exercise to Logical Analysis. *Philosophy of Science, 4*: 427-455.

Black, M. (1963) Reasoning with Loose Concepts. *Dialogue, 2*:1-12.

Braae, M. & Rutherford, D. (1979). Selection of parameters for a fuzzy logic controller. *Fuzzy Sets and Systems, 2*: 185-199.

Daft, R.L. & Noe, R.A. (2001) *Organizational Behavior.* Harcourt, Inc.

Gilat, A. (2008) *MATLAB: An Introduction with Applications.* Wiley. ISBN: 978-0-470-10877-2.

ITU-T (2000) Principles for a telecommunications management network. *Recommendation M.3010.* International Telecommunication Union.

Jager, R. (1995) Fuzzy Logic in Control. *PhD Thesis.* Delft University of Technology, Electrical Engineering Dept., Delft, The Netherlands.

Karwowski, W. & Mital, A. (1986) *Applications of Fuzzy Set Theory in Human Factor - Advances in Human Factors/Ergonomics*, Vol.6. Elsevier Science Publishers.

King, P.J. & Mamdani, E.H. (1977) The application of fuzzy control systems to industrial processes. *Automatica, 12*: 301-308.

Klir, G.J. & Folger, T.A. (1988) *Fuzzy Sets, Uncertainty, and Information.* Englewood Cliffs, N.J: Prentice Hall.

Kuo, B.C. (1995) *Automatic Control Systems.* Prentice Hall, 7th edition.

Lee, C.C. (1990) Fuzzy Logic Control Systems: Fuzzy Logic Controllers – Part I and II. *IEEE Transactions on Systems, Man and Cybernetics, vol.20 (2)*: 404-435.

Li, H. & Gatland, H. (1995). A new methodology for designing a fuzzy logic controller. *IEEE Transactions on Systems, Man and Cybernetics, 25(3)*: 505-513.

MacVicar Whelan, P.J. (1976) Fuzzy sets for machine interaction. *International Journal of Man-Machines Studies, 8*: 687-697.

Nobre, F.S. (1997) Design and Analysis of Fuzzy Logic Controllers. *M.Sc. Thesis Dissertation*, 110 pages. Faculty of Electrical and Computer Engineering / State University of Campinas (UNICAMP), Brazil.

Nobre, F.S. & Nakasone, J. (1999) A Fuzzy Computational Approach for Evaluating Process Control Quality. *IEEE Proceedings of the International Conference on Fuzzy Systems* (pp. 1701-1706). Seoul, Korea.

(Nobre, F.S. & Volpe, R. (1999) SEI-CMM Implementation at the NEC Brasil S.A. *Proceedings of the International Conference on Software Technology: Industrial Track* (pp. 45-72). Curitiba, Brazil.

Nobre, F.S. *et al* (2000) Fuzzy Logic in Management Control: A Case Study. *IEEE Proceedings of the International Engineering Management Conference* (pp. 414-419). Albuquerque-NM, USA.

Nobre, F.S. & Steiner, S.J. (2001a) Fuzzy Logic in Organization Analysis and Control. *Proceedings of the International Conference in Fuzzy Logic and Technology* (pp. 126-129). Leicester, England.

Nobre, F.S. (2005) On Cognitive Machines in Organizations. *PhD Thesis*, 343 pages. University of Birmingham / Birmingham-UK. Birmingham Main Library. Control Number: M0266887BU.

Pedrycz, W. & Gomide, F. (1998) *An Introduction To Fuzzy Sets: Analysis and Design*. The MIT Press.

Pedrycz, W. & Gomide, F. (2007) *Fuzzy Systems Engineering: Toward Human-Centric Computing*. Wiley-IEEE Press.

Wang, L. (1994) *Adaptive Fuzzy Systems and Control: Design and Stability Analysis*. PTR Prentice-Hall.

Zadeh, L.A. (1965) Fuzzy Sets. *Information and Control*, *8*: 338-353.

Zadeh, L.A. (1973) Outline of a New Approach to the Analysis of Complex Systems and Decision Process. *IEEE Transactions on Systems, Man, and Cybernetics*, *3 (1)*: 28-44.

Zadeh, L.A. (1996a) Fuzzy Logic = Computing with Words. *IEEE Transactions on Fuzzy Systems*, *4 (2)*: 103-111.

Zadeh, L.A. (1999) From Computing with Numbers to Computing with Words – From Manipulation of Measurements to Manipulation of Perceptions. *IEEE Transactions on Circuits and Systems, 45 (1)*: 105-119.

Zadeh, L.A. (2001) A New Direction in AI: Toward a Computational Theory of Perceptions. *AI Magazine. Spring*: 73-84.

ENDNOTES

[1]   Rational, natural and open systems, along with combinations of open-rational and open-natural systems, are proposed in (Scott, 1998) and introduced in Appendix C of this book.

[2]   State variables are set of variables that describe the state of a dynamical system.

[3]   Linguistic variables are synonymous with fuzzy variables when they are represented by fuzzy sets.

Chapter XI
Findings for the Industrial Case Study

INTRODUCTION

Chapter XI presents results, analyses, and conclusions about the industrial case study.

From a micro perspective, it presents findings of the management control system of the organization process performance. In particular, it gives special attention to the analysis of data of a set of five successive large-scale software projects which were engineered and managed in the Telecommunications Management Networks (TMN) Section of NEC of Brazil (NOB). These data include project cost (C) and project requirements completeness (R) and they represent the state variables of the software process of the TMN Section. C and R are fed into the cognitive machine which performs the computation of performance indexes of the software process of the TMN Section. The performance indexes include Customer Satisfaction (CS) and Project Management Quality (PMQ). The process of mapping the inputs (C and R) to the outputs (CS and PMQ) was illustrated earlier in Figure 10.2. In this perspective, organization process performance is synonymous with the TMN Section's process performance.

From a macro perspective, this chapter presents analysis and conclusions about the main correlations between measures of organization process improvement and organizational cognition. Findings indicate that improvements in the level of organization process performance are associated with improvements in the level of organization process maturity. Proceeding further, we associate these results with improvements in the degree of organizational cognition. Chapter XI also outlines the main contributions and limitations found with the implementation of The Capability Maturity Model in the organization of study.

THE ORGANIZATION PROCESS

The TMN Section's Software Process

From the micro perspective presented in the introduction of this chapter, the organization process is represented by the TMN Section's process. Therefore, the management control system, and thus the cognitive machine, is responsible to evaluate the performance of the TMN Section's process which is the representation of the Project's Defined Software Process (PDSP) in the Radio Systems Division. The PDSP of the TMN Section was mostly specified and constituted by engineering and management policies whose procedures were mainly based on the Organization's Standardized Software Process (OSSP). The OSSP was mostly written as a tailored version of the Process Maturity Level 2 of The Capability Maturity Model (CMM) guidelines. A top-down structure of these processes in the organization (NOB) was illustrated in Figure 9.2.

From the implementation of the CMM Level 2 in NEC of Brazil (NOB), its four divisions and thus the TMN Section expected to improve their software process and to achieve success through discipline and experience accumulated with similar projects or projects of similar complexity. For this purpose, Projects' Defined Software Processes were written in the TMN Section with basis on engineering and management procedures in order to reach the necessary specification and maturation of the CMM Process Maturity Level 2.

Large-Scale Software Projects

The data about this investigation was gathered from five successive, large-scale and discrete software projects which were developed in the Telecommunications Management Networks (TMN) Section of the Engineering Department of the Radio Systems Division of NEC of Brazil (NOB). These software projects belong to the class of Telecommunications Management Networks of International Telecommunication Union (ITU) standards – where ITU is the United Nations Specialized Agency in the field of Telecommunications (ITU-T, 2000). They were developed in the period between 1997 and 2000 and they were similar in their scope of application and complexity. According to the guidelines of the CMM, the organization that achieves Process Maturity Level 2 can repeat success in their projects findings through disciplined processes and accumulation of experience for a line of similar software projects. Therefore, such findings with repletion of success were expected for the TMN Section's software projects.

Participants in the Software Projects

The participants or employees in the TMN Section included a manager and ten engineers of software and electronics engineering background – including the first author among them. They were trained in the CMM guidelines and appraisal framework, and they remained together in the TMN Section in the period between 1997 and 2000 when they were working on software project engineering and management.

Source of Data of Software Projects

Most of the data about this investigation were selected from internal reports and database of NEC of Brazil and they were published in (Nobre, 2005; Nobre *et al*, 2000; Nobre & Volpe, 1999; Nobre & Nakasone, 1999; and Volpe & Nobre, 2000).

Such publications include:

i. Data about project cost (C), project schedule (T) and project requirements completeness (R) of five successive, large-scale and discrete software projects. The recording of this data had been done according to procedures of the PDSP for software project planning, tracking and oversight in the TMN Section. Such data are further fed into a cognitive machine in the form of input variables for the computation of performance indexes of the TMN Section's process.
ii. Feedback information from internal and external clients of software projects and software products. It was used to derive the concept of Customer Satisfaction (CS). CS is a performance index of the TMN Section's process. Such feedback information had been collected by Software Engineering Process Groups across NEC of Brazil (NOB) during meetings between them and internal and external clients of NOB.
iii. Feedback information from engineers and managers of software projects within the TMN Section. It was used to derive the concept of Project Management Quality (PMQ). PMQ is a second performance index of the TMN Section's process. Such feedback information had also been collected by a Software Engineering Process Group of the Radio Systems Division during meetings between them and participants in the TMN Section of NOB.

DATA OF THE ORGANIZATION PROCESS

This section presents the data gathered from a set of five successive large-scale software projects of Telecommunication Management Networks which were developed in the TMN Section of NOB during the years from 1997 to 2000.

The data include a set of planning information (T_o, C_o and R_o) as well as a set of actual information (T_A, C_A and R_A) about the TMN Section's process which were sampled at time $t = T_A = T_o$. We recall that C, R and T are defined in Appendix F.

Tables 11.1 and 11.2 contain the set of planning data (T_o, C_o and R_o) and the set of actual data (T_A, C_A and R_A) respectively for the five software projects. The software projects are enumerated chronologically to their development and they are abbreviated by $SP_{(i=1,...,5)}$, where SP_i is the designation of Software Project i.

Table 11.3 contains the performance indexes (CS and PMQ) for the TMN Section's process. CS and PMQ were computed by the cognitive machine from input information about the planning and actual data of the software projects of Tables 11.1 and 11.2. The symbol OPP in the Table 11.3 abbreviates Organization Process Performance and it was calculated by the arithmetic average between the performance indexes of CS and PMQ.

It is important to understand that CS, PMQ and OPP are performance indexes of the TMN Section's process which represents the organization of study in this micro perspective and application. However, a similar approach of management control with

Table 11.1. Planned data of software projects

Projects	C_o (US$. 10^6)	R_o	T_o (years)
SP_1	0.2	50	0.4
SP_2	0.5	100	0.9
SD_3	1	150	1
SP_4	1.2	180	1.5
SP_5	2	300	2

Table 11.2. Actual data of software projects

Projects	C_A (US$. 10^6)	R_A	T_A (years)
SP_1	0.3	40	0.4
SP_2	0.65	85	0.9
SD_3	1	135	1
SP_4	1.44	180	1.5
SP_5	1.9	300	2

Table 11.3. Performance indexes

Projects	CS	PMQ	OPP
SP$_1$	5	2	3.5
SP$_2$	6.25	2.8	4.52
SD$_3$	7.5	5	6.25
SP$_4$	10	6	8
SP$_5$	10	10	10

other performance indexes could be defined and applied in the evaluation of other units of the organization and even in the assessment of the whole enterprise.

DATA ANALYSIS

A graphical representation of the results of Table 11.3 is illustrated in Figure 11.1, where the continuous real scale [0,10] denotes measurements of the level of Customer Satisfaction (CS), Project Management Quality (PMQ) and Organization Process Performance (OPP).

Graphical results show that as we move from the chronological order of projects SP$_1$ to SP$_5$, the performance indexes CS, PMQ and OPP grow in the continuous real

Figure 11.1. Organization's performance indexes (CS, PMQ and OP)

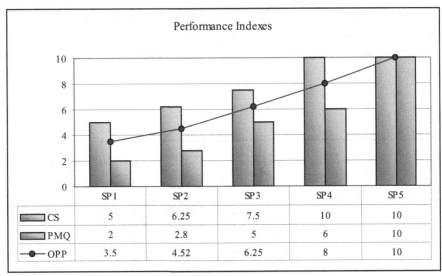

scale of [0,10] until they reach the maximum value given by 10. From another view of analysis, these results indicate that the Organization's Standardized Software Process (OSSP), and thus the Project's Defined Software Process (PDSP) of the TMN Section, contributed to improve the performance indexes (CS, PMQ and OPP) of the TMN Section's process. Such results are associated with the implementation of engineering, management and organizational processes of The Capability Maturity Model (CMM) in the organization (NOB).

Therefore, improvements in the level of organization process performance are associated with improvements in the level of organization process maturity. While the former level is represented in the continuous real scale of [0,10], the latter is levered in the integer real scale of [1,5]. This association confirms proposition 9.4.

Consequently, and according to Propositions 9.3 and 9.5, we can assert that such improvements in the levels of organization process maturity and performance are associated with improvements in the degree of organizational cognition. Therefore, degrees of organizational cognition can be represented in the continuous real scale of [0,10] when organizational cognition is associated with organization process performance. Additionally, degrees of organizational cognition can be represented in the integer real scale of [1,5] when organizational cognition is associated with organization process maturity.

Additional analysis of the results of Table 11.3 is presented in Table 11.4 by comparing planning and actual data of the five software projects. We recall that these data were sampled at time $t = T_o$ and $SP_{(i=1,...,5)}$ enumerates the software projects. The symbols ↑ and ↓ denote up and down respectively.

It can be observed that the actual cost (C_A) of software project SP_1 is 50% higher than the planning cost (C_o) and that the actual requirements (R_A) which were successfully implemented represents 80% of the total of the planning requirements (R_o). On the other hand, the actual cost (C_A) of the TMN software project SP_5 is 5% lower than the planning cost (C_o) and the actual requirements (R_A) which were successfully implemented represents 100% of the total of the planning requirements (R_o).

Table 11.4. Analysis of the performance indexes

Software Projects	Analysis
SP1	C_A is 50% ↑ to C_o and R_A is 80% of R_o
SP2	C_A is 30% ↑ to C_o and R_A is 85% of R_o
SP3	C_A is equal to C_o and R_A is 90% of R_o
SP4	C_A is 20% ↑ to C_o and R_A is 100% of R_o
SP5	C_A is 5% ↓ to C_o and R_A is 100% of R_o

ORGANIZATIONAL FINDINGS

This section presents a postscript of macro results of the implementation of the CMM in the organization of study. It overlooks findings at different levels of analysis.

Levels of Analysis of the CMM in the NOB

- **Technical Level:** The technical level of NEC of Brazil (NOB) which is related with the CMM consists of the set of Project's Defined Software Processes (PDSP) in the Divisions of Radio, Transmission, Switching and Wireless Communications Systems.
- **Managerial Level:** The managerial level consists of the Organization's Standardized Software Process (OSSP) which was used for tailoring the PDSP in the four divisions of NOB.
- **Institutional Level:** The institutional level is concerned with the alignment of the CMM guidelines and goals with the organization processes and goals. It involves a tailoring process to map the CMM to OSSP, and OSSP to PDSP. At this level, managers execute programs of organization design and strategic planning; they pursue new solutions, services and products to the market; they create new processes for organizational and technological innovation, among other tasks.

The Bottom-Up Strategy for Process Improvement

The idea of implementation of the Capability Maturity Model (CMM) in NEC of Brazil (NOB) was paved and proposed by engineers and managers who played operational and management roles in the technical level of the organization hierarchy. Therefore, their purpose and program for software process improvement in the organization (NOB) was approved by managers who occupied positions at the managerial and institutional levels of NOB. Therefore, the initiative and the initial efforts of implementation of the CMM followed a bottom-up path in the organization hierarchy.

Nevertheless, despite being approved by managers of higher hierarchic levels at the managerial and institutional layers of the organization, the CMM program and its goals were not well aligned with those goals of NEC of Brazil (NOB). The CMM comprises a set of goals at the various organizational levels of analysis. The organization that aims to achieve success and to benefit from such a continuous process improvement model needs to align its goals and sub-goals with those of the CMM for all the layers in the organization hierarchy.

In such a way, despite being accepted and institutionalized in the NOB, the practice CMM was not regularly done at the higher levels of the organization. Processes and strategies of areas such as supply chain, production, marketing, human resources and organizational strategic planning were not aligned with the CMM proposal for continuous process improvement.

Effects of a Stationary Environment

As a result, the CMM was a successful program at the technical level of the organization. It guided the organization software projects to a continuous process improvement path during a period characterized by a stationary environment. On the one hand, it was stationary because since its foundation, NEC of Brazil (NOB) had had the ability to hold its main customers (Brazilian governmental telecommunications companies) for almost 30 years. Additionally, the software projects developed in the divisions and units of NOB had similar requirements and thus similar levels of complexity when compared to previous projects. Hence, these projects could be well engineered and managed with basis on the guidelines of CMM Process Maturity Level 2 since it gives repeatability of performance under these circumstances. In such a way, success could be repeated with similar software projects. Hence, NOB had accumulated experience and learning. On the other hand, a stationary environment was characterized by the inability of NOB to attract new customers and to expand its frontiers to new markets through an effective and efficient strategy.

Effects of a Dynamic Environment

However, in between August of 1995 and July of 1997, the national congress of Brazil approved a set of new constitutional laws which allowed the Brazilian government to begin a new era of privatization of the Brazilian market of telecommunications with concessions to worldwide competitors. This process was completed in July of 1998 after the privatization of EMBRATEL which used to be the biggest Brazilian enterprise in the area of telecommunications (ANATEL). This privatization yields the Brazilian government more than 22 billions of Real (which is the Brazilian currency[1]).

From the year of 2000, NOB began to feel drastic modifications in its wealth scenario caused by economic and political transformations of the telecommunications business environment. NOB lost most of its main customers and thus it was forced to re-design its goals, social structure and business areas. Such changes affected its participants (employees) drastically. In between 1997 and 2002, the number of participants in NOB was reduced by 80% approximately.

SUMMARY

Chapter XI showed results, analyses and conclusions about the industrial case study.

From a micro perspective, it presented findings of the management control system of the organization process performance. In particular, it gave special attention to the analysis of data of a set of five successive large-scale software projects which were engineered and managed in the Telecommunications Management Networks (TMN) Section of NEC of Brazil (NOB). In this perspective, organization process performance was synonymous with the TMN Section's process performance.

From a macro perspective, Chapter XI presented analysis and conclusions about the main correlations between measures of organization process improvement and organizational cognition.

Findings indicated that improvements in the level of organization process performance were associated with the implementation of engineering, management and organizational processes of The Capability Maturity Model (CMM) in the organization (NOB). Therefore, improvements in the level of organization process performance were associated with improvements in the level of organization process maturity. Proceeding further, we associated such improvements in the levels of organization process maturity and performance with improvements in the degree of organizational cognition.

Improvements in the level of organization process performance were represented in the continuous real scale of [0,10], while improvements in the level of organization process maturity were represented in the integer real scale of [1,5]. Consequently, degrees of organizational cognition could be represented in the continuous real scale of [0,10] when organizational cognition was associated with organization process performance. Additionally, degrees of organizational cognition could be represented in the integer real scale of [1,5] when organizational cognition was associated with organization process maturity.

Chapter XI also outlined the main contributions and limitations found with the implementation of The Capability Maturity Model in the organization of study. This was done through different levels of analysis.

The CMM arose in NOB from a top-down approach whose initiative and proposals emerged with the participants in the technical level. At this level, the CMM gave the organization prominent results through new engineering, managerial and organizational software processes. However, the organization NOB did not provide the necessary institutionalization for the CMM in upper layers of its hierarchical structure. Consequently, it had not worked the appropriate alignment of its strategies with the CMM goals at the levels of business areas which related the organization NOB to the market. Therefore, the CMM found serious limitations to progress in those areas at higher levels, such as in the managerial and institutional layers of the organization.

REFERENCES

ANATEL. National Agency of Telecommunications of Brazil: http://www.anatel.gov.br

ITU-T (2000) Principles for a telecommunications management network. *Recommendation M.3010*. International Telecommunication Union.

Nobre, F. S., & Nakasone, J. (1999). A Fuzzy Computational Approach for Evaluating Process Control Quality. *IEEE International Conference on Fuzzy Systems.* Proceedings: 1701-1706. Seoul, Korea.

Nobre, F. S., & Volpe, R. (1999). SEI-CMM Implementation at the NEC Brasil S. A. *Proceedings of the International Conference on Software Technology: Industrial Track* (pp. 45-72). Curitiba, Brazil.

Nobre, F. S. *et al* (2000). Fuzzy Logic in Management Control: A Case Study. *IEEE Proceedings of the International Engineering Management Conference* (pp. 414-419). Albuquerque-NM, USA.

Nobre, F. S. (2005). On Cognitive Machines in Organizations. *PhD Thesis*, 343 pages. University of Birmingham / Birmingham-UK. Birmingham Main Library. Control Number: M0266887BU.

Volpe, R., Nobre, F. S., *et al* (2000). The Role of Software Process Improvement into TQM: An Industrial Experience. *IEEE Proceedings of the International Engineering Management Conference* (pp. 29-34). Albuquerque-NM, USA.

ENDNOTE

[1]   During 1997, one US$ was equivalent to two Brazilian Real approximately. Ratio of 1:2.

Section VI
Implications and the New Organization

Imagination is more important than knowledge.

Albert Einstein (1879-1955)

Section VI contributes by outlining implications of cognitive machines for organizations and it derives important concepts towards new organizations whose main participants comprise cognitive machines and cognitive information systems. Part VI constitutes of chapters XII, XIII, and XIV.

Chapter XII analyses the impact of cognitive machines on organizational design and upon the elements of the organization which subsume goals, social structure, inducements and contracts, technology, and participants.

Chapter XIII outlines limitations of past and current manufacturing organizations and it presents concepts and features of new models of organizational production systems through perspectives of management, socio-technology and organizational systems theory. From these perspectives, it proposes a background to customer-centric systems which represent a new organizational production model with capabilities to manage high levels of environmental complexity, to pursue high degrees of organizational cognition, to operate with high levels of mass customization, and to provide customers with immersiveness.

From all this background, Chapter XIV proposes the definition, the structure and the processes of Computational Organization Management Networks (COMN) which are new organizations whose principles of operation are based on the concepts of Organization Functional Layers (proposed in this chapter), Hierarchic Cognitive Systems (proposed in Chapter III) along with those of Telecommunications Management Networks of the International Telecommunication Union. Structured with functional layers and the cognitive roles which range from technical and managerial to institutional levels of analysis, and also equipped with technological, operational, managerial and business processes, the concept of Computational Organization Management Networks (COMN) plays an important part in the developments of future organizations where cognitive machines and Cognitive Information Systems (CIS) – that is information management systems with high degrees of cognition, intelligence and autonomy - are prominent actors of governance, automation, and control of the whole organization. Additionally, it introduces the concept of immersive systems in order to provide the new organization with the capability of immersiveness.

Chapter XII
Implications of Cognitive Machines for Organizations

INTRODUCTION

Analyses and predictions about the implications of cognitive machines for organizations are a topic of further research which demands a high level of imagination in connection with the knowledge available in the literature of interdisciplinary fields of research. Under such a perspective, this chapter presents an outline of some possible implications. It starts by discussing literature results on the benefits of information technology (IT) to organizations. It proceeds by associating IT with cognitive machines, and thus it presents some implications of cognitive machines for organizations.

ON INFORMATION TECHNOLOGY AND ECONOMIC GROWTH OF ORGANIZATIONS

Investments in information technology (IT), which involves computers, software programs and communication systems, have demonstrated to be associated with improvements in tangible and intangible outcomes of organizations such as profitability and performance, knowledge management, quality of services and goods. Results of case studies at the firm level of analysis have shown that the impact of IT on economic growth of organizations is relevant and quite large when compared to their share of capital stock or investment, and this impact is likely to grow more in the next years (Brynjolfsson & Hitt, 2000).

Improvements in organizations due to investments in IT are associated with:

a.   Reduction of costs of coordination, communications and information process-
     ing. It is quite reasonable to assert that nowadays managers make decisions
     which involve much more inter-dependent variables than in the pre-computer
     era (Simon, 1977 and 1982b). In a metaphorical way, computers play the role
     of manipulation of variables behind the curtain of managerial complex deci-
     sions.
b.   Complementary investments in organizational and management processes
     which also lead the organization to improve intangible outcomes such as
     human capital, quality of services and goods, satisfaction of customers and
     employees (Brynjolfsson & Hitt, 2000).

ON INFORMATION TECHNOLOGY AND COGNITIVE MACHINES

Cognitive machines are special classes of information technology (IT) and thus
they represent potential candidates which can provide organizations with additional
improvements in those areas where IT has already demonstrated its strengths.

ON COGNITIVE MACHINES IN ORGANIZATIONS

Herbert A. Simon's Statement on Computers in Organizations

*In our fascination with change, we must keep firmly in mind that the structures of
effective organizations are at least as much shaped by the tasks they are designed
to perform as by the nature of the human and computer resources available for
performing them. The permanence of most of these tasks constitutes the most important reason for predicting that the organizations of the future will, in most respects,
resemble the organizations of the past and present. They will retain the familiar
shape of a hierarchy of semi-independent components and sub-components.* Herbert
A. Simon (1916-2001), published in (Augier and March, 2002: 404-418).

This book supports such a statement and it extends the term "computer resources"
to include cognitive machines. Moreover, it discusses in the following some implications that cognitive machines may have upon organization design and on the
elements of the organization.

Organization Design

The perspective of organization design as a process of choice of organizing models will not change in the future – either for organizations or computational organization models. The strategic selection of the goals, social structure, participants and technology of the organization will remain contingent upon the environment with which the organization relates. The characteristics of the elements of the organization will change, evolve and develop continuously, towards higher levels of complexity, but the purpose of existence of the organization will remain the same or will not change in the same proportion of its elements.

Goals

Might cognitive machines be able to have their own motives and to pursue organization's goals? The answer could be yes if we considered the cognitive machines as carriers of people's motives and organization's goals. In such a perspective the cognitive machines could be implemented through software agents governed and coordinated by normative, structural and ontological concepts of computational organization models (Prietula *et al*, 1998). Therefore, they could follow and create strategies and tactics in order to satisfy (satisfice) organization's goals and to support people in the achievement of their own motives[1].

Social Structure

A social structure comprises normative and behavioral parts as defined in Appendix C. While a normative structure consists of institutionalized rational procedures and prescriptions for behaviour, a behavioural structure consists of actual behaviour which emerges from non-procedural processes and social relations.

The introduction of cognitive machines in organizations, with no (or little) attention to emotions, will provide the organization with higher levels of rationalization since its normative structure will overcome non-procedural behaviour. This phenomenon can lead the organization to higher levels of predictability of outcomes which depend on prescriptive behaviour.

Participants

According to the Cambridge International Dictionary of English, a participant is "a person who takes part in or becomes involved in a particular activity".

By assuming the perspective that computer systems take part in and are involved in activities of information processing and communications in organizations of today, then it is reasonable to assert that cognitive machines, like people, are participants within the organization.

However, by considering that participation in the organization involves consciousness of the participant, we might question whether cognitive machines are able to be conscious. This is another controversial subject in the fields of artificial intelligence, cognition and social sciences which demands further investigation. Nevertheless, it was defined in Chapter VII that:

Definition 7.3: Machine consciousness represents the awareness of its designer in relation to the cognitive processes and abilities that the machine carries on during task execution.

Inducements (Rewards and incentives) and Contracts

From the perspective that cognitive machines are carriers of people's motives and organization's goals, it is plausible to assume that they do not need to be induced by the organization directly, but the designers of these machines are who do need to receive incentives. Therefore, a contract must exist between the organization and the machine designer. In Chapter VII, we propose a definition that supports this perspective:

Definition 7.4: The work relationship between the machine designer and the organization can be regularized by a contract which makes explicit the cognitive abilities of the machine; the tasks that the machine can perform within the organization; the roles that the machine fulfils in the organization; and also the designer and the organization attestation (or signatures).

Technology

Cognitive machines might demand investments in alternative business processes and technologies from the organization. Such investments can bring important competitive advantages in order to improve tangible and intangible outcomes of the organization such as demonstrated in the literature of economic perspectives of information technology in organizations (Brynjolfsson & Hitt, 2000).

Cognition as an Agent of Organization Change

I believe that at the end of the century the use of words and general educated opinion will have altered so much that one will be able to speak of machines thinking without expecting to be contradicted. (Turing, A. 1950, p.442)

We believe that much of what the brilliant mind of Alan Turing thought in the 1950's, as written in the above quotation of him, will approach to a more real statement as we discover more and more about cognition.

While the structure or anatomy of the organization of the future might remain similar to the models of the past and today, its processes or physiology might change in greater proportions. Advancements in the science of cognition will continue to represent an important agent of organizational change.

Developments in cognition provide researchers with a better understanding of the organization of the human brain and its processes, and discoveries in this field contribute to extend other disciplines to new frontiers. In the area of organizations, for instance, researchers will be able to provide the organization with alternative processes of learning, problem-solving and decision-making, and thus with more complex models of organizational learning and organizational cognition. Advancements in cognition will also provide cognitive machines with more realistic models of the human mind, and thus with the ability to solve more complex problems which involve natural or fuzzy concepts. Moreover, education might be the area of foremost transformation as more developments in cognition are reached.

The New Enterprise of Telecommunications Management Networks

The idea of the new organization resembling principles of Telecommunications Management Networks of the International Telecommunications Union (ITU-T, 2000) was touched upon in (Nobre & Simon, 2001b and 2002a). It assumes a high level of automation for the new organization, where machines and information management systems will perform most of the technical, managerial and institutional activities in the organization. Viewed as information processing and management agents, these machines will need to interact with each other via standardized protocols of communication systems. Such interactions will need to be governed by processes and structures organized into hierarchic layers.

We put forwards this perspective in Chapter XIV where we propose the concept of Computational Organization Management Networks – which are new organizations whose main participants comprise cognitive machines and cognitive information systems.

SUMMARY

This chapter outlined important implications of cognitive machines for organizations. It asserted that cognitive machines are special classes of information technology

(IT) and thus they represent potential candidates which can provide organizations with additional improvements in those areas where IT has already demonstrated its strengths. It provided analyses about the impact of cognitive machines on organizational design and upon the elements of the organization - comprising goals, social structure, inducements and contracts, technology and participants. It pointed out the importance of advancements in cognitive sciences associated with developments in organizations and cognitive machines. It concluded by touching upon the concept of computational organization management networks which are new organizations further proposed in details in Chapter XIV.

REFERENCES

Augier, M., & March, J. G. (2002). *The Economics of Choice, Change and Organization: Essays in Memory of Richard M. Cyert*. Edward Elgar,

Brynjolfsson, E., & Hitt, L. M. (2000). Beyond Computation: Information Technology, Organizational Transformation and Business Performance. *The Journal of Economic Perspectives*, *14*(4), 23-48.

ITU-T (2000). Principles for a telecommunications management network. *Recommendation M.3010*. International Telecommunication Union.

Nobre, F. S., & Steiner, S. J. (2001b). Towards Intelligent and Immersive Manufacturing Systems. *Proceedings of the UK Workshop on Computational Intelligence* (pp. 232-236). Edinburgh, UK.

Nobre, F. S., & Steiner, S. J. (2002a). Beyond the Thresholds of Manufacturing: Perspectives on Management, Technology and Organizations. *Proceedings of the IEEE International Engineering Management Conference* (pp. 788-793). Cambridge-UK.

Prietula, M. J., Carley, K., & Gasser, M. (1998). *Simulating Organizations: Computational Models of Institutions and Groups*. AAAI Press / The MIT Press.

Simon, H. A. (1977). *The New Science of Management Decision*. Prentice-Hall, Inc.

Simon, H. A. (1982b). *Models of Bounded Rationality: Behavioral Economics and Business Organization, 2*. The MIT Press.

Turing, A. M. (1950) Computing Machinery and Intelligence. Mind - *A Quarterly Review of Psychology and Philosophy, LIX (236)*, 433-460.

ENDNOTE

[1] People's motives in organizations involve consciousness. *"To be conscious that we are perceiving or thinking is to be conscious of our own existence"*: Aristotle (384BC – 322BC).

Chapter XIII
Beyond the Thresholds of Manufacturing Organizations

INTRODUCTION

The major contributions of this chapter are concerned with:

a. Analysis of the limitations of past and current manufacturing organizations (and operations management systems).
b. Definition of concepts and features for new manufacturing organizations through perspectives of management, socio-technology and organizational systems theory. From these perspectives we derive the concept of a new organizing and production model that we call customer-centric organizations.

MOTIVATIONS

The technological and organizational developments presented in this book inspired the writing of this chapter. After reviewing the literature, problem analyses have been understood and solutions design have been proposed.

Our point of departure is that despite some academic and industrial efforts to add performance criteria such as quality, flexibility and agility to manufacturing and operations management systems[1] (Steiner *et al*, 2001), they still are a long way from being classified as "customer-centric systems" – which are organizational systems with high maturity levels of management of complex environments, with capabilities to pursue high degrees of mass customization, and with the ability to provide customers with immersiveness – where the concept of immersive systems is defined in Chapter XIV.

To be in conformance with the property of customer-centric systems, we propose that new capabilities need to be embedded into the current manufacturing and operations management systems of the organization. For this purpose, our task is threefold, and therefore we propose three complementary perspectives on management, socio-technology and organizational systems theory respectively in order to introduce concepts towards new manufacturing organizations.

The first perspective is concerned with the concept of environmental management - which comprises customer relationship and supply chain management, and the development of organizational learning, value chain and competitive advantage processes for the organization.

The second perspective is concerned with the design of machinery and management systems with high degrees of cognition, intelligence and autonomy. These systems are supposed to operate at the technical (shop floor), managerial and institutional levels of the manufacturing organization. Moreover, and most importantly, these systems have to be equipped with structures, processes, goals, agents and technologies which are able to provide the organization with the capability to pursue high levels of immersiveness – where immersiveness represents the ability of an organizational system to interact with customers (either people or machines) in a friendly way, by immersing them into the organization through approaches such as virtual reality, simulation or real world operations.

The third perspective is concerned with organizational systems theory. Analyses of manufacturing organizations from the past and the present time to the future are introduced through organization theories developed by organizational schools of the 20th century, as well as by the concept of hierarchical levels of complexity and cognition of organizational systems.

A REVIEW OF MANUFACTURING ORGANIZATIONS

During the 20th century, manufacturing organizations have evolved from mass to batch production systems. These systems entered the 21st century moving towards a new production model called mass customization. With such a new model, information management systems have been playing an increasing and dominant role. A representation of such a transition from mass and batch production to mass customization processes was presented by Monfared & Steiner through a mathematical model of paradigm shift (Monfared & Steiner, 1997). In their work, they argued that the current and dominant scientific principles of the time are incompatible with the emerging needs of the present and future of manufacturing systems. To support the new trends of their own manufacturing model, these authors have emphasized that some new dimensions of human intelligence need to be captured, represented, modelled and applied in activities such as design, inspection, planning, scheduling, decision-making and control. They proposed that fuzzy logic, neural networks and genetic algorithms are the main tools which can be used to handle the uncertainties and dynamics inherent to the new manufacturing systems of mass customization operations. In such a direction, Rao *et al* (1993) has presented the concept, methodology and implementation techniques of an integrated and distributed intelligent system. Rao and his colleagues introduced applications of design, operation, control, planning and maintenance of what they called intelligent manufacturing and they put emphasis on the integration and the management of such activities. Moreover, Kusiak (2000) has presented new advances in model construction and application of computational intelligence approaches to solve problems across many areas of an enterprise, with emphasis on design and manufacturing. This author has focused mainly on knowledge-based systems for automated decision-making; planning, testing and diagnostic systems; treatment of ambiguous, complex, incomplete and conflicting data; technology integration, material handling and storage, information systems and knowledge management. As a result of such an application, Kusiak argues that the manufacturing enterprises of the future will be better represented with the attributes of adaptability, agility, modularity, standardization, collaboration, distribution, simplicity, knowledge orientation, human orientation and environment awareness, where the latter is concerned with the use of less consumable resources and the generation of less waste.

This chapter supports all these works, and additionally, it extends their concepts by proposing some new features to manufacturing and operations management systems, moving towards the concept of "customer-centric systems" – which are organizational systems with the ability to manage complex environments, and with capabilities to operate through intensive mass customization processes and to provide immersiveness to their customers. To begin, to make progress in, and to realize such a transition, managerial, technological and organizational innovations have to be developed in order to satisfy the requirements of new manufacturing organizations in the 21st century. For such a purpose, we introduce perspectives of management, socio-technology and organizational systems theory on the new organizational production model that we have called customer-centric systems. Most of the managerial, technological and organizational features of such a model play an important role in the proposal of the structure and the processes of the new Computational Organization Management Networks (COMN) further introduced in Chapter XIV.

The next section introduces the features of customer-centric systems.

CUSTOMER-CENTRIC SYSTEMS

The idea behind "Customer-centric systems" was first described in (Nobre & Steiner, 2001b, 2001c and 2002a). We can define them as organizational models with capabilities to:

i.   Manage high levels of environmental complexity - which include the management of customers relashionship and supply chain, the development of competitive advantage[2], value chain[3] and organizational learning processes.
ii.   Operate with high levels of mass customization – where mass customization is a business model which allows any customer to buy goods or services that have been pre-designed (customized) to fit a customer's exact needs (Pine 1999).
iii. Pursue high degrees of organizational cognition, intelligence and autonomy, and consequently, high degrees of flexibility and agility.
iv.   and provide customers with immersiveness.

To empower the understanding of these features, we contribute by introducing in the next sections of this chapter three complementary perspectives on management, socio-technology and organizational systems theory.

MANAGEMENT PERSPECTIVES

Historical Transition

There was a time in the past when manufacturers used to interact with their customers in a personal way, i.e. human to human interaction. Every customer had a distinguished treatment since they had different needs of services and goods[4]. In such a way, manufacturers were able to learn and to evolve with their customers. That was a craftsman era.

With the emergence of modern and industrial organizations - in the early period of apogee of the Industrial Revolution (centuries 18th and 19th), and latterly in the 20th century - new organizational models, managerial processes and technological systems were developed in order to support new business challenges and to manage higher levels of complexity of the environment. In between the innovations which emerged in the beginning of the 20th century, there was the concept and the practice of mass production system - whose purpose and development was concerned to provide manufacturers with processes and technologies capable to produce higher volumes of products and to reach a broader market than any other production model could make before it. At that time, special attention and contributions were received from the school of scientific management, and thus by the studies proposed by Frederic Taylor (1911) and later put in action by Henry Ford. With the scientific management approaches, the activities of both managers and workers were pragmatically separated, defined and rationalized. Interchangeable components and standardized products, manufactured with minimal cost for mass markets, were some of the strategies adopted in that period.

The gradual transition occurred during the 20th century from mass production systems to a model characterized by versatile products in smaller numbers established what is known today as batch production. This production model offers some level of customization, and thus it provides the organizations with capabilities to produce more variety of products than older approaches. Batch production models were the "levers" for the study of both flexible (Toni & Tonchia, 1998) and agile (Lee, G.H. 1998) manufacturing systems and they were supported by the concepts of integrated and cellular manufacturing, just-in-time (JIT), statistical sampling and quality control which emerged around the 1940's in the United States of America - with progresses made by the American Society for Quality Control (ASQC) - and later put in action in Japan - by Japanese organizations and the Japanese Union of Scientists and Engineers (JUSE).

The Management Threshold Principle

The gradual migration of the current organizational production systems to the proposed customer-centric model is a continuous process that causes some managerial implications to the new manufacturing organizations. These implications can be summarized by the premise (definition) and proposition stated in the following:

Definition 13.1. The Management Threshold Principle: The gradual transition of manufacturing organizations from mass and batch production systems to customer-centric models - which are characterized by a continuous growth in the level of customization - will reach a threshold where customers will be part of the design, production and management of their own needs – resulting in the generation of highly personal and customized services and goods.

Level of Customization vs. Level of Environmental Complexity

By considering The Management Threshold Principle of Definition 13.1, we propose that:

Proposition 13.1: The higher the level of customization of the manufacturing organization, the higher is the level of environmental complexity.

This proposition is concerned with the level of environmental complexity that the manufacturing organization has to deal with in order to complete tasks, to control production demand, and to manage customers, supply-chain, along with its core elements of technology, social structure, goals and participants.

New Management Perspectives of Customer-Centric Systems

Therefore, to evolve to such a new dynamic and more complex environment, besides higher degrees of flexibility and agility, the manufacturing organization (and the operations management system) has to present the capability to interact with its customers by capturing their particular needs, resulting in the production of their goods and services according to their requirements. Organizational learning, competitive advantage and value chain processes, along with customer relationship and supply chain management will play an increasing and important part with such a new customer-centric organizational model. Additionally, more emphasis will be needed and taken for management of the organizational system environment, by considering for example the management of customers' requirements and needs, along with the coordination of supply chain and inter-organizational networks. The Capability Maturity Model Integration (CMMI) for Systems Engineering, Software Engineering, Integrated Product and Process Development, and Supplier Sourcing, as proposed by the Software Engineering Institute of the Carnegie Mellon University (CMU-SEI, 2002), appears as a powerful and important organizational model which can be applied to the processes and technological change management of this new organizational production system. Such capabilities for the management of processes and technological changes are necessary tools to support the dynamics of a new organizational model which is being defined as "customer-centric systems" and characterized with high levels of mass customization.

Figure 13.1 illustrates the Management Threshold Principle - where the threshold line illustrates the transition point from batch production systems towards the customer-centric model. In this transition, manufacturing organizations move towards higher levels of customization and higher capabilities of mass customization.

It can be observed that the migration of the organizations from mass and batch production to the customer-centric model moves towards the values of the customer relationship management (CRM) paradigm (Brown, 2000) which is motivated in part by the human aspects provided by the craftsman era. In essence, the CRM strategy is concerned with the attraction, acquisition, retention and satisfaction of

Figure 13.1. The management threshold principle

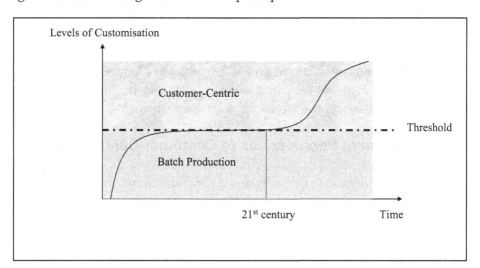

customers. Its main goal is to contribute to the company's success, since customer satisfaction is a key factor that makes organizational results successful.

Figure 13.2 illustrates the convergence of mass and batch production systems towards the new organizational production model of customer-centric properties - which is characterized by higher capabilities of customization and higher levels of customer satisfaction.

Table 13.1 describes a summary of the management principles of organizational production models, where the dotted arrow points out the direction of higher levels of customization.

SOCIO-TECHNOLOGICAL PERSPECTIVES

Historical Transition

The emergence of mass production systems during the beginning of the 20th century was encompassed by the consolidation of more structured manufacturing organizations, and therefore, new machinery and management technologies were introduced for the analysis and design of such enterprises. Pneumatic tools and analogue machinery systems were used to support shop floor operations and processes. The interdependence between the manufacturing organization and the environment was neither treated with the necessary relevance nor too much considered by the organizations at that time. Static and linear modelling were the main mathematical

Figure 13.2. The managerial transition of organizational production models

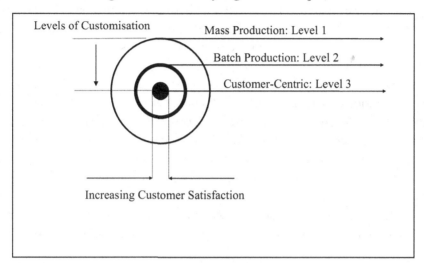

Table 13.1. Management principles of organizational production models

Levels of Customization	Management Principles
Mass Production: Level 1	Interchangeable components, standardized products, minimal cost and mass markets (Scientific Management – F. Taylor)
Batch Production: Level 2	Versatile products in smaller quantities (Integrated and Cellular Manufacturing, Just in Time, Statistical Sampling and Quality Control Management)
Customer-Centric: Level 3	Higher levels of customization, mass customization capability, management of the environment, focuses on customers and competitors (Organizational Learning, Competitive Advantage and Value Chain Processes, Supply Chain and Customer Relationship Management, and CMMI Model)

tools used for the analysis of such systems. Human presence was mainly on the shop floor level and new management processes and roles started to be structured in the organizations. Therefore, humans with years of experience in shop floor activities used to play an important part in that period, where they could use their skills to execute tasks such as adjusting appropriately to differences in the size, shape and orientation of production systems' parts (Kusiak, 2000).

The transition from mass to batch production systems was empowered by the emergence and application of digital computers. Such technology provided a shift from single-purpose machines to multi-purpose and more flexible machinery systems. Programmable systems arose and evolved in such a way that many functions and tasks could be performed on a single hardware platform. More variables, more complex dynamics and behaviour were incorporated into the manufacturing systems of batch production. The interdependence of the organization with the environment has grown in relevance and complexity. Cybernetics models have been used for the analysis of such systems, and in particular, concepts of information and feedback control with self-regulation have been used for this purpose. Stochastic and non-linear systems accompanied by operational research and artificial intelligence techniques have been the mathematical and logical tools used for the analysis of such organizational systems of batch production. Human presence has grown in the higher layers of the organization in order to occupy the new management roles and to execute managerial tasks at the shop floor. Therefore, humans with experience in the management of shop floor activities - such as in process planning, equipment selection, cellular configuration, facility layout, suppliers coordination and workers supervision, and material resources planning - as well as in the operation of computer integrated manufacturing systems (CIM) - have played an important role for the transition from mass to batch production models (Wu, 1994).

The Socio-Technological Threshold Principle

The gradual migration of mass and batch production systems to the proposed customer-centric model has some socio-technological implications to the new manufacturing organizations. This transition generates a continuous growth in the dynamics and in the level of complexity of the environment. Consequently, a growth in the level of environmental complexity demands from the organization the design or acquisition of new elements that comprise machinery systems along with manufacturing and operations management processes. These new elements are supposed to provide the organization with higher degrees of flexibility and agility in order to produce and to satisfy customers' exact needs and also to attend the growth in market demand for new solutions and products. These implications can be summarized by the premise (definition) stated in the following:

Definition 13.2. The Socio-Technological Threshold Principle: The gradual transition of organizations from mass and batch production systems to customer-centric models - which are also characterized by a continuous growth in the degrees of flexibility and agility - will reach a threshold where the current (and the dominant) technological state of the art will found their limits of contribution.

The incompatibility between the growth in the level of environmental complexity and the current technological state of the art in organizations will continuously motivate researchers to develop new technologies and management processes in order to reach new solutions. The Socio-Technological Threshold Principle of Definition 13.2 is one among the main motivations that researchers and industrials have had to empower the gradual transition in history from old to new technologies in organizations and society.

Level of Customization vs. Degree of Machine Cognition

Therefore, by considering The Socio-Technological Threshold Principle, and Proposition 13.1, we state that:

Proposition 13.2: The higher the level of customization of the manufacturing organization, the higher is the degree of machine cognition (needed) in order to improve the level of organizational cognition.

This proposition associates improvements in the degree of organizational cognition with growth in the degree of cognition of machines that participate in the manufacturing organization. Therefore, it is concerned with the degree of organizational cognition that the manufacturing organization needs to pursue in order to deal with the level of environmental complexity.

New Socio-Technological Perspectives of Customer-Centric Systems

Figure 13.3 illustrates the Socio-Technological Principle – where the threshold line illustrates the point of change from batch production to customer-centric systems. In this transition, technology and organizational processes move towards higher degrees of flexibility and agility along with cognition, intelligence and autonomy. Therefore, it would be also plausible to propose that:

Proposition 13.3: The higher the degree of cognition of a system, the higher is its degree of agility and flexibility.

where flexibility means capability to reconfigure and to adapt to new operational and management conditions; and agility means the ability to manufacture a variety of products at low cost and in a short period of time.

Figure 13.4 depicts the convergence of mass and batch production systems towards the customer-centric model, under this socio-technological perspective. The term technological cognition used in this figure is synonymous with degrees of cognition of machines and management systems.

Table 13.2 describes a summary of the socio-technological principles of organizational production models, where the dotted arrow points out the direction of higher degrees of technological cognition. The abbreviations SC, FS, CTP, VR, AT,

Figure 13.3. The technological threshold principle

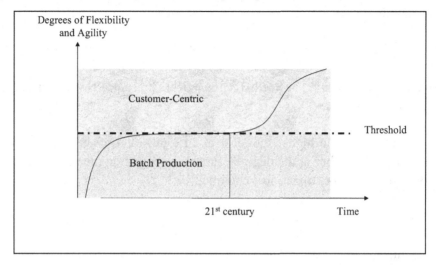

Figure 13.4. The socio-technological transition of organizational production models

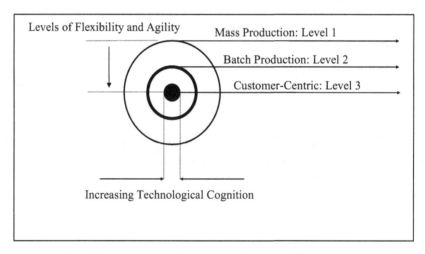

Table 13.2. Socio-technological principles of the manufacturing systems

Levels of Customization	Technological Principles
Mass Production: Level 1	Manual and Single Purpose Machines (Pneumatic Tools and Analogue Machinery)
Batch Production: Level 2	Programmable Systems – Computer Integrated and Flexible Manufacturing Systems (Digital Computers and Machines)
Customer-centric: Level 3	Cognitive Machines, Cognitive Information Systems, Immersiveness, Agile and Flexible Machinery and Management Systems (SC, FS, CTP, VR, AT, DAI, COT and Internet)

DAI and COT indicate soft computing, fuzzy systems, and computational theory of perceptions, virtual reality, agent technology, distributed artificial intelligence, and computational organization theory respectively.

ORGANIZATIONAL SYSTEMS THEORY PERSPECTIVES

Historical Transition

The gradual transition from a non-industrial to an industrial society has marked the frontiers between the periods of evolution and development of organizations and thus manufacturing systems.

Modern organizations and manufacturing systems emerged after the Industrial Revolution and they were challenged by new political, economic and social contexts. Thus, schools of organizations and management were developed in order to support the analysis of the new organization, the design of new organizational structures and processes, and the conception of new production models. The schools of organizations emerged in the first decade of the 20th century and they contributed towards the maturation of the disciplines of organization theory and management sciences. They started chronologically by proposing theories of bureaucracy and principles of scientific management and administrative theory, and they received new insights from the experiments of the human relations school. However, organizations and manufacturing systems of today have been closer to the contributions provided by the schools of administrative behaviour (and decision-making), systems theory, contingency theory and organizational learning.

In this section, we have given more attention to the school of systems theory because we have used concepts of hierarchic levels of complexity to derive analyses and conclusions about the evolution and developments in manufacturing organizations.

The analysis of organizations as cybernetic systems received its first contribution after Norbert Wiener's work published in 1948: Cybernetics, or control and communication in the animal and the machine (Wiener, 1948). Such systems present the capability of self-regulation in terms of some externally prescribed target or criterion (Boulding, 1956), and they are suitable for the analysis of any type of organizations, including manufacturing systems. Self-regulation means the ability of a system to maintain its steady states by sensing and by responding to its environment. Self-regulating systems encompass processes which work according to some artificial or natural law of behaviour, and they are supported by the principle of feedback. Therefore, they play a fundamental role in control theory, and thus in management control of organizational processes (Anthony, 1984), administrative decision-making (Simon, 1982a), organization design (Haberstroh, 1965), organizational change (Sundarasaradula *et al*, 2005) and adaptive learning cycles of learning organizations (Daft & Noe, 2001).

Organizations and thus manufacturing can also be analysed according to the operations and properties of systems of higher levels of complexity than cybernetics, such as open systems and social systems. By considering these organizational systems perspectives, we provide in the next sections analyses for past, current and future models of manufacturing organizations.

The Organizational Threshold Principle

The gradual migration of mass and batch production systems to the proposed customer-centric model has some organizational implications to the new manufacturing systems. This transition causes a continuous growth in the level of environmental complexity and it demands for higher degrees of organizational cognition in order to improve the computational capacity of the manufacturing organization along with its ability for knowledge and uncertainty management.

These implications can be summarized by the premise (definition) stated in the following:

Definition 13.3. The Organizational Threshold Principle: The gradual transition of manufacturing organizations from mass and batch production systems to customer-centric models - which are also characterized by a continuously growth in the levels of organizational and environmental complexity - will reach a threshold where current (and dominant) models of organizing will found their limits of contribution.

The incompatibility between a high level of environmental complexity and current organizing models of manufacturing systems will continuously motivate researchers to investigate new organizational theories and models in order to reach new solutions. The Organizational Threshold Principle of Definition 13.3 is one among the main motivations that researchers and industrials have had to empower the gradual transition in history from old to new models of organizing.

Level of Customization vs. Degree of Organizational Cognition

Therefore, by considering The Organizational Threshold Principle, and Propositions 13.1 and 13.2, we state that:

Proposition 13.4: The higher the level of customization of the manufacturing organization, the higher is the degree of organizational cognition (needed) in order to manage the level of environmental complexity.

New Organizational Perspectives of Customer-Centric Systems

Figure 13.5 illustrates the Organizational Threshold Principle - where the threshold line illustrates the transition point from batch production systems towards the customer-centric model. In this transition, manufacturing organizations move towards higher degrees of organizational cognition.

Figure 13.6 illustrates the convergence of mass and batch production systems towards the new organizational production model of customer-centric properties. By observing it, we can state that the levels of complexity of manufacturing organizations and their respective environments evolves as we move from level 1 to level 3. These three levels are not mutually exclusive. Indeed, each higher level system incorporates the features of those below it. In level 1, the system structure is highly rigid, more constrained and limited. As we progress from level 1 to 3, the system structure becomes somewhat less constrained and the connections among the interacting parts become relatively loose, where less constraint is placed on the behaviour of one element by the condition of the others; the manufacturing organization and its environment becomes more interdependent, and therefore, the evolving of one affects the other. Additionally, according to the concept of hierar-

Figure 13.5. The organizational threshold principle

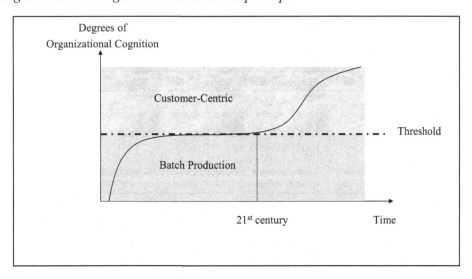

Figure 13.6. The organizational transition of production models

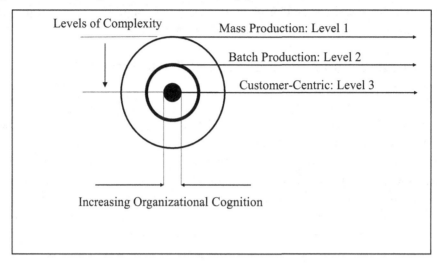

chic levels of cognition introduced in Chapter III, we can assert that the degrees of cognition of these systems and of their elements increase as we move from level 1 to 3. Consequently, there is also growth in their degrees of intelligence, autonomy, flexibility and agility.

Table 13.3 presents a summary of the organizational principles of production models, where the dotted arrow points out the direction of higher degrees of organizational cognition.

Table 13.3. Organizational principles of production systems

Levels of Customization	Organizational Principles
Mass Production: Level 1	Rational Systems with: Static, rigid and constrained structures; low level of environmental complexity and interaction.
Batch Production: Level 2	Cybernetics Systems with: Time-varying parameters and non-linear structures, capability of self-regulation; and medium level of environmental complexity and interdependence.
Customer-centric: Level 3	Open, Social and Learning Systems with: High level of environmental complexity and interdependence, high degree of organizational cognition, capability of self-maintenance and sustainable development, loosely connected parts with high degrees of flexibility and agility.

SUMMARY

Chapter XIII examined limitations of past and current manufacturing organizations (and operations management systems) and it contributed by proposing concepts and features towards new organizational production models through perspectives of management, socio-technology and organizational systems theory. From these perspectives, it introduced the concept of customer-centric systems which represents a new organizational production model with capabilities to manage high levels of environmental complexity, to operate with high levels of mass customization, and to provide customers with immersiveness. Additionally, these new systems pursue higher degrees of organizational cognition, intelligence and autonomy than past and current manufacturing organizations, and consequently, they also are characterized by higher degrees of agility and flexibility.

According to the perspectives of Chapter XIII, it was stated that:

For the Management Perspective:

Definition 13.1. The Management Threshold Principle: The gradual transition of manufacturing organizations from mass and batch production systems to customer-centric models - which are characterized by a continuous growth in the level of customization - will reach a threshold where customers will be part of the design, production and management of their own needs – resulting in the generation of highly personal and customized services and goods.

For the Socio-Technological Perspective:

Proposition 13.1: The higher the level of customization of the manufacturing organization, the higher is the level of environmental complexity.

For the Socio-Technological Perspective

Definition 13.2. The Socio-Technological Threshold Principle: The gradual transition of organizations from mass and batch production systems to customer-centric models - which are also characterized by a continuous growth in the degrees of flexibility and agility - will reach a threshold where the current (and the dominant) technological state of the art will found their limits of contribution.

Proposition 13.2: The higher the level of customization of the manufacturing organization, the higher is the degree of machine cognition (needed) in order to improve the level of organizational cognition.

Proposition 13.3: The higher the degree of cognition of a system, the higher is its degree of agility and flexibility.

For the Organizational Perspective

Definition 13.3. The Organizational Threshold Principle: The gradual transition of manufacturing organizations from mass and batch production systems to customer-centric models - which are also characterized by a continuously growth in the levels of organizational and environmental complexity - will reach a threshold where current (and dominant) models of organizing will found their limits of contribution.

Proposition 13.4: The higher the level of customization of the manufacturing organization, the higher is the degree of organizational cognition (needed) in order to manage the level of environmental complexity.

REFERENCES

Anthony, R. N., Dearden, J., & Bedford, N. M. (1984). *Management Control Systems*. Richard D. Irwin, Inc.

Brown, S. A. (2000). *Customer Relationship Management: Linking People, Process and Technology*. John Wiley Trade.

CMU-SEI (2002). CMMI for Systems Engineering, Software Engineering, Integrated Product and Process Development, and Supplier Sourcing: Staged Representation. Version 1.1. CMMI/SE/SW/IPPD/SS. *Technical Report CMU/SEI-TR-012*. Carnegie Mellon University. http://www.sei.cmu.edu.

Daft, R. L., & Noe, R. A. (2001). *Organizational Behavior*. Harcourt, Inc.

Haberstroh, C. (1965). Organization Design and Systems Analysis. In J.G. March (Ed.), *Handbook of Organizations*, (pp. 1171-1211). Rand McNally & Company.

Krajewski, L. J., & Ritzman, L. P. (2004). *Operations Management: Strategy and Analysis*. Prentice Hall.

Kusiak, A. (2000) *Computational Intelligence in Design and Manufacturing*. John Wiley & Sons, Inc.

Lee, G. H. (1998). Designs of Components and Manufacturing Systems for Agile Manufacturing, *International Journal of Production Research*, 4(36), 1023-1044.

Monfared, M. A. S., & Steiner, S. J. (1997). Emerging Intelligent Manufacturing Systems. *International. Journal of Flexible Automation and Integrated Manufacturing, 5*, 151-170.

Nobre, F. S., & Steiner, S. J. (2001b). Towards Intelligent and Immersive Manufacturing Systems. *Proceedings of the UK Workshop on Computational Intelligence* (pp. 232-236). Edinburgh, UK.

Nobre, F. S., & Steiner, S. J. (2001c). Towards Customer Centred Manufacturing Systems. *Proceedings of the 7th Postgraduate Research Symposium*, (pp.75-77). School of Manufacturing Engineering / University of Birmingham, England. ISBN: 0704423057.

Nobre, F. S., & Steiner, S. J. (2002a). Beyond the Thresholds of Manufacturing: Perspectives on Management, Technology and Organizations. *Proceedings of the IEEE International Engineering Management Conference* (pp. 788-793). Cambridge-UK.

Pine, B. J. (1999). *Mass Customization: The New Frontier in Business Competition.* Harvard Business School Press.

Porter, M. E. (1998). *Competitive Advantage: Creating and Sustaining Superior Performance.* The Free Press.

Rao, M. *et al* (1993). *Integrated Distributed Intelligent Systems in Manufacturing.* Chapman & Hall.

Simon, H. A. (1982a). *Models of Bounded Rationality: Economic Analysis and Public Policy, 1.* The MIT Press.

Steiner, S., A. de Vicq, & Medland, A. (2001). A Background to the ARMMS Programme – Agile Reconfigurable Manufacturing Machinery Systems – A Project of the European Thematic Network. *World Manufacturing Congress (WMC).* In the Proceedings. Rochester-NY, USA. Postponed to April 2-5th 2002.

Sundarasaradula D., Hasan H., Walker D. S., & Tobias A. M. (2005). Self-Organization, Evolutionary and Revolutionary Change in Organizations. *Strategic Change, 14*(7), 367-380.

Taylor, F. W. (1911). *The Principles of Scientific Management.* New York: Harper.

Toni, A., & Tonchia, S. (1998). Manufacturing Flexibility: A Literature Review, *International Journal of Production* Research, *6*(36), 1587-1617.

Wu, B. (1994). *Manufacturing Systems Design and Analysis: Context and Techniques.* Second edition. Chapman & Hall.

Scott, W. R. (1998). Organizations: Rational, Natural, and Open Systems. Prentice Hall, Inc.

ENDNOTES

[1]   Manufacturing (from Latin *manu factura*, "making by hand") is the use of tools and labor to make things for use or sale. Operations management is a business area of the organization which is concerned with the efficient and effective production of goods and services (Krajewski & Ritzman, 2004). Therefore, operations management can subsume manufacturing processes.

[2]   Competitive advantage is a position that a firm occupies in its competitive environment. It involves managerial and business processes that provide the organization with the capability to create superior value for its customers and superior profits for itself (Porter, 1998).

[3]   Value chain categorizes the generic value-adding activities of an organization supply chain.

[4]   Definitions of services and goods, as well as their differences and similarities are encountered in (Krajewski & Ritzman, 2004).

Chapter XIV

The New Organization:
Towards Computational Organization Management Networks

INTRODUCTION

This chapter contributes by proposing the definition, the structure and the proc-esses of Computational Organization Management Networks (COMN) which are new organizations whose principles of operation are based on the concepts of Hierarchic Cognitive Systems (as proposed in Chapter III) along with those of Tel-ecommunications Management Networks of the International Telecommunication Union (ITU-T, 2000). Structured with functional layers and the roles which range from technical and managerial to institutional levels of analysis, and also equipped with technological, operational, managerial and business processes, the concept of Computational Organization Management Networks (COMN), as proposed in this chapter, plays an important part in the developments of future organizations where cognitive machines and Cognitive Information Systems (CIS) are prominent ac-tors of governance, automation and control of the whole enterprise. Moreover, this chapter introduces the concept of immersive systems in order to provide the new organization with the capability of immersiveness.

THE SCOPE OF THE NEW ORGANIZATION

As introduced in Chapter XIII, customer-centric systems are new models of manufacturing organizations with capabilities to pursue high degrees of organizational cognition, intelligence and autonomy, and consequentely, they also are characterized by high degrees of agility and flexibility. Additionally, they also have the capabilities to manage high levels of environmental complexity, to operate with high levels of mass customization, and to provide customers with immersiveness.

From such a perspectice, this book advocates that such a kind of new organization has to be equiped with high levels of automation in order to pursue the necessary capabilities to govern, to coordinate and to control cognitive tasks in the technical, managerial, institutional and worldwide levels of the whole enterprise.

This chapter focuses attention to the conception of organizations of this type.

COGNITIVE INFORMATION SYSTEMS (CIS)

This is into such a domain and perspective of new organizations that we need to concentrate efforts in the design and engineering of information management systems with high degrees of cognition, intelligence and autonomy. These systems are hereafter called Cognitive Information Systems (CIS).

Definition 14.1: Cognitive Information Systems (CIS) are Information Management Systems (IMS) that pursue high degrees of cognition, intelligence and autonomy. They are particular classes of cognitive machines, and they are designed to participate in the organization by performing cognitive tasks and by fulfilling managerial roles in all the levels and layers of the whole enterprise.

PARTICIPATION OF CIS IN THE ORGANIZATION

Cognitive Information Systems (CIS) participate in the organization by performing cognitive tasks and by fulfilling technical, managerial and institutional roles in all the organizational layers. From this point of view, this book identifies four major areas of CIS application in the whole enterprise. These areas are classified into four organizational layers:

i)   Element Layer (Operational Level).
ii)   Network Management Layer (Primary Managerial Level).
iii)   Service Management Layer (Secondary Managerial Level).
iv)   Business Layer (Institutional Level).

ORGANIZATION FUNCTIONAL LAYERS: THE NEW ORGANIZATION

Functional layers play the fundamental part in the definition of the structure and processes for the new organization of Computational Organization Management Networks (COMN). Their concepts are based on the definition of Hierarchic Cognitive Systems which were introduced in Chapter III, along with the principles of Telecommunications Management Networks (TMN) architectures which have been proposed by International Telecommunication Union (ITU-T) - where ITU-T is the designation of the United Nations Specialized Agency in the field of telecommunications (ITU-T, 2000). In the organizational architectures of TMN, agents execute tasks in all hierarchic layers of the organization. Similarly, agent technology (Bradshaw, 1997; and Watt, 1997) plays an important task in the functional layers of the new organization – where agents are also synonymous with cognitive machines and Cognitive Information Systems (CIS).

This section proposes four functional layers for the new organization. It also introduces the roles of the agents - the Cognitive Information Systems (CIS) - that participate in the new organization by governing, controlling and coordinating cognitive tasks in all the levels and layers of the whole enterprise.

CIS in the Element Layer of the Organization – The Operational Level

The Element Layer (EL) comprises a Network Element Layer (NEL) and an Element Network Layer (ENL). The former part (NEL) comprises functional elements that work upon an individual basis, and, therefore, each individual element carries its own motives and fulfils micro-roles. The latter part (ENL) comprises a set of interconnected functional elements that work in group, and, therefore, they carry common motives and sub-goals, and they also fulfil micro-roles. In this kind of organization, an element is synonymous with an agent, and an agent is synonymous with a cognitive machine; and thus, a group of interconnected elements is synonymous with a group of agents that has the same meaning of a group of interconnected cognitive machines. Figure 14.1 illustrates the two parts of an Element Layer (EL), where $a_{(1...n)}$ denotes agents, for n integer.

The roles of Cognitive Information Systems (CIS) in the Element Layer (EL) are concerned with the execution of cognitive tasks of operation and control of individual elements as well as of groups of interconnected elements. These elements, as individuals and groups, participate in the technical, managerial and institutional levels of the organization; they perform cognitive tasks and fulfil technological, operational, managerial, and business roles in the whole enterprise. Therefore, in this particular case, the CIS provide operational and control processes to individual agents and group of agents that participate in the organization.

Figure 14.1. NEL as a controller of individual agents $a_{(1...n)}$ and ENL as a controller of a group of integrated agents $a_{(1...n)}$

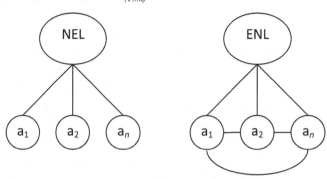

The Element Layer (EL) demands high degrees of cognition, intelligence and autonomy from the individual machines as well as from the groups of machines. For these requests, the technology of cognitive machines, along with the methodologies of Soft Computing (SC) (Zadeh, 1994), Fuzzy Logic (FL) (Zadeh, 1973), Computing with Words (CW) (Zadeh, 1996b), and Computational Theory of Perceptions (CTP) (Zadeh, 2001), play an important part in the conception of Cognitive Information Systems (CIS).

Applications at the level of Element Layer (EL) have received some attention, for instance, by researchers who have developed information and decision-support systems for manufacturing operations through the background of fuzzy logic, neural networks and genetic algorithms (Rao *et al*, 1993; Wu, 1994; Chang & Yih, 1998; Min *et al*, 1998; Perego & Rangone, 1998; Rajasekharan *et al*, 1998; Webster *et al*, 1998; Kusiak, 2000; Monfared & Steiner, 2000; and Morshed & Meeran, 2001). Nevertheless, despite achieving some successful results, these managerial and decision-support tools of mathematical and computational background have been constrained by the limitations of cognition, intelligence and autonomy of the existing machines which are mostly encountered in the organizations of today. The application of these machines in Flexible Manufacturing Cells and Systems (FMS) and their coordination through Computer Integrated Manufacturing (CIM) technology, have reached thresholds and limitations of contributions because of their low degrees of cognition, intelligence and autonomy (Nobre & Steiner, 2002a).

CIS in the Network Management Layer of the Organization – The Primary Managerial Level

The united work of individual agents and groups of agents in the Element Layer (EL) forms a set of patterns or clusters which represent the main macro-roles in the organization. Each pattern or cluster is synonymous with a functional network.

The Network Management Layer (NML) comprises the set of individual functional networks in the organization; and it is equipped and organized with normative structure, processes, technologies, agents and sub-goals, in order to provide management for each functional network upon an individual basis. Therefore, the NML provides the individual functional networks with managerial systems in order to coordinate and to control processes, operations and information that flow through the clusters of agents and groups of agents that participate in the whole enterprise. Figure 14.2 illustrates an NML managing individual Functional Layers $FL_{(1...m)}$, for m integer.

The roles of Cognitive Information Systems (CIS) in the Network Management Layer (NML) is concerned with the execution of cognitive tasks of coordination, control and thus management of the functional networks upon an individual basis; where, in this case, a functional network is synonymous with a network of agents and also with a network of cognitive machines that work together according to an organizational system equipped with normative structure, processes, technologies and sub-goals. Into such a perspective, functional networks (and thus networks of cognitive machines) participate in the technical, managerial and institutional levels of the organization; they perform cognitive tasks and fulfil technological, operational, management, and business roles in the whole enterprise.

It is important to emphasize that while Cognitive Information Systems (CIS) participate in the Network Management Layer (NML) by managing each individual functional network in the organization, they participate in the Element Layer (EL) by operating and controlling individual agents and groups of agents that participate in the functional networks of the organization. Therefore, the NML comprises the management of the EL in the organization.

This book assumes that the performance of managerial roles in the organization is contingent upon the capabilities of the managers and also upon the capabilities of the individuals and groups that the managers supervise. Therefore, it states that:

Figure 14.2. NML as the manager of individual $FL_{(1...m)}$

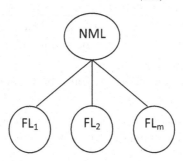

Proposition 14.1: The higher the degree of cognition, intelligence and autonomy of Cognitive Information Systems (CIS), the higher is their capability to manage Functional Networks (FN) in the organization.

Proposition 14.2: The higher the degree of cognition, intelligence and autonomy of the elements of a Functional Network (FN), the higher is the capability of CIS to manage the FN.

CIS in the Service Management Layer of the Organization – The Secondary Managerial Level

The set of functional networks in the organization forms vertical and horizontal processes constituted by sub-goals and goals, where sub-goals represent means for the achievement of more complex goals. Therefore, a managerial system is needed in order to coordinate, to control and to mediate all the operations, processes and information in between the functional networks in the organization.

The Service Management Layer (SML) comprises the set of functional networks in the organization; and it is equipped and organized with normative structures, processes, technologies, agents, goals and sub-goals, in order to provide management for the set of functional networks. Therefore, the SML provides the organization with a managerial system with the capability to integrate, to coordinate, to control and to mediate all the operations, processes and information in between the functional networks in the whole enterprise. Figure 14.3 illustrates an SML managing a set of integrated Functional Layers $FL_{(1...m)}$.

The roles of Cognitive Information Systems (CIS) in the Service Management Layer (SML) is concerned with the execution of cognitive tasks of integration, coordination, control and thus management of the relations, operations, processes and information in between the functional networks in the organization; where, in this case, the set of functional networks is synonymous with the set of networks of agents and consequently with the set of networks of cognitive machines in the organization.

In this application layer, the organization of the functional layers and thus the shape and the structure of the enterprise can be chosen according to the different organizational design models presented in the literature (Galbraith, 2002). Into such a domain, each functional network can be synonymous with a cluster of services, or in short, a service. Therefore, the Cognitive Information Systems (CIS) in the Network Management Layer (NML) can also be viewed as agents of management of the whole services in the organization.

It is important to emphasize that while CIS participate in the Service Management Layer (SML) by managing the operations, processes and information

Figure 14.3. SML as the manager of integrated FL$_{(1...m)}$

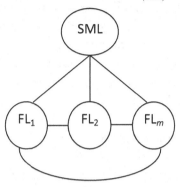

between all the functional networks in the organization, they participate in the Network Management Layer (NML) by managing each functional network upon an individual basis. Therefore, the SML comprises the management of the NML in the organization.

Applications at the SML and NML have received some contributions with the advances in Enterprise Resources Planning and Management Systems (EPR) that emerged from the 1970's. ERP are classes of information technology and management systems which are applied to, and implemented in the whole organization with the purposes of integration, control and automation of data, information and processes. Examples of areas of application of an ERP system include: Manufacturing, Supply Chain, Financials, Customer Relationship Management (CRM), Human Resources, Warehouse Management and Decision Support System (Brady *et al*, 2001). Applications in the level of the Service Management Layer (SML) will receive greater contributions in the proportion of the continuous advancements in Cognitive Information Systems (CIS) of high degrees of cognition, intelligence and autonomy; and thus CIS will play an important role in the SML of new organizations.

CIS in the Business Management Layer of the Organization – The Institutional Level

The Business Management Layer (BML) comprises all the operations, management processes and services of the previous layers, i.e. the EL, NML and SML respectively; and it is equipped and organized with a normative structure, processes, technologies, agents and goals, in order to provide the organization with capabilities to manage the environment. More specifically, the BML provides the enterprise with a managerial system with the capability to coordinate, to control and to mediate the operations, processes and information between the organization and the environment. Figure 14.4 illustrates the role of the BML in the organization.

The roles of Cognitive Information Systems (CIS) in the Business Management Layer (BML) are less obvious and less present in the organizations of today. It is concerned with the execution of cognitive tasks of coordination, control and thus management of the relations, operations, processes and information in between the organization and the environment. To empower this application this research proposes the concept of immersiveness whose idea was first spoken in (Nobre & Steiner, 2001b, 2001c and 2002a).

The Concept of Immersiveness

It was stated in this chapter that the new organization has to be equipped with structure, processes, goals, agents and technologies which are able to provide them with the capability to pursue high levels of immersiveness.

Definition 14.2: Immersiveness represents the ability of the organization to interact with its customers (either humans or machines) in a friendly way, by immersing them into the organization's operations through approaches such as virtual reality, simulation or via real world protocols; in order to satisfy customers by capturing their exact needs, by customizing and managing the design, engineering and production of their goods and services, and by delivering their products with efficacy and effectiveness.

More specifically, either a manufacturing or a service organization, it can immerse its customers by providing them with the scope to interact with some of the life cycle stages of its processes of design, engineering and production, including those processes of requirements analysis, product design, test, prototyping, demand

Figure 14.4. BML as the manager that mediates between the organization and the environment

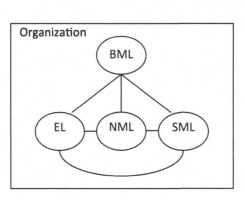

specification, volume and variety choice. Under this perspective, virtual reality will play an important task in the customer immersiveness; the technologies of cognitive information systems and cognitive machines will provide important contributions in the execution of cognitive tasks such as pattern recognition and vision, natural language processing, decision-making, problem-solving, learning, and management; additionally, the internet will play an important part in the connection of customers into the new organization. This perspective is illustrated in Figure 14.5 and it assumes that such an illustrative immersive system can be configured to provide customers with different levels of interaction to the technical and managerial operations of the processes of design, engineering and production in the organization. The dotted lines symbolize the internet which connects customers within the organization; and the continuous lines denote the system operational levels that customers can interact with, in order to capture their exact needs and even emotions, to customize and to manage the design, engineering and production of their goods and services.

DEFINITION OF COMPUTATIONAL ORGANIZATION MANAGEMENT NETWORKS (COMN)

The scope of the new organization, the definition of Cognitive Information Systems (CIS), and the concept of Functional Layers, as presented in previous sections of

Figure 14.5. Illustration of an Immersive System

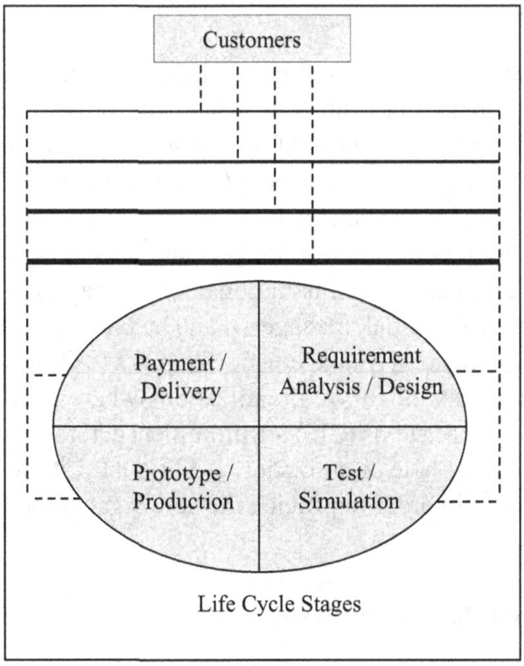

this chapter, form the base for the definition of Computational Organization Management Networks (COMN).

Definition 14.3: Computational Organization Management Networks (COMN) are organizations whose structure, processes, participants, goals and technologies are designed according to the concepts of Functional Layers which comprise Element Layer, Network Management Layer, Service Management Layer and Business Management Layer. COMN pursue high degrees of organizational cognition and their main participants comprise Cognitive Information Systems (CIS) and cognitive machines.

STRUCTURE AND PROCESSES OF COMPUTATIONAL ORGANIZATION MANAGEMENT NETWORKS (COMN)

Figure 14.6 illustrates the structure of a Computational Organization Management Network (COMN) composed by the four functional layers that comprise operational, managerial and institutional tasks. Hence, the organizational layers of the COMN and their cognitive roles follow the definitions and concepts of Element Layer (EL), Network Management Layer (NML), Service Management Layer (SML) and Business Management Layer (BML) respectively.

SUMMARY

Chapter XIV contributed by proposing the definition, the structure and the processes of Computational Organization Management Networks (COMN) which are new organizations whose principles of operation are based on the concepts of Organization Functional Layers, Hierarchic Cognitive Systems along with those of Telecommunications Management Networks of the International Telecommunication Union. Structured with functional layers and the cognitive roles which range from technical and managerial to institutional levels of analysis, and also equipped with technological, operational, managerial and business processes, the concept of Computational Organization Management Networks (COMN) plays an important part in the developments of future organizations where cognitive machines and Cognitive Information Systems (CIS) are prominent actors of governance, automation and control of the whole organization. Additionally, it introduced the concept of immersive systems in order to provide the new organization with the capability of immersiveness.

In Chapter XIV, it was proposed that:

For **Cognitive Information Systems** (CIS):

Figure 14.6. Structure of Computational Organization Management Networks – COMN

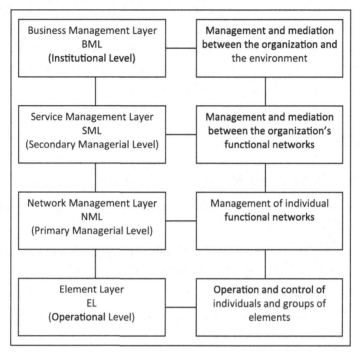

Definition 14.1: Cognitive Information Systems (CIS) are Information Management Systems (IMS) that pursue high degrees of cognition, intelligence and autonomy. They are particular classes of cognitive machines, and they are designed to participate in the organization by performing cognitive tasks and by fulfilling managerial roles in all the levels and layers of the whole enterprise.

For **Immersiveness**:

Definition 14.2: Immersiveness represents the ability of the organization to interact with its customers (either humans or machines) in a friendly way, by immersing them into the organization's operations through approaches such as virtual reality, simulation or via real world protocols; in order to satisfy customers by capturing their exact needs, by customizing and managing the design, engineering and production of their goods and services, and by delivering their products with efficacy and effectiveness.

And for **Computational Organization Management Networks** (COMN):

Definition 14.3: Computational Organization Management Networks (COMN) are organizations whose structure, processes, participants, goals and technologies are designed according to the concepts of Functional Layers which comprise Element Layer, Network Management Layer, Service Management Layer and Business Management Layer. COMN pursue high degrees of organizational cognition and their main participants comprise Cognitive Information Systems (CIS) and cognitive machines.

REFERENCES

Bradshaw, J.M. (1997) *Software Agents*. AAAI Press.

Brady, J., Monk, E. & Wagner, B. (2001) *Concepts in Enterprise Resource Planning*. Course Technology.

Chang, T,-M. & Yih, Y. (1998) A fuzzy rule-based approach for dynamic control of kanbans in a generic kaban system. *International Journal of Production Research, (36) 8*: 2247-2257.

Galbraith, J.R. (2002) *Designing Organizations - An executive guide to strategy, structure, and process*. Jossey-Bass.

ITU-T (2000) Principles for a telecommunications management network. *Recommendation M.3010*. International Telecommunication Union.

Kusiak, A. (2000) *Computational Intelligence in Design and Manufacturing*. John Wiley & Sons, Inc.

Min, H.-S. *et al* (1998) A competitive neural network approach to multi-objective FMS scheduling. *International Journal of Production Research, (36) 7*: 1749-1765.

Monfared, M.A.S. & Steiner, S.J. (2000) Fuzzy Adaptive Scheduling and Control Systems. *Fuzzy Sets and Systems, 115*: 231-246.

Morshed, M.S. & Meeran, S. (2001) Job Shop Scheduling: A Brief Survey. *Proceedings of the Seventh Annual Research Symposium of Postgraduate Research* (pp. 78-82). School of Manufacturing and Mechanical Engineering / University of Birmingham UK.

Nobre, F.S. & Steiner, S.J. (2001b) Towards Intelligent and Immersive Manufacturing Systems. *Proceedings of the UK Workshop on Computational Intelligence* (pp. 232-236). Edinburgh, UK.

Nobre, F.S. & Steiner, S.J. (2001c) Towards Customer Centred Manufacturing Systems. *Proceedings of the 7th Postgraduate Research Symposium*, (pp.75-77).

School of Manufacturing Engineering / University of Birmingham, England. ISBN: 0704423057.

Nobre, F.S. & Steiner, S.J. (2002a) Beyond the Thresholds of Manufacturing: Perspectives on Management, Technology and Organizations. *Proceedings of the IEEE International Engineering Management Conference* (pp. 788-793). Cambridge-UK.

Perego, A. & Rangone, A. (1998) A reference framework for the application of MADM fuzzy techniques to selecting AMTS. *International Journal of Production Research*, (36) 2: 437-458.

Rajasekharan, M. *et al* (1998) A Genetic algorithm for facility layout design in manufacturing systems. *International Journal of Production Research*, (30) 1: 95-110.

Rao, M. *et al* (1993) *Integrated Distributed Intelligent Systems in Manufacturing.* Chapman & Hall.

Watt, S.N.K. (1997) Artificial Societies and Psychological Agents. In Nwana and Azarmi (Ed.), *Software Agents and Soft Computing: Towards Enhancing Machine Intelligence* (pp. 27-41). Springer.

Webster, S. *et al* (1998) A genetic algorithm for scheduling job families on a single machine with arbitrary earliness/tardiness penalties and unrestricted common due date. *International Journal of Production Research*, (36) 9: 2543-2551.

Wu, B. (1994). *Manufacturing Systems Design and Analysis: Context and Techniques.* Second edition. Chapman & Hall.

Zadeh, L.A. (1973) Outline of a New Approach to the Analysis of Complex Systems and Decision Process. *IEEE Transactions on Systems, Man, and Cybernetics, 3 (1)*: 28-44.

Zadeh, L.A. (1994) Soft Computing and Fuzzy Logic. *IEEE Software, November*: 48-56.

Zadeh, L.A. (1996b) The Evolution of Systems Analysis and Control: A Personal Perspective. *IEEE Control Systems, June*: 95-98.

Zadeh, L.A. (1997) The Roles of Fuzzy Logic and Soft Computing in the Conception, Design and Development of Intelligent Systems. In Nwana and Azarmi (Ed.), *Software Agents and Soft Computing: Towards Enhancing Machine Intelligence* (pp. 183-190). Springer.

Zadeh, L.A. (2001) A New Direction in AI: Toward a Computational Theory of Perceptions. *AI Magazine. Spring*: 73-84.

Section VII
General Conclusions

Never discourage anyone...who continually makes progress, no matter how slow.

Plato (427 BC – 347 BC)

Section VII provides general conclusions about this research book and it comprises Chapter XV only.

This chapter highlights the core contributions of this book; it points out alignments between proposals and findings; and it concludes by indicating topics of further research.

Chapter XV
Contributions and Extensions

INTRODUCTION

This book has provided many contributions to the concepts of organizational cognition and cognitive machines, but most importantly, we have to acknowledge that this work has put forwards new challenges and new perspectives to our understanding on the participation of cognitive machines in organizations. It introduced analyses on the implications of cognitive machines for organizations and it proposed the concept of Computational Organization Management Networks – whose structure, processes and agents form the base of new organizations.

The contents of such contributions are presented in the next sections of this chapter.

ON THE UNIFICATION OF ORGANIZATIONAL AND TECHNOLOGICAL THEORIES

Firstly, this book was largely influenced by the scientific works of Herbert A. Simon (on Bounded Rationality, Administrative Behaviour and Organizations) and Lotfi A. Zadeh (on Fuzzy Systems Theory and its derivatives on Computational Theory of Perceptions and Words) respectively. In such a way, this book played an important part as a bridge between these brilliant theories of these two researchers. It has brought to light the richness that exists in the unification of such organizational and technological theories, and most important, it has proposed new concepts from these backgrounds. The unification of theories, as exploited in this book, has formed the core element of contribution to the design and analysis of cognitive machines, and also to understand their implications for organizations.

ON ORGANIZATIONAL COGNITION

Through Section II, this book put forward cognition as a fundamental element of the organization. It explained why cognition plays an important part in organizational design and also in the analyses of the organization, the environment, and their relations. In summary, it set up that:

- A theory of organizational cognition is important and necessary when we decide to design organizations with higher capabilities of information processing and uncertainty management. In such a way, organizational cognition is a discipline which contributes to improve the computational capacity of the organization along with its ability for knowledge management.
- The theory of organizational cognition as proposed in this book plays an important part, and introduces a new perspective, in the analysis of the relations between the organization, its elements and the environment.

To support such statements and conclusions, this book contributed with definitions, premises and propositions towards a theory of organizational cognition which comprises concepts of intelligence, cognition, autonomy and complexity of the organization and the environment along with their relations. It proposed ten principles about organizational cognition and it clearly distinguished organizational cognition from the concept of organizational learning. It also outlined the concept of hierarchic levels of cognition in organizational systems and thus it proposed cognition as a fundamental element of the organization.

ON THE DESIGN OF COGNITIVE MACHINES

In Chapter V, it was defined that:

Definition 5.1: Cognitive machines are agents whose processes of functioning are mainly inspired by human cognition. Therefore, they have great possibilities to present intelligent behaviour.

In such a connection of cognition and machines, this book played an important part by selecting technologies of machines and by relating them to the discipline of cognition. The technologies behind cognitive machines were selected through some criteria and they include the disciplines of fuzzy systems, computing with words and computational theory of perceptions.

In his work on a computational theory of perceptions (which is a derivative of fuzzy systems), Zadeh introduced ideas and definitions that associate elements of his theory with the process of perception (Zadeh, 1999 and 2001). In this book, we extended such association by relating his ideas and definitions to additional elements of cognition such as natural concepts and levels of information-processing.

From such a background, Chapter VI contributed by presenting a framework of cognitive machines with the ability to manipulate complex symbols which are representations of percepts (and thus concepts) along with mental models described by words, propositions and sentences of natural language. The ability of these machines to manipulate natural concepts provides them with higher levels of information-processing than other symbolic-processing machines; and according to the theory of levels of processing in cognition (Reed, 1988), these machines mimic (even through simple models) cognitive processes of humans.

ON COGNITIVE MACHINES AND ORGANIZATIONAL COGNITION

This book relied on the premise that cognitive machines can improve the cognitive abilities of the organization. Therefore, it was proposed in Chapter VII that:

Proposition 7.1: Cognitive machines increase the level of complexity of the organization, and thus it improve the degree of cognition of the organization.

Organizational cognition is concerned with the processes which provide agents and organizations with the ability to learn, to make decisions and to solve problems. The main agents of organizational cognition are the participants within the organization and the social networks which they form. Additionally, in such a perspective, the participants within the organization comprise humans and cognitive machines and they are supposed to act as decision-makers in the name of the organization. Therefore, cognitive machines are also agents of organizational cognition.

ON COGNITIVE MACHINES IN CONFLICT RESOLUTION: ANALYSIS

The premise that cognitive machines can improve the cognitive abilities of the organization was associated with the assertion that such machines can reduce or solve intra-individual and group dysfunctional conflicts which arise from decision-making processes in organizations. This assertion was supported by the analyses introduced in Chapter VII through theories of bounded rationality, economic decision-making and conflict resolution along with perspectives about the participation of cognitive machines in organizations.

It was proposed that cognitive machines can reduce intra-individual conflicts by solving the problems of uncertainty, incomparability and unacceptability which pervade alternatives and the processes of decision-making of the participants in the organization. It was also proposed that such machines can reduce group conflicts by integrating the different views or opinions of the participants in the group (within the organization); and by storing the group's perspectives into a commonsensical knowledge base; and thus by making a commonsensical decision[1].

ON ORGANIZATIONAL COGNITION AND ENVIRONMENTAL COMPLEXITY

This book borrowed the picture of organizations as contingent upon the environment from the perspective of organization design and contingency theory as proposed by Galbraith (1973, 1977 and 2002). Moving further, it also relied on the proposition that an increase in organizational cognition reduces the relative levels of uncertainty and complexity of the environment with which the organization relates. Such perspectives were summarized in one theorem proposed in Chapter III and reprinted in the following.

Theorem 3.1: The higher the degree of cognition of the organization, the lower is the relative level of environmental complexity and uncertainty that the organization confronts and needs to manage.

According to the concept of Hierarchic Levels of Cognition presented in Chapter III, organizational systems grow in complexity as they move from frameworks to social systems. It was defined that cognition, and thus degree of cognition, is the main element which makes such organizational systems distinct from each other in terms of complexity and behaviour. Organizations with higher degrees of cognition have higher levels of complexity along with higher degrees of intelligence and autonomy. Therefore, in this book, organizational complexity was defined as synonymous with (and contingent upon) organizational cognition; and environmental complexity was defined as synonymous with (and contingent upon) environmental uncertainty.

Moreover, it was defined that organizational cognition is a matter of degree which is contingent upon organization design – i.e. the choice of the elements of the organization such as its goals, social structure, participants and technology. Therefore, organizational cognition differs from human cognition if we consider the perspective that the former is part of an artificial process of design, and the latter is part of a natural kind or a biological evolutionary process.

Additionally, as a consequence of the contingency of the organization upon the environment, it was stated that organizations have different degrees of cognition when they operate in different environments.

ON COGNITIVE MACHINES, ORGANIZATIONS AND THE ENVIRONMENT

This book contributed by associating the premises and propositions on cognitive machines, organizational cognition and environmental complexity, and thus by concluding that:

Theorem 7.1: The technology of cognitive machines increases the degree of organizational cognition, and it relatively reduces the level of environmental complexity and uncertainty that the organization needs to manage.

ON THE PARTICIPATION OF COGNITIVE MACHINES IN ORGANIZATIONS

In this book, it was assumed that, if the cognitive roles in organizations, as fulfilled by agents, have performance and outcomes which can be attributed to humans or machines, without any distinction, then machines can be considered as participants within organizations.

Besides analyzing the participation of cognitive machines in conflict resolution of decision-making processes in organizations, this book proposed definitions about the relationships between the cognitive machine, its designer and the organization. It was defined that:

Definition 10.5: The organization is responsible for the assignment of roles to the cognitive machine, and the machine is responsible for the roles it fulfils in the organization. However, the machine designer and the organization are the main parts responsible for the machine results and performance. If the machine exhibits deviant behaviour during task execution or performance below specified criteria, then the contract between the organization and the machine designer is the object of analysis and judgement.

ON THE INDUSTRIAL CASE

This book introduced in Section V additional contributions to organizational cognition and cognitive machines. It presented evidence about the alignment of its premises and propositions with results of an industrial case study. The central point of contribution of part V was concerned with the development of approaches and measures to evaluate the degree of organizational cognition. Such developments had three major complementary activities.

The first activity was about the implementation of The Capability Maturity Model in the organization of study. From this investigation, we defined measures of organization process improvement and we proposed correlations between them and organizational cognition. Among these measures were included organization process maturity, capability and performance. From such correlations, we also defined an association between organizational cognition and organizational learning.

The second activity was about the development of an approach for the evaluation and management control of the organization process performance. For this purpose, we proposed a management control system which included a cognitive machine among its elements. The computation of performance indexes of the organization process was executed by the cognitive machine which was engineered through a set of criteria of design along with qualitative and quantitative analysis.

The third activity highlighted data analysis and findings of the industrial case study which opened new directions to evaluate, to assess and to measure degree of organizational cognition from appraisal methods of organization process improvement models.

On Organizational Cognition and Organization Process Maturity

Results of the industrial case study which were concerned with organization process improvement in the NOB indicated that:

- Organizational cognition can be associated with organization process maturity. Hence, the degree of organizational cognition can be represented by level of organization process maturity.

Therefore, in this application we contributed by deriving a proposition that correlates organizational cognition with organization process maturity:

Proposition 9.3: The higher the degree of organizational cognition, the higher is the level of process maturity of the organization.

On Organizational Cognition, Organization Process Capability and Performance

Results of the industrial case which were concerned with organization process capability and performance in the NOB indicated that:

- The level of organization process capability and performance can be associated with the level of organization process maturity. Therefore, the degree of organizational cognition can also be associated with the level of organization process capability and performance.

Therefore, in this application we contributed by deriving a proposition that correlates organizational cognition with organization process capability and performance:

Proposition 9.5: The higher the degree of organizational cognition, the greater is the chance of the organization to achieve high levels of process capability and performance.

On Organizational Cognition and Organizational Learning

Additionally, by associating conclusions of the industrial case with results in the literature, we stated that:

- Improvements in organizational cognition can be associated with improvement in organizational learning. This assertion is reinforced in the literature when improvements in organization performance and productivity are associated with the practices of organizational learning (Argote, 1999; and Brynjolfsson & Hitt, 2000).

Therefore, in this application we also contributed by associating improvements in organizational cognition with organization learning:

Proposition 9.6: The higher the degree of organizational cognition, the higher is the level of organizational learning.

Where, the higher level of organizational learning, the higher is the capability of the organization to learn.

On Measurements of Organizational Cognition

The associations of degree of organizational cognition with levels of organizational process maturity, capability and performance along with organizational learning, have provided this research with important directions to assess and to measure the degree of organizational cognition with basis on appraisal methods of continuous process improvement models such as those of The Capability Maturity Model.

Practical results with data analysis of the industrial case presented two methods of quantitative measurement that indicated improvements in the levels of organization process maturity and organization process performance which were associated with improvements in the degree of organizational cognition.

Therefore, this book also contributed by pointing out new directions to tailor and to derive approaches to measure the degree of organizational cognition.

On the Participation of a Cognitive Machine in the Organization NOB

Results of the industrial case which were concerned with the participation of the cognitive machine in the NOB indicated that:

i.   Cognitive machines can support managers in decision analysis and management control processes in the organization. The execution of these tasks involves a combination of manipulation of natural concepts with arithmetic and analytical computation.
ii. The engineering of such machines comprises the design of a commonsensical knowledge base which integrates different perspectives, opinions and perceptions of the participants in a group. Additionally, the ability of these machines to represent natural concepts and to manipulate mental models through rules of approximate reasoning makes them agents with capabilities to reduce intra-individual and group dysfunctional conflicts which arise from decision-making processes in the organization.

On the Analysis of the Technical, Managerial and Institutional Levels of NOB

Observations about the organization levels of analysis of NOB indicated that:

i.   The Capability Maturity Model (CMM) provided the technical level of NOB with successful results which could be observed through improvements in the levels of organization process maturity and performance of software projects.

ii. The CMM found limitations to progress in those areas at upper levels of management such as at the managerial and institutional levels. It was caused by the lack of alignment between the organization goals with those of the CMM at the levels and areas which related the organization NOB to the market. Therefore, the organization NOB as a whole failed in the implementation of the CMM, but not the CMM itself.

On Organizational Cognition and the Environmental Complexity of NOB

It was also observed that during the period between 1995 and 1998 the Brazilian telecommunications market, and thus the environment of NOB, passed through a drastic transformation as a result of a constitutional process of privatization. In between 1997 and 2002, the number of participants (employees) in NOB was reduced by 80% approximately.

These additional observations about NOB lead to the conclusions that:

i.   The alignment of the technical, managerial and institutional levels of the organization represents a necessary process for its survival and sustainable development. Such a process involves the alignment of organization goals and social structure.

ii. Organizational cognition is an organizational capability. Therefore, organizations presenting only satisfactory degree of cognition in isolated parts of their hierarchy levels will have a great chance to fail in their development and survival.

ON THE IMPLICATIONS OF COGNITIVE MACHINES FOR ORGANIZATIONS

Investigations on the implications of cognitive machines for organizations contribute to the analysis of organizational change and to the design of new organizations. This book contributed with analyses about the impact of cognitive machines on organizational design and upon the elements of the organization. It was concluded that, while the characteristics of the elements of the organization will change, evolve and develop continuously towards higher levels of complexity, the purpose of existence of the organization will remain the same or will not change in the same proportion of its elements.

ON THE THRESHOLDS OF MANUFACTURING ORGANIZATIONS

This book introduced perspectives of management, socio-technology and organizational systems theory in order to investigate limitations of past and current manufacturing organizations and to propose new concepts and features towards customer-centric systems which represent a new organizational production model with capabilities to pursue high degrees of organizational cognition, intelligence and autonomy, and consequentely, they also are characterized with high degrees of agility and flexibility. Additionally, they also have the capabilities to manage high levels of environmental complexity, to operate with high levels of mass customization, and to provide customers with immersiveness.

Such a kind of new organization has to be equiped with high levels of automation in order to pursue the necessary capabilities to govern, to coordinate and to control cognitive tasks in the technical, managerial, institutional and worldwide levels of the whole enterprise.

It was based on this view that this book proposed the concept of Computational Organization Management Networks.

ON THE COMPUTATIONAL ORGANIZATION MANAGEMENT NETWORKS

This book proposed that:

Definition 14.3: Computational Organization Management Networks (COMN) are organizations whose structure, processes, participants, goals and technologies are designed according to the concepts of Functional Layers which comprise Element Layer, Network Management Layer, Service Management Layer and Business Management Layer. COMN pursue high degrees of organizational cognition and their main participants comprise Cognitive Information Systems (CIS) and cognitive machines.

Such a kind of new organization will play a fundamental part in the processes of engineering, production, logistics and management of goods and services along with the processes of management of transactions, business and electronic commerce in the future organizations. Such new enterprises will be governed according to the structure and processes of Computational Organization Management Networks; they will be legally supported with nexus of contracts that assign the responsibilities to, and agreements between, the organization and the designer of the cognitive machines (and cognitive information systems) which are the main participants in the layers and levels of the whole organization. The roles of these participants can be defined in the normative structure of the organization.

FURTHER EXTENSIONS

On Cognitive Machines and Learning

The design of a framework of cognitive machines introduced in Part III was mainly concerned with perception, concept identification, categorization, memory and decision-making processes. The topics on learning and emotions were left to further research.

The field of machine learning is concerned with the engineering of computational systems that automatically change and improve with experience (Mitchell, 1997). Neural computation (Hertz, 1991), soft computing (Zadeh, 1994), adaptive fuzzy systems (Wang, 1994), evolutionary computation and genetic algorithms (Back, *et al*, 2000; and Fogel, 2000), along with genetic programming (Koza, J.R. 1992) are among the main disciplines which can be used to design and to aggregate learning processes to machines.

The computational processes and algorithms of learning introduced by Wang (1994) represent potential candidates for such a purpose – i.e. to provide the cognitive machines of this book with the capability to learn. The framework of cognitive machines introduced in Chapter VI has structure and processes which are similar to those of the fuzzy systems adopted by Wang. Therefore, similar algorithms of learning could de embedded into such machines.

On Cognitive Machines and Emotions

The topic of machines with emotions and emotional processes was also left for further research. However, it deserves some comments due to its importance in the literature.

Whether machines should exhibit emotional behaviour, and whether they are able to have emotions or not, are controversial topics among the researchers of artificial intelligence, cognition and social sciences.

By assuming that machines may indeed be able to have emotional processes and emotional behaviour, the question of whether emotions are important to machines or not depends on the motivations of their designers and upon the environment with which they relate. On the one hand, machines with emotions, or emotional machines, might form better relations and social networks with humans in organizations than other machines. In such a view, machine emotion would be relevant for researchers on organizational behaviour. On the other hand, machines with emotions might have their own motives and might represent additional agents of dysfunctional conflicts in organizations. In such a view, machine emotion would be a problem for researchers of rational theories.

Among the institutions which have been researching the field of emotional machines include The MIT Artificial Intelligence Laboratory at Massachusetts (USA) which has carried out a project called Sociable Machines (Breazeal, 2000).

On Cognitive Machines *vs.* Humans in Organizations

Are cognitive machines better agents of organizational cognition and organizational learning than humans? Are they better agents of organization performance and productivity than humans? Such questions rely on the statement that: if we assume that the cognitive roles in organizations have performance and outcomes which can be attributed to either humans or machines, without any distinction, then we are ready to consider machines as participants within the organization similarly to people. This perspective involves a rational comparison of machines with human's performance and thus they compete for the same role in the organization.

Another formulation for such a problem consists of asking whether cognitive machines can satisfy (satisfice) cognitive roles and goals in the organization or not. In this perspective, machines are not competing with humans directly, but with the organization criteria of satisfying (satisficing) roles and goals. Both perspectives need to be further investigated in order to derive conclusions about the economic, political, social and technological implications of cognitive machines for the society.

ON THE FUTURE OF ORGANIZATIONS

We authors have said that while the characteristics of the elements of the organization will change, evolve and develop continuously towards higher levels of complexity, the purpose of existence of the organization will remain the same or will not change in the same proportion of its elements.

The former part, which is concerned with the elements of the organization, will move towards high levels of automation – mainly in those areas at upper layers and levels of the organization, and thus their integration will provide organizations with more capabilities of computational capacity along with knowledge and uncertainty management. Therefore, new organizations of this kind will be able to operate in, and to manage higher levels of environmental complexity than the organizations of today. These transformations in the new organizations will have implications for the society and this is a topic of further research. Nevertheless, we can preview and assert that new classes of jobs will emerge in order to attend a new demand for designers of the new elements of the new organizations – where in between such elements are included cognitive machines.

The latter part, which is concerned with the purpose and the existence of organizations, will remain the same and for sure will not change in the same proportions to the evolutions in the organization elements. This is because the individual motives and the organizational goals which are pursued by human kind will not change over time into the political, economical and social facets of this world.

SUMMARY

This book contributed with interdisciplinary and fundamental concepts on organizational cognition and cognitive machines along with studies on the implications of cognitive machines for the new organization. It puts forward a set of contributions that comprise:

i.   The Unification of Organizational and Technological Theories: that contributes to the conception of cognitive machines.
ii. The Foundation of a Theory on Organizational Cognition: that contributes to the pursuit of improvements in the computational capacity of the organization along with its capability for knowledge and uncertainty management.
iii. The Design and Analysis of Cognitive Machines: that contributes to the pursuit of the extension of the human boundaries of computational capacity along with knowledge and uncertainty management to more advanced models of cognition or information processing.

iv.   The Association of Cognitive Machines with Organizational Cognition: that contributes to understand how cognitive machines can improve the cognitive capabilities of the organization.

v.   The Roles of Cognitive Machines in Conflict Resolution: that contributes to understand how cognitive machines can solve or reduce intra-individual and group dysfunctional conflicts that emerge in decision-making processes in organizations.

vi.   The Relations of Organizational Cognition and Environmental Complexity: which state that the higher the degree of organizational cognition, the lower is the relative level of environmental complexity; and thus the more is the capability of the organization to manage complex environments.

vii. The Relations of Cognitive Machines, Organizations and the Environment: which state that cognitive machines can improve the degree of organizational cognition, and consequently it provides the organization with more capabilities to manage the level of environmental complexity and uncertainty.

viii. The Participation of Cognitive Machines in Organizations: which is governed by a contract that specifies the work responsibilities between the organization and the designer of the cognitive machine; and that also describes the roles of the cognitive machine in the organization.

ix.   The Study of an Industrial Case with NEC of Brazil (NOB) which contributed with:

    a.   Correlations between degree of organizational cognition and measures of organization process improvement.

    b.   Associations between organizational cognition and organization maturity, process capability and performance.

    c.   Relations between organizational cognition and organizational learning.

    d.   Measurements of degree of organizational cognition.

    e.   The participation of a cognitive machine in the organization of study NOB.

    f.   The analysis of technical, managerial and institutional levels of NOB.

    g.   Relations of organizational cognition and environmental complexity of NOB.

x.   The Implications of Cognitive Machines for Organizations.

xi.   The Analysis of Thresholds of Manufacturing Organizations.

xii. The Definition of Computational Organization Management Networks.

REFERENCES

Argote, L. (1999). *Organizational Learning: Creating, Retaining and Transferring Knowledge*. Kluwer Academic Publishers.

Bäck, T., Fogel, D. B., & Michalewicz, Z. (2000). *Evolutionary Computation: Part I and II*. Institute of Physics Publishing.

Breazeal, C. (2000). Sociable Machines: Expressive Social Exchange between Humans and Robots. *Sc.D. Dissertation*, Department of Electrical Engineering and Computer Science, MIT.

Brynjolfsson, E., & Hitt, L. M. (2000). Beyond Computation: Information Technology, Organizational Transformation and Business Performance. *The Journal of Economic Perspectives, 14*(4), 23-48.

Fogel, D. B. (2000). *Evolutionary computation: toward a new philosophy of machine intelligence*. IEEE Press.

Galbraith, J. R. (1973). *Designing Complex Organizations*. Addison-Wesley.

Galbraith, J. R. (1977). *Organization Design*. Addison-Wesley.

Galbraith, J. R. (2002). *Designing Organizations - An executive guide to strategy, structure, and process*. Jossey-Bass.

Hertz, J., Palmer, R., & Krogh, A. (1991). *Introduction to the Theory of Neural Computation*. Westview Press.

Koza, J. R. (1992). *Genetic Programming: On the programming of computers by means of natural selection*. The MIT Press.

Mitchell, T. M. (1997). *Machine Learning*. The McGraw-Hill Companies, Inc.

Reed, S. K. (1988). *Cognition: Theory and Applications*. 2nd Ed. Brooks-Cole Publishing Company.

Wang, L. (1994). *Adaptive Fuzzy Systems and Control: Design and Stability Analysis*. PTR Prentice-Hall.

Zadeh, L. A. (1994). Soft Computing and Fuzzy Logic. *IEEE Software, November*, 48-56.

Zadeh, L. A. (1999). From Computing with Numbers to Computing with Words – From Manipulation of Measurements to Manipulation of Perceptions. *IEEE Transactions on Circuits and Systems, 45*(1), 105-119.

Zadeh, L. A. (2001). A New Direction in AI: Toward a Computational Theory of Perceptions. *AI Magazine. Spring*, 73-84.

ENDNOTE

[1]   A commonsensical knowledge base consists of a set of rules (conditional statements), and its design involves the integration and storage of propositions and mental models of the participants in the group into a common memory (storage device). It represents an attempt to satisfy (satisfice) the perspectives of a group and to attend some criteria of design. A commonsensical decision involves a process with access to a commonsensical knowledge base. It attempts to make choices and to provide outcomes which satisfy (satisfice) the opinions of the group and the criteria of design.

Appendix Section

"To live effectively is to live with adequate information."

(Wiener, N. 1954)

The Appendixes included in this book were written in order to provide readers with complementary and additional information on the main disciplines, concepts, and data of the book.

Appendix A introduces the concept of process of theorizing as used in the book.

Appendixes B, C, and D introduce a survey on the subject of organizations. It was written for those readers who are not familiar with the field of organizations; as for those who want to refresh some concepts on organizations; and as for those who want to understand the broad perspective on organizations as we put forward in our book.

Appendix E presents an overview on the subject of technology. It was written with the same purpose we wrote Appendixes B, C, and D, but now for the field of technology with emphasis on information and cognitive machines.

Appendixes F, G, and H present definitions, models, data, and theorem proof of Part V on the industrial case study.

APPENDIX A:
ANALYSIS AND DESIGN OF THEORY

INTRODUCTION

This appendix presents a definition of theory and it describes the process of theorizing which is used in this book. Proceeding further, it introduces the criteria used to select the approaches to the study of organizations as followed in this book.

NATURE OF THEORY

Developing a theory is a scientific enterprise. It is designed to explain phenomena. If the phenomena can be explained by a theory, then the theory can facilitate predictions about the future behaviour of the phenomena. The theory gets confirmed once explanations and predictions are borne out, and this gives the scientist greater control over the domain of the phenomena (Khandwalla, 1977).

Therefore, first of all theories consist of a formal background that explains past and current phenomena with a subject of study. Secondly, in addition to explanations, a theory has also to provide knowledge to support predictions. Thirdly, theories have to provide evidence in order to support their explanations and predictions.

Explanatory studies attempt to answer why and how things happened, but not only to tell what happened as descriptive studies do. Explanation and prediction are complementary processes. The former takes place after the event has occurred, and the latter extends the former to the control of events that may occur.

COMPONENTS OF THEORY

The basic components of theory are variables, propositions and reasoning processes. The former can assume concepts of mental images or perceptions, words of a natural language, numbers and general symbols. The second is simply a statement about one or more variables and it defines the relationships between the variables of study (Bailey, 1982). The latter can be synonymous of logic and cognitive mechanisms used to deduct and to induct new propositions from either previous propositions or qualitative and quantitative data analysis.

Propositions encompass hypothesis, axioms, postulates and theorems. Hypotheses are often defined alone and they can be used to induct new hypotheses by either generalisation or analogy. On the other hand, axioms and postulates are provided in the form of a set of statements whose combination can be used to deduct through syllogism additional propositions called theorems.

On Hypothesis and Inductive Reasoning

A hypothesis is a proposition that is stated in testable form and predicts a particular relationship between two or more variables.

Inductive reasoning works basically in two ways. Firstly, it moves from specific observations, qualitative and quantitative data, statistical analysis results and thus hypotheses, towards broader results and theories similarly to a bottom-up approach. The generalization of a hypothesis is an attempt to assert that it holds in all cases, or in most of the cases under investigation. Hence, this process is also called induction by enumeration, or, more commonly, generalisation. Secondly, inductive reasoning can also draw conclusions and hypotheses about things based on their similarities to other things, and thus this process is called induction by analogy.

Figure A.1 illustrates the primary steps of an inductive process. It begins with specific observations, proceeds with data analysis to detect patterns and regularities, formulates some tentative hypotheses that can be explored, and finally ends up developing some general conclusions, hypotheses and theories. A horizontal way is also drawn to show the process of induction by analogy.

Figure A.1. Inductive processes of generalisation and analogy

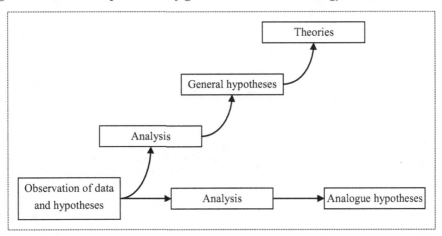

On Axioms, Postulates, Theorems and Deductive Reasoning

On the other hand, deductive reasoning works from the more general to the more specific, similarly to a top-down approach. We might begin with a theory and propositions about a specific topic. We then may narrow them down into more specific propositions called theorems that we can test. We narrow down even further when we collect observations and data to address the theorems. This ultimately leads us to be able to test the theorems with specific data, providing evidence to the original theory. Figure A.2 illustrates such a process of deductive reasoning.

Axioms, postulates and theorems are components of axiomatic or deductive theory, which takes the form of a set of interrelated propositions as in the following example.

Proposition 1: If A then B

Proposition 2: If B then C

Therefore,

Proposition 3: If A then C

In such a theory, if propositions 1 and 2 are true statements, it follows by deduction that proposition 3 is also true. Such true statements are called axioms and

Figure A.2. Deductive process

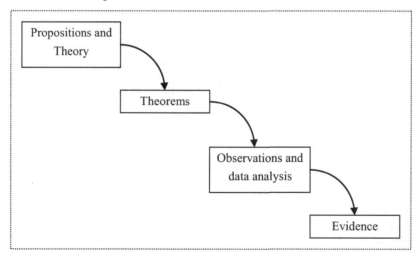

postulates, and other statements can be deduced from them. Thus propositions 1 and 2 of the previous example are axioms and postulates. Nevertheless, axiom has a mathematical connotation and is used more often for statements that are true by definition and for propositions involving highly abstract concepts. Postulate is more often used for statements whose truth has been demonstrated empirically. Additionally, a proposition that can be deduced from a set of statements is called theorem. Proposition 3 in the previous example symbolises a theorem deduced from the statements 1 and 2. As an example, consider the propositions settled in the following where postulates 1 and 2 are used to derive theorem 1 by deductive syllogism.

Postulate 1: The better the incentives and reward systems, the more productive the workers of an organization are.

Postulate 2: The more productive the workers are, the higher is the probability of an organization to satisfy its goals.

Therefore,

Theorem 1: The better the incentives and reward systems, the higher is the probability of an organization to satisfy its goals.

Since postulates are considered to be true, there is little reason to treat them as testable hypothesis. However, it makes often necessary to write the deduced proposition - i.e. the theorem - as a hypothesis and test it, as this is the main mean of testing the entire theory.

Despite distinct, inductive and deductive processes complement each other. The former can be used to the exploration of new theories and broader results. The latter can be used to the exploitation of propositions and theories, providing them with refinements and more precise results.

Table A.1 summarises the different types of propositions and their scope of application.

A PROCESS OF THEORIZING

Theorizing is a process which involves the explanation and prediction of natural and artificial phenomena, and it encompasses evidence (Bailey, 1982).

In order to formulate a theory, firstly we need to choose a problem among alternatives in order to proceed with the analysis of its domain. Secondly, after

Table A.1. Types of propositions

Propositions	Derivation	Testable
Hypothesis	Induced by generalization or analogy	Yes
Axiom	True by definition	No
Postulate	Assumed to be true	No
Theorem	Deduced from axioms or postulates	Yes

analysing the problem, we need to select the set of variables that represent the domain of interest. Moreover, we need to decide how to measure such variables and also to design propositions that define the relationships among them. Thirdly, we need to gather data about the variables from a sample. Fourthly, after gathering the data we need to analyse them. Moreover, we have to add meaning to them and to the relationships among them. Fifthly and lastly, we need to provide evidence which supports the theory. It is done by testing propositions and by analysing the results.

Such a process can provide a theory with better results as we follow the circle from the first to the fifth stages continuously. At the end of step 5 we may need to analyse the problem again, to redesign its variables and propositions, to refine the gathered data and to analyse them again, and finally to review the evidence and results. Figure A.3 depicts such a continuous process.

Figure A.3. Process of theorizing

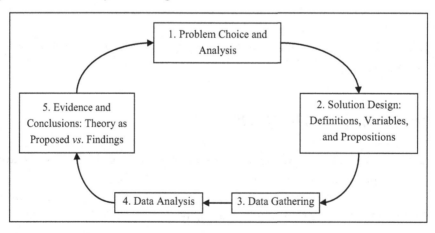

APPROACHES TO ORGANIZATION STUDIES

This section presents some of the main methods for studying organizations, and in particular, those methods which provide a theory on organizations with data and evidence (Khandwalla, 1977). For the purpose of this book, such a set of methods will be also called "approaches to organization studies".

Case Studies

The researcher interviews a few individuals to determine the organization background and history. The interview can include questions on: age, size, structure and wealth of the organization; number of employees, markets of action, goals, strategies, strikes and conflicts; levels of centralization and decentralization; specialization; the technology employed by the organization; authority, power and responsibilities with the organization; reward systems; the processes with the organization; the relationship between the organization and the environment; and so on.

Case studies are likely to yield incomplete information because of the few individuals interviewed and also due to it involves the study of only one or a very few organizations.

Field Studies

Shortly speaking, field studies and case studies are alike. However, field studies are usually much more time consuming than case studies since the researcher tries to interview a more significant sample of organization members.

Participant Observation

This method, and the two previous ones, can be classified within the broad spectrum of field approaches (Scott, 1965). The researcher is a member of the organization, and being a participant, he derives data and conclusions by observing facts within the organization behaviour.

The researcher can join the organization with the purpose of observing its behaviour, like a consultant for instance. Nevertheless, despite his comfortable position to observe how those around him really feel and what really go on within the organization, this method also results in serious drawbacks. People within the organization can feel constrained with the researcher's presence, and emotional involvement with them may also give the researcher certain biases.

On the other hand, if the researcher is a current or previous member of the organization, thus he can provide a formal study on it without any of the problems of feelings as mentioned before. Nevertheless, his experience may be limited to a specific department or division of the organization and it should be considered when addressing and reporting his research. Therefore, the more access and participation within the different departments and activities of the organization, the broader and richer can be the researcher's investigation and conclusions.

Questionnaire Survey

It consists of gathering information from the organization (or from a sample of organizations) by interviewing its members and by requesting their answers to questionnaire surveys. If quantitative data are provided with the surveys, thus this method makes possible the development of statistical analysis. This method can also be used to support the previous approaches.

Field Experiment

In this approach, the researcher tries to manipulate some variables in order to observe their effects on other variables which affect the functioning of the organization. Field experiments are not appropriate to organizations since they can put them in situations of risk. Nevertheless, such a method can be used in laboratories in order to simulate the behaviour of the organization.

Literature Review

It consists of a review of published material on the subjects of organizations which matches the interest of the researcher - such as decision-making and problem solving, the exercise of power and authority, and so on. March and Scott provide a distinguished literature review on organizations, including various levels of organization analysis (March, 1965; and Scott, 1998). Literature review is an important method which supports the researcher in the proposal of new theories on organizations.

Information Survey

It consists of gathering information about a representative number of organizations from literature and consistent databases. Literature examples include The Journal of Economic Perspectives and The American Economic Review, and other sources of information comprise The United Nations and World Bank databases. Information survey is an important approach to provide researchers with qualitative and quantitative data which can be used to justify theories, generalize results and also to derive new propositions on theories.

Information survey differs from literature review since it is concerned with data collection about organizations and markets, including return on investment and gross domestic income of a country for instance. On the other hand literature review is more concerned with the study of principles and theories of organizations.

Analytical Research

It consists of building mathematical models of organizations and it has been a common approach used by economists to the analysis and design of processes within organizations and between networks of organizations (Shy, 2001). Such an approach provides reductionism by the nature of mathematics, since the problem under analysis is usually formulated by considering a set of constrains (Helm, 2000). However, it brings clarification and accuracy to the domain of the problem under analysis (Simon, 1957; and Starbuck, 1965).

Nevertheless, organizations hold properties of dynamic and non-linear systems (Parker *et al*, 2000), coupled with the environment, with capabilities to adapt and to evolve, and whose behaviour results from interactions among a variety of adaptive agents and other factors. Therefore, organizations seem to be poor candidates for analytical approaches. Such behaviour characterizes organizations as complex systems whose degree of complexity can only be poorly modelled by analytical approaches (Prietula *et al*, 1998).

Computational Modelling and Simulation

The approach to computational modelling and simulation of organizations has received new insights mainly from the 1990's (Carley & Gasser, 1999), and thus special attention is devoted to this subject in the following.

Models are simplified representations of objects and phenomena encountered within the world. Therefore, as analytical models are, computational models are also characterized by reductionism, since they include constrains and approximations of the problem under analysis. Nevertheless, computational modelling has developed as an alternative and powerful tool to support the analysis and design of systems of higher magnitude of complexity than those treated by analytical methods.

The capability of computational models to overcome the limitations of analytical approaches in the modelling of complex behaviour in organizations is only one of its main advantages. Compared with experiments using human subjects, computational models are generally less noisy, easier to control, more flexible, and can be used to the analysis of a larger variety of factors within less time. Furthermore, computational models may be larger, to include more agents, and may cover a longer period with more tasks than can be covered in a human laboratory experiment.

In the same way as analytical modelling, computational modelling tries to achieve more precise and well-defined results for organizations than theories which involve vague and intuitive propositions. Additionally, computational modelling and simulation can be seen as a hypothesis generator system with capabilities to derive propositions and to verify their consistency to theoretical conclusions. Hence, theories can be confronted with organizations, and new theories can also be derived from simulations of computational models.

The pioneer applications of computational modelling to the analysis of organizations appeared in the second half of the 20th century (Cyert & March, 1963; and Cohen & Cyert, 1965). Computational modelling of organizations advanced after the development of digital computers, and most importantly, it received new insights with the advent and maturation of the disciplines of artificial intelligence, cognitive science and information processing systems, social psychology and multi-agent systems. Perspectives on organizations resembling cognitive and information processing systems with computational agents of bounded rationality emerged during that period (Simon, 1947; and March & Simon, 1958), and thus they opened new doors to the research of new areas like computational organizational theory.

Computational Organization Theory (COT) has emerged as a scientific base to study organizations as distributed computational agents (Prietula *et al*, 1998). COT encompasses distributed artificial intelligence, agent technology, software engineering and organization theory as its principal disciplines, where the latter involves mainly the domains of organization behaviour, sociology, economy, psychology and political sciences.

Within the field of COT, computational analysis is used to develop a better understanding of the fundamental principles of organizing multiple information processing agents and the nature of organizations as computational agents. Research in this area has two focuses. The first has to do with building new concepts, theories and knowledge about organizing and organizations. The second has to do with developing tools and procedures for their validation.

CRITERIA OF CHOICE OF RESEARCH METHODS

Each research method or approach to organization studies presented in the previous section has its advantages and disadvantages. Therefore, it makes necessary to define a set of criteria in order to support the researcher to choose one or more methods among the set of available alternatives. Table A.2 presents a set of criteria

Table A.2. Criteria of choice of research methods

a. How much control does the researcher have on the manipulation of the variables? (criteria of control)
b. How much can the results acquired through the use of the method be generalised to other organizations? (criteria of generalisation)
c. How valid and reliable are the measurements of organization variables? (criteria of reliability)
d. How economically can the researcher get the necessary information? (criteria of economy)
e. How speedily can the researcher get the necessary information? (criteria of speedy)
f. How much knowledge does the researcher have on the method? (criteria of application)

adapted from (Khandwalla, 1997), which are useful in the selection of approaches to the study of organizations.

Table A.3 presents the results of application of each criteria of Table A.2 to the research methods.

It must be considered that different researchers may have distinct opinions on the application of the criteria of Table A.2 to the set of research methods shown in Table A.3. Criteria (f) for instance, that concerns application, depends on the knowledge of the researcher about each method, and thus it plays an important role in the process of choice.

Table A.4 was designed to add quantitative meaning to the results of Table A.3 and to reduce their subjectiveness. For such a task, the values 1, 2 and 3 were attributed to the labels low, medium and high respectively, and thus a weight could be computed to each research method according to the average of such values.

$$w_i = \frac{\sum_{j=1}^{n} c_j}{j}, \text{ for } i = 1,\dots,9 \text{ and } j = 1,\dots,n \qquad (A.1)$$

where w_i denotes the weight computed to each respective research method i; c_j represents the values attributed to each criteria; and n is the number of criteria applied to account the average. It must be observed that $n = 5$ for the methods of computational simulation and analytical research only, since N.A. cannot be accounted. On the other hand, $n = 6$ for all of the others.

Table A.3. Application of criteria to research methods

Research Method	control	generality	reliability	economy	speedy	application
Case Study	low	low	low	high	high	low
Field Study	low	low	high	medium	low	low
*Participant Observation	medium	low	high	high	high	high
Questionnaire Survey	low	high	medium	medium	medium	medium
Field Experiment	medium	low	high	low	low	low
*Literature Review	low	medium	medium	high	medium	high
*Information Survey	low	high	high	high	high	high
*Analytical Research	high	low	N.A.	high	medium	medium
*Computational Simulation	high	medium	N.A.	high	medium	medium

Selected research methods to the study of organizations within this book.

Low, medium and high denote the magnitude of application of each criteria to the research methods.

N.A. means not applicable.

Table A.4. Attribution of weights to research methods

Res. Method	control	generality	reliability	economy	speedy	application	weight
Case Study	1	1	1	3	3	1	1.7
Field Study	1	1	3	2	1	1	1.5
*Part. Observ.	2	1	3	3	3	3	2.5
Quest. Survey	1	3	2	2	2	2	2.0
Field Exper.	2	1	3	1	1	1	1.8
*Literat. Rev.	1	2	2	3	2	3	2.2
*Info. Survey	1	3	3	3	3	3	2.7
*Analyt. Res.	3	1	N.A.	3	2	2	2.2
*Comp. Simul.	3	2	N.A.	3	2	2	2.4

Selected research methods to the study of organizations within this book.

Low =1, medium =2 and high = 3.

N.A. is not accounted to the average.

Figure A.4 depicts a graphical representation of the weights computed to each research method. CS, FS, PO, QS, FE, LR, IS, AR, and CM abbreviates the respective research methods.

Figure A.4. Applied criteria and computed weights to research methods

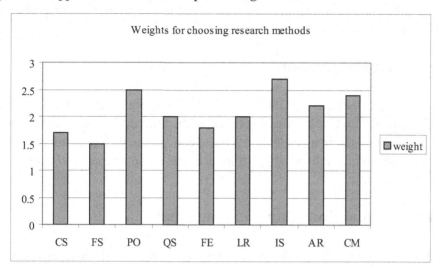

SELECTED APPROACHES TO ORGANIZATION STUDIES WITHIN THIS BOOK

It can be asserted that the higher the weight value of a research method, the more likely is it to be chosen among the set of alternatives. By observing Figure A.1, it can be stated that the approaches to participant observation (PO), literature review (LR), information survey (IS), analytical research (AR) and computational modelling and simulation (CM), are the stronger candidates for the study of organizations within this book. Hence, such methods were selected according to these criteria. Moreover, the analysis in the following provides additional rationales for these choices.

Literature Review

Literature review is fundamental to support a new theory on organizations. After providing an overview on organizations, thus current principles and theories can be selected, unified and extended to form new concepts. That is the main point, i.e. to understand the past and the current trends on organizations in order to propose new ones.

Analytical Research

Analytical research is used within this book when analysis needs to be reduced to accurate models of organizations. This approach is mainly used to support some of the definitions of organizations as exposed in Part II, and also to demonstrate and to prove the consistency of qualitative and quantitative analysis and the design of a computational model as proposed in Part V.

Participant Observation

Studies about a distinguished industrial and business organization are provided in Part V since the first author was a member of this firm during the period between 1997 and 2000. Such an investigation is broad enough to conclude results to distinct levels of the organization, ranging from technical and managerial to institutional analysis.

Computational Modelling and Simulation

Computational modelling and simulation is used to support the analyses provided by the approach to participant observation. Through this method, models can be built and tested, and variables can be manipulated in order to derive new conclusions on the whole analysis.

Information Survey

Information survey provides a basis to support conclusions and to give evidence. It provides the book with a large amount of data about its domain of investigation - i.e. organizations and technology - in order to measure the alignment of the book proposal and data of the market.

SUMMARY

Appendix A presented a definition of theory and it described the process of theorizing used in this book. Proceeding further, it defined some criteria to select approaches to the study of organizations as followed in this book. The chosen approaches are Literature Review, Analytical Research, Participant Observation, Computational Modelling and Simulation, and Information Survey.

REFERENCES

Bailey, K. D. (1982). *Methods of Social Research*. The Free Press.

Carley, K. M., & Gasser, L. (1999). Computational Organizational Theory. In G. Weiss (Ed.), *Multiagent Systems: A Modern Approach to Distributed Artificial Intelligence* (pp. 299-330). The MIT Press.

Cohen, K. J., & Cyert, R. M. (1965). Simulation of Organizational Behavior. In J.G. March (Ed.), *Handbook of Organizations* (pp. 305-334). Rand McNally & Company.

Cyert, R. M., & March, J.G. (1963). *A Behavioral Theory of the Firm.* 1st Ed. Blackwell Publishers.

Helm, C. (2000). *Economic Theories of International Environmental Cooperation: New Horizons in Environmental Economics.* Edward Elgar.

Khandwalla, P. N. (1977). *Design of Organizations.* Harcourt Brace Jovanovich.

March, J. G. (1965). *Handbook of Organizations.* Rand McNally & Company.

March, J. G., & Simon, H. A. (1958). *Organizations.* 1st Ed. John Wiley & Sons, Inc.

Parker, D., Whitby, S., & Tobias, A. M. (2000). Improving our Understanding of Competitive Dynamics: A Nonlinear Model of Duopolistic Competition, *Economic Issues,* 3(5), 27-44.

Prietula, M. J., Carley, K., & Gasser, M. (1998). *Simulating Organizations: Computational Models of Institutions and Groups.* AAAI Press / The MIT Press.

Scott, W. R. (1965). Field methods in the study of organizations. In J.G. March (Ed.), *Handbook of Organizations* (pp.261-304). Rand McNally, Chicago, IL.

Scott, W. R. (1998). *Organizations: Rational, Natural, and Open Systems.* Prentice Hall, Inc.

Shy, Oz (2001). *The Economics of Network Industries.* Cambridge University Press.

Simon, H. A. (1947). *Administrative Behavior: A Study of Decision-Making Processes in Administrative Organization.* New York, NY: Macmillan.

Simon, H. A. (1957). *Models of Man: Social and Rational.* John Wiley & Sons.

Starbuck, W. H. (1965). Mathematics and Organization Theory. In J.G. March (Ed.), *Handbook of Organizations* (pp. 335-386). Rand McNally & Company.

APPENDIX B:
ORGANIZATION THEORY

INTRODUCTION

This appendix surveys organization theory and it puts such a multi-disciplinary field into the context of the book. It starts by presenting a historical perspective on the evolution and development of organizations and it describes the roles of organizations of today. It overlooks and reviews the schools of organizations which emerged during the 20th Century.

ORGANIZATIONS IN HISTORY

The synthesis about the history of organizations presented in this section represents a survey about the literature, and therefore it is not an invention. Nevertheless, it contributes by unifying peaces of information gathered from selected references about: the history of Europe (Delouche, 2001); the history of management thought (George, 1972; and Wren, 1987); organizations (Scott, 1998); and global analyses of economic and social benefits of organizations and technology (Easterlin, 2000; Gordon, 2000; and Johnson, 2000).

Organizations have gradually grown in importance within the economic, social and political worldwide contexts according to the evolution and development of the human history. They found their maturation after the Industrial Revolution originated in Europe in the 18th century and later spread in the United States of America in the 19th century. The gradual transition from a non-industrial to an industrial society has marked the frontiers between the periods of evolution and development of organizations.

The term evolution is usually used when changes in the society assume relatively unpredictable forms. Instead, development follows a more predictable sequence of stages deliberately planned with some form of modernisation as the intended end (Richter, 1982). The former encompasses the processes of organizing provided by ancient and the Middle Ages civilizations. Nevertheless, the flourishing of the Renaissance in Europe emerged as a gear lever to support the latter, and thus the development of the Industrial Revolution in Europe.

Old Organizations: Ancient Civilizations and the Middle Ages

Many principles of today about organizing emerged during ancient civilizations (5.000 B.C. - 500 A.C) among Sumerians, Egyptians, Babylonians, Hebrews,

Chinese, Greeks and Romans. It is highly probable that organizing processes first began in the family, later expanding to the tribe, and finally pervaded the formalized political units (Wren, 1987).

After the fall of the Roman Empire in A.D. 476 and the subsequent emergence of the Feudalism in Europe during the Middle Ages, new principles of organizing evolved as solutions to the economic and political crises in Europe. Although organised in a feudal structure, man began to take significant steps in his thinking about organization and management. An increasing record of writings about the discipline of organizing also characterized the Middle Ages. Nevertheless, economies and societies were essentially static, management practices were still largely antihuman, and political values involved unilateral decisions by some central authority. All of these conditions were not favourable to develop an industrialized society with some liberty and market ethic.

Pre-Industrial Organizations: The Renaissance and the Enlightenment Age

The crises in Europe during the 14th and 16th centuries paved a revolution in thinking, together with religious, social, economic and political strife, giving genesis to the period of Renaissance in the 16th century. The Renaissance brought a new focus on reason, discovery, exploration and science, and thus a revolution in scientific thought began in the 16th and 17th centuries. The overseas expansion of Europe between the 16th and 18th centuries strengthened the integration of cultures of different continents giving genesis to the Mercantilism. Such revolution with the strengthening of globalization and characterised by a world scale economy, requested the development of more complex principles of organizing.

Additionally, in the period of Renaissance there was increasingly a need and call for practices that could bring ethics to the liberty and to the market, forming the philosophy of the Age of Enlightenment. At that time, political philosophers began to stimulate the thoughts of people by disseminating new ideas about equality, justice, the rights of citizens, notions of a republic governed by the consent of the people, and to deliberate concepts such as decentralization rather then centralization of power.

In the 18th century new economic theories emerged to challenge Mercantilism and the controlling power of the landed aristocracy. In his work on *Wealth of Nations*, Adam Smith (1723-1790) established the classical school of liberal economics and he proposed that only the market and competition would be the regulators of economic activity. The Enlightenment Age had then opened the doors towards a new era called Industrial Revolution.

Modern Organizations: Post-Industrial Revolution

The transition from pre to post-industrial organizations was not sudden but gradual. Such a transition created new social, economic and political conditions, and brought new challenges to society as a whole. The continuous advances in science and technology made possible large combinations of humans and machines, giving the genesis for a new generation of organizations. Therefore, principles of organization and management had to be revised, improved and extended to a new cultural environment.

The post-industrial generation of organizations was characterised by the agglomeration of people into a central place, and also by the introduction of machines to minimize the work of human's muscles. Such organizations received new insights on organization design - like those of division of labour, departmentalization, centralization and decentralization of decisions, incentive and reward systems, and so on. Scientific management thoughts were developed at the same time in order to integrate functions of planning, leading, coordinating and controlling to the whole organization (George, 1972; and Wren, 1987).

Therefore, organizations gradually started to liberate people from the primitive use of muscles as an essential condition for survival. Machines provided people with economy in time and strength, and thus extra efforts could be devoted to the exercise and exploration of more complex cognitive tasks in organizations. However, modern organizations increasingly started to depend on the use of additional resources such as energy in order to feed their electrical, combustion and steam engines. Moreover, little attention was given to the organization's environment until the late 1940s.

ORGANIZATIONS OF TODAY

Similarly, the transition from post-industrial to the organizations of today has been defined gradually.

Organizations have been shaped by advances in computers, communication networks and general information technologies. Moreover, they also have been influenced by cultural, normative and regulative institutional processes.

Tracing back to the 18th, 19th and 20th centuries, organizations (of manufacturing) have gradually replaced muscular activities of humans with machines. This was possible after the invention and commercialization of internal combustion engines, electricity and electric motors. Since the second half of 20th century, organizations have replaced some cognitive abilities of humans with new machines. The use of these machines to support and to carry out mental tasks in organizations of today has given people additional resources to expand the frontiers of the organization. Economy of time and energy (both physical and mental) has led people to overlook the organization at upper levels of analysis. Hence, they have developed new processes for the peripheral components of the organization, and in particular to the levels that connect the organization to the environment.

As in the post-industrial era, organizations of today still demand, and depend on, energy-based technologies. However, with advancements in information-processing technologies, the demand for information has become relatively greater than energy. Therefore, organizations have continuously shifted attention from energy to information.

The gradual transition from energy to information management has motivated researchers to develop theories and perspectives on organizations as cognitive and learning systems (Carley & Gasser, 1999; Dierkes *et al*, 2003; March & Simon, 1958). In these perspectives, the environment is viewed as a dynamic and complex system that influences the organization (and vice-versa).

SCHOOLS OF ORGANIZATIONS: THE 20TH CENTURY

Theories of organizations have been properly developed since the beginning of the 20th century. Their initial ground was mainly prepared from previous theories in philosophy and social sciences. However, organization theorists simultaneously advanced in knowledge with the development of new theories and sciences. This book asserts that organization theory has matured with the chronological developments in management, psychology research and general systems theory (Nobre, 2003d).

Organization theory constitutes a multi-disciplinary field and thus it has received contributions from scientists of diverse areas and different backgrounds. The literature has classified the major contributors of organization theory in different schools, according to their lines of investigation (Grusky & Miller, 1981; Pugh, 1997; and Scott, 1998).

The schools presented in this section follow a chronological order of development back through the 20th century. However, administrative behaviour (within decision-making and bounded rationality), general systems, socio-technical systems, contingency theory and organizational learning are the schools of organizations which play the most influential part in this research. Table B.1 names the schools as described in this section in order.

Table B.1. Major schools of organizations of the 20ᵗʰ century

Year of Publication	Schools of Organizations (and some Major Contributors)
1924	Bureaucracy (Max Weber)
1911	Scientific Management (Frederick Taylor)
1916	Administrative Theory (Henri Fayol)
1945	Human Relations (Elton Mayo)
1947 / 1958	Administrative Behaviour and Decision-Making (Herbert Simon and James March)
1966 /1968	Systems Theory (Daniel Katz and Robert Kahn / W. Buckley)
1959 / 1981	Socio-Technical Systems (Eric Trist and Fred Emery / Tavistock Institute)
1967 / 1973	Contingency Theory (Paul Lawrence and Jay Lorsch / Jay Galbraith)
1963 / 2001	Organizational Learning (R. Cyert and J. March / M. Dierkes *et al*)

Organizations like Instruments

This subsection presents three schools of organizations and management. They are symbolically classified as "Organizations like Instruments" because they concern the organization as a complex device which can operate with maximal efficiency. Little importance (if any) is given to human needs, motives, behaviour and to the cognitive limits of the participants in the organization. Moreover, these schools are alike in that they give little attention (if any) to the environment.

- **Bureaucracy School:** The bureaucracy school is one of the approaches to the study of organization structure. It was founded by the social scientist Max Weber in the first decade of the 20ᵗʰ century. Nevertheless, Weber's works on bureaucracy just became well known after their translation from German into English in the 1940's (Pugh, 1997).

Weber's works on organizations include the description of administrative structures characterized by three different forms of authority (Scott, 1998). Briefly, they are traditional authority, which relies on sanctity, beliefs and traditions; charismatic authority, which is synonymous with the ability of people to influence others; and rational-legal authority, which is established according to the normative rules of a social structure.

Although Weber's works are considered broad enough to encompass the analysis of administrative structures of different types and cultures, his theories were mainly proposed to investigate structures which could better serve and explain organizations of west civilizations. Among his analyses, Weber emphasized that in modern society of continuous growth of rationalization, and capitalism, the bureaucracy form of organization had become preponderant because of its technical superiority and greater efficiency. Therefore, rational-legal authority becomes the main structure of analysis within the bureaucracy school.

First and foremost, bureaucracy is synonymous with hierarchy of authority and it includes: delegation of authority; specification of roles and departmentalization; division of labour and specialization; payment of wages based on hierarchical positions; reward systems based on technical skills and knowledge; and normative rules and standard procedures. Following such attributes, the organization of the bureaucracy school appears to be efficient, rational and robust, with this latter representing the capability of the organization to replace its participants without major effects over its whole structure and performance.

Nevertheless, although being one of the pioneer schools with distinguished contributions to organization theory, the bureaucracy school has received many critics. Among them, the literature has mentioned that this school regards the organization as a type of instrument designed to pursue its maximal efficiency, and to achieve goals. The participants in the organizations are assumed to be passive instruments, and thus little attention (if any) is given to their motives, rational limitations and social behaviour. Moreover, little emphasis (if any) is attributed to the environment.

- **Scientific Management School:** The scientific management though emerged during the apogee of the Industrial Revolution in the United States of America, in the late nineteenth and early twentieth centuries (George, 1972). It developed mainly from the prominent work of Frederick Taylor on The Principles of Scientific Management (Taylor, 1911). Taylor was an engineer from Philadelphia with pragmatic ideas on both shop floor and management activities.

The scientific management school is mainly concerned with the rationalization of technical and managerial tasks. It invokes the replacement of rules of thumb with scientific methods which are supposed to provide organizations with measurements and standardization procedures of maximal efficiency, i.e. the production of maximum output through minimum input of resources.

The scientific management though provided the field of organizations with important contributions and new requirements, among those of:

- The development of procedures for hiring and training the participants in the organization.
- The payment of higher wages in return to higher productivity.
- The specification of methods of management, like planning, coordination and control.

- The equal division of work between technical and management activities.
- The introduction of standard procedures and products; the concepts of quality control; and the basic principles for the subsequent era of mass production.

Although accepted by many industrialists as an innovative approach for management, the scientific management school had its principles rejected by many workers, managers and researchers who did not accept the idea of an organization functioning as an efficient instrument of rational procedures (Scott, 1998). Similarly to the Weber's school, the scientific management gives little attention (if any) to human needs, social behaviour and cognitive limitations; and thus it considers the participants in the organization as passive instruments. Moreover, little emphasis (if any) is given to the environment.

- **Administrative Theory School:** The administrative theory school was developed simultaneously with scientific management. Among its proponents was the French industrialist Henry Fayol. However, his work on General and Industrial Management (published in 1916) was only translated from French into English in the late of 1940's (Scott, 1998).

The administrative theory school is concerned with the prescription of general principles of management and it includes (Pugh, 1997): division of work (specialization, role specification and departmentalization); authority and responsibility; discipline (obedience to general agreements between the organization and its participants); unity of command (each employee should receive orders from one superior only); unit of direction (the use of a single plan to coordinate a group of activities having the same objective); subordination of individual interest to the general interest (the interest of the organization should come always before that of its single participants, groups and units); remuneration of personnel (including reward systems, and also different methods of payment: time-rates, job-rates and piece-rates); degrees of centralization and decentralization; scalar chain (hierarchy of authority); order (the efficient allocation of human resources in the social positions of the organization); equity (a combination of justice and kindliness); stability of tenure of personnel (the minimum period of an employee to learn the activities of his new job and to give successful results in doing it); initiative (proactive); and e*spirit de corps* (union of the participants in the organization).

The Fayol's school of administrative theory along with the Taylor's principles of scientific management and the Weber's theory on bureaucracy have similarities in the sense that they concern the organization as an instrument which can operate with maximal efficiency, no matter how significant are human needs, motives, behaviour and the cognitive limitations of the participants in the organization.

Moreover, they are alike since they give little attention (if any) to the environment (e.g. its influence on the organization, its dynamics and resources). However, while the theories of Fayol and Weber analyse the organization from a top-down approach, at the structural level of analysis, the Taylor's school establishes principles to rationalize the organization from a bottom-up perspective (Scott, 1998). Additionally, the work of Fayol on administrative theory is more concerned with the design of processes - among those of planning, specialization, leading, coordinating and controlling - which cut across the structure of the organization; while Weber's work on bureaucracy is more related to the design of the anatomy or structure of the organization.

Organizations like Behavioural and Cognitive Processes

This subsection presents two schools. The first is called human relations, and it concerns not only behavioural and social aspects of people in organizations, but also ergonomics. The second is called administrative behaviour and decision-making school, and it involves not only the study of behaviour in organizations, but also some cognitive processes within the organization. These schools do not resemble organizations as instruments, but they concern the organization as a system which can operate with efficiency when behavioural and cognitive processes are understood, planned and coordinated.

Although representing a breakthrough in the field of organizations, the human relations movement gives little (if any) attention to the environment. However, it was the school of administrative behaviour and decision-making that gave new insights on the importance of the environment as a stimulus to the organization response and behaviour.

- **Human Relations School:** The human relations school flourished in a period between the 1920's and 1940's, simultaneously with the development and apogee of theories on behavioural and social psychology. Although it received contributions from the analyses of various researchers, the school of human relations was greatly influenced by the work of the industrial psychologist Elton Mayo (Scott, 1998).

This school conducted much of its work from the results of a series of studies carried out at the Hawthorne plant of the Western Electric Company, located in the western suburbs of Chicago, during the late 1920's and early 1930's. These studies were accompanied by various experiments based on stimuli-responses and reward methods in order to analyse workers' behaviour and productivity under different circumstances.

Among these studies are: the Illumination Experiment; the Relay Assembly Room; and the Bank Wiring Room (Vecchio, 1995). The first and the second studies were intended to analyse whether changes in the work setting would influence the behaviour and productivity of the employees. The third study was intended to analyse the social behaviour of groups under the eyes of a supervisor.

The Illumination Experiment was concerned with the effects of different intensity of light (stimuli) on the behaviour and productivity of workers (responses). The researchers could observe an increase in productivity not only in the rooms of high intensity of illumination, but also in those rooms with low intensity of light.

Within the experiments of the Relay Assembly Room, the investigators introduced new conditions in the work setting of a group of female employees such as rest periods, free mid-morning lunch, a five-day workweek and variations in methods of payment. As a general result, the investigators observed a gradual increase in productivity over the course of the entire study, and also a lower rate of absenteeism.

The Bank Wiring Room was concerned with the investigation of the behaviour of a group of men in their standard conditions of work, but when supervised by an observer. The investigators could notice that informal structures of behaviour had emerged and became patterned among the workers of the group under supervision. Such behavioural structures were developed (and shaped by internal conflicts) in order to regulate the behaviour, the attitudes and thus the productivity of the workers. Hence, no disparity of productivity could be observed by the supervisor.

Conclusions on these studies showed that:

- Organizations are arenas of emotions and feelings.
- Participants in organizations have motivations which are influenced not only by economic interests, but also by their values, sentiments and by the behaviour of others.
- Organizations shape participants' behaviour (from a top-down view), but participants also shape organizations (from a bottom-up view).
- Normative structures shape behaviour as behavioural structures shape norms.
- Leadership characterized by attention and equality can give better results than authoritarian structures.

The school of human relations was criticized in different ways. One of the main reasons lies in the lack of evidence about the relation between worker satisfaction and productivity. However, in its broad sense the human relations school represented a re-orientation on the research of management and organizations, since it provided an initial background towards the discipline of organizational behaviour.

- **Administrative Behaviour and Decision-Making School:** The administrative behaviour (and decision-making) school emerged during the 1940's with the prominent work of Herbert Simon who was awarded in 1978 the Nobel Prize in Economics (Simon, 1997b).

In summary, administrative behaviour describes and explains organizations in terms of cognitive processes (with special attention for decision-making). This school is less prescriptive than the previous schools. It describes management and organization processes as they really like to happen in practice, and not what and how they ought to be.

The central contribution provided within the school of administrative behaviour is concerned with the concept of bounded rationality and its implication for organization behaviour. Shortly speaking, bounded rationality designates theories of rational choice which recognize the cognitive limitations of the decision maker - limitations of both knowledge and computation. Therefore, the concept of satisfying (satisficing) criteria and goals is applied instead of optimizing (or maximizing) them. In such a way, theories of bounded rationality extend classical economic theories of rational choice to a more realistic perspective on human decision-making as supported by cognitive psychology research. Among the implications of bounded rationality for the literature of social sciences are the development of the discipline of behavioural economics (Simon, 1997a) and other branches combining psychology and economics (Rabin, 2002).

Simon's work on administrative behaviour was influenced by some other authors on management science (Barnard, 1938); decision-making in organizations (March, 1994; and March & Simon, 1958 and 1993); artificial intelligence and cognitive science (Newell and Simon, 1972); and it has also influenced many other researchers of different areas raging from artificial intelligence, psychology and computer science (Carley & Gasser, 1999) to economics (Cyert & March, 1963).

In 1958 March and Simon authored a remarkable book titled "Organizations", which was latter revised in 1993 (March & Simon, 1958 and 1993). They introduced concepts of administrative behaviour into organizations, and then they proposed a new theory on organizations. Some of their contributions are enumerated in the next paragraphs.

Firstly, March and Simon viewed organizations like vertical and horizontal structures constituted by sub-goals and goals. Sub-goals are formed at lower levels and they represent means for the achievement of more complex goals (ends) at upper levels. In such a view of structures of goals and sub-goals, the organization selects and allocates specific sub-goals for its participants and units; and such a procedure can be understood as synonymous with the cognitive process of attention which plays the role of directing and focusing certain mental efforts of the participants in the organization to enhance perception, performance and mental experience during task execution. Moreover, high mental processes of cognition (such as decision-making and problem-solving) play an important task in the organization by providing means for planning and achievement of sub-goals, moving towards more complex goals. Hence, the processes of attention (selection) and division of work (specialization) in the organization can reduce the amount of information which has to be processed by the participants. Consequently, these processes reduce the amount of uncertainty within the organization which emerges from the more complex goals at upper levels and from the influence of the environment.

Secondly, March and Simon provide the literature with the perspective of the organization as a set of programs which can be evoked due to an individual, organizational or environmental stimulus. These programs are classified into programmed and non-programmed decisions (Simon, 1977). The former type plays an important part in the processes of coordination of recurring or repetitive tasks; and the latter applies to planning, innovation and learning practices in organizations. Since programmed decisions are recurrent programs for repetitive stimulus, they provide the organization with predictability; they reduce the amount of information to be processed by individuals when taking decisions and solving problems; and thus they contribute to reduce the amount of uncertainty that the organization confronts.

Thirdly, March and Simon has also provided the literature with the perspective of the organization as an information-processing system constituted by distributed computational minds and agents. In such a view, communication plays an important part by: transmitting decisions from one agent to another; channelling information; and controlling the flow of decisions. This perspective has been further explored and extended to a new research on computational organization theory (Carley & Gasser, 1999; and Prietula *et al*, 1999).

The school of administrative behaviour not only represents a re-orientation in organization theory, but also the emergence of a body of concepts which play the most important part in the functioning of organizations of today. Among these concepts is the perspective of organizations as cognitive systems with the ability to learn.

Re-orientation concerns mainly the transition of emphasis given to the participants in the organization. The schools of bureaucracy, scientific management, administrative theory and human relations do give attention to either the structure of organizations or the management processes within the organization, but they seriously understate the cognitive abilities and limitations of the participants in the organization. The administrative behaviour school emerged to extend these schools to a theory which describes and explains organizations (and thus their structure, management processes and behaviour) in terms of processes of cognition - e.g.

perception, attention, memory and communication, decision-making, problem-solving and learning.

Moreover, we would like to add important conclusions on this school:

- Processes of information and knowledge management play the most important role in organizations of today. These processes comprise cognitive tasks of (Reed, 1988): selecting information (perception and attention), recording (memory), forming and organizing knowledge (concept formation and categorization), information-processing (decision-making), planning and innovating (problem solving and learning) and acting (response). Hence, theories of administrative behaviour play an important part in organizations of today; no matter whether among the participants in the organization are machines that pursue cognitive abilities for autonomous and intelligent action.

- The school of administrative behaviour gives some attention to the environment and it treats it mainly as a source of stimulus for evoking programs, decisions and actions within the organization. However, this school gives more emphasis on the individual and the organizational levels of analysis. The subsequent schools of systems theory, contingency theory and organizational learning emerged to give greater attention to the environment, and then to open new perspectives on organizations, the environment and population of organizations.

- The school of administrative behaviour flourished in a period of both: transformation of psychology research and apogee of general systems theory. It is highly probable that Herbert Simon was influenced by the new theories of cognitive psychology which emerged during the 1950's; and most importantly by the advent of digital computers which played an important part as metaphors for the development of a theory on information-processing systems (Newell & Simon, 1972; Reed, 1988; and Reisberg, 1997).

- In another context, bounded rationality and general systems theorists played a counterpart task in the literature by proclaiming the lack of mathematical tools for coping with more complex problems (where human behaviour, emotions and cognition are key factors). On the one hand, the theory of bounded rationality (Simon, 1997a) called for new approaches which could extend the methods of statistical decisions analysis used by economic theorists to a more realistic scenario about human decision-making (Simon, 1997a). On the other hand, general systems theory pointed out the need for new mathematics in order to narrow the gap of understanding between the analysis of non-living and living systems (Zadeh, 1962). This book advocates that such a new approach (as proclaimed by bounded rationality and general systems theorists) emerged with the advent of fuzzy systems theory (Zadeh, 1965 and 1973) and its derivatives on computing with words and perceptions (Zadeh, 1996a and 2001).

Administrative behaviour plays an important task with the concepts of organizational cognition as we propose in Part II.

Organizations like Systems: Analysis and Design

The schools presented in this subsection give special attention to the environment. They are called schools of systems theory, socio-technical systems, contingency theory and organizational learning. They emerged during the second half of the 20th century and they were mostly inspired by many of the concepts proposed and exploited by general systems theorists. The core of these schools is the analysis and design of organizations.

*   **Systems Theory School:** The school of systems theory provides a picture of organizations as systems with input and output relations to the environment[1] (Silverman, 1970).

Systems theorists have the perspective on the environment as a source of resources which are necessary for the organization survival, evolution and development. The environment shapes the organization and it influences the elements of the organization (such as its social structure, technology and goals along with the motives, perception, emotions and behaviour of its participants). Moreover, organizations also influence the environment; they influence the economic, political and social contexts of the environment.

Systems theorists have attempted to describe organizations as processes of organizing which fall in two main domains. The first domain concerns those processes which lead the organization to adapt to its environment; and they involve the concepts of learning, information-processing, open systems, entropy, self-regulation and homeostasis (Scott, 1998). The second domain involves the dynamic processes of interaction between the elements of the organization and they can be stimulated by internal and external sources. Hence, a change in one or more of the elements affects the whole organization. Systems theorists also regard organizations as hierarchical and loosely coupled systems (Scott, 1998).

Not only have the principles and concepts within general systems theory influenced the school of systems theory, but also the mathematical and computational tools which emerged during its development and apogee. Among the mathematical background used for the analysis of general systems (and thus organizations) are theories of linear and non-linear systems, stochastic and learning systems, optimal systems and fuzzy systems (Zadeh and Polak, 1969; and Zadeh, 1973). Some of these mathematical concepts (supported by computer simulation) have been largely used for instance by The MIT System Dynamics Group of the Sloan School of Management since the 1960's. The main purpose of this group has been the analysis and design of complex systems (including organizations), and also the prediction of behaviour of industrial, social and general systems (Forrester, 1961 and 1973).

With the advent and popularization of digital computers, new tools emerged in order to support the analysis and design of processes and systems of higher order of complexity. Among these tools are distributed artificial intelligence (Bond and Gasser, 1988), software agents and multi-agent systems (Nwana & Azarmi, 1997; and Weiss 1999) and soft computing (Zadeh, 1994). Such mathematical and computational tools have stimulated the development of new approaches for the: simulation of organizations and social networks; analysis and design of organizations; and test-generation of propositions and theories of organizations. Following this direction, the multi-disciplinary centre for Computational Analysis of Social and Organizational Systems of the Carnegie Mellon University emerged to carry out research towards the discipline of Computational Organization Theory (COT) (Carley & Gasser, 1999; and Prietula *et al*, 1998).

Among the prominent contributors to the school of systems theory are the names of (Khandwalla, 1977):

- D. Katz and R. Kahn, who provided a theory about the cycle of input-through-put-output in organizations.
- T. Parsons, who has defined the technical, managerial and institutional sub-systems of the organization.
- F. Emery and E. Trist, who defined the organization as a system composed by subsystems (divisions) which are influenced by technical, economic and social forces.
- H. Leavitt, who described a model of the organization and the process of interaction between the elements of the organization. A change in one or more of these elements affects the others and thus the whole organization.

Although providing organizations with new insights on the environment and with general principles of organizing and models of organization, the school of systems theory did not escape criticism. Most of the critics advocate that the concepts, principles and theories of organizations provided by the school of systems theory are too generalist to address the particular features of different organizations which are contingent on the situation or context in which they exist.

Systems theory (within the broad context of general systems theory) plays an important role in Part II.

- **Socio-Technical Systems Theory:** The school of socio-technical systems theory emerged from studies of a research team with the Tavistock Institute of Human Relations in London, with early development during the 1940's and 1950's. Its main contributors include sociologists and psychologists such as Eric Trist and Fred Emery who participated and coordinated research in the Tavistock Institute (Scott, 1998).

The main perspective of social-technical systems theory refers to the interrelation and combination of the technological and social elements of the organization. It proposes that the technological subsystems affect the social subsystems (and vice-versa) in the whole organization and thus the choice of one element influences the choice of the other part. The concept of mutual relation and integration between technology and social elements can lead the organization to efficient and efficacious results under a rational systems perspective, and it also can lead the organization to equilibrium between its goals and the participants' motives.

The technological subsystem refers to the machines, tools, processes, activities, workplace, layout, task performance, production system, and other sub-elements of the organization.

The social subsystem refers to the people that participate in the organization, the social relations that they form, and thus it is highly influenced by the social structure of the organization.

The socio-technical systems theory views the organization as an open system whose operations are based on Figure B.1. It includes:

- the acquisition or importation of resources from the environment,
- the processing of resource and their transformation to services and goods,
- and the exportation of results, services and goods to the environment.

For a review on socio-technical systems, we recommend the reading of (Trist, 1981). Socio-technical systems theory plays an important part in this book, specifically in Parts II, IV and VI.

Figure B.1. Input and output relations between the organization and the environment

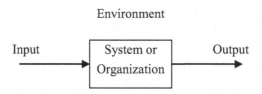

- **Contingency Theory School:** The core of contingency theory is concerned with the design of organizations and its basic premises assume that (Galbraith, 1973 and 1977):

- *There is no one best way to organize.*
- *Any way of organizing is not equally effective.*

The first premise asserts that there is no general principle for organizing. Instead, principles of organizations and processes of organizing are contingent upon the situation, context or environment. The second premise complements the first one and it asserts that different structures of the organization and different processes of organizing lead the organization to different results (subsuming behaviour, performance, efficiency, efficacy, and so on).

The practice of designing organizations can be traced back to ancient and medieval civilizations, but it only developed as a discipline of organization theory during the 20th century. The schools of organizations previously presented in this section were the first schools to provide principles of design to organizations. These principles can be classified in structural and processes design. However, although most of the previous schools had developed principles of organization and organizing which were contingent on particular contexts, they published their results in the form of general concepts, propositions and theories. These generalizations mark the foremost line of separation between previous schools of organizations and contingency theory.

The school of contingency theory concerns the organization (and thus its elements), the features of the organization (like its size) and also the processes (of management) as objects of design which are dependent upon the environment (i.e. its cultural, technological, economic, political and social contexts). Moreover, contingency theory concerns the organization as a dynamic system (which changes over time). A change in one of the elements of the organization influences the other elements. Hence, the organization needs to be redesigned periodically.

Contingency theory is not only a qualitative and prescriptive school, but also quantitative and descriptive. Many of its results are derived from large-scale empirical research. Although being classified as distinct, the approach to comparative studies (or comparative analysis) of organizations has provided and influenced the school of contingency with a broad spectrum of practical results (Blau, 1981; Blau & Scott, 1963; and Scott, 1998).

Among the prominent contributors to the school of contingency theory are the names of (Galbraith, 1973; and Khandwalla, 1977):

- T. Burns and G. Stalker, who observed two distinct forms of management in a set of 20 British and Scottish firms. These were called mechanistic and organic styles. Burns and Stalker identified that both styles were effective, but in different contexts. The mechanistic form was associated with a more stable environment and the organic form with a more dynamic environment of technology innovation.

- J. Woodward, who studied 100 British firms, observed relationships between the form of technology used by the organization and its structure. Among the results, Woodward concluded that different firms with different levels of technological complexity of production had distinct spans of control[2] and distinct hierarchies of authority, with the latter being characterized by the number of managerial levels in an organization of scalar principle[3].

- J. Thompson, who, among other contributions, proposed that the different levels or layers of the organization can have distinct behaviour, and thus distinct social structures. Thompson uses the definitions of organizational levels of analysis as proposed by Parsons (1960) and he explains that (Scott, 1998): on the one extreme is the technical level which resembles the concept of rational systems. This level is more like a closed system of normative structure which tries to protect the organization from uncertainties of the environment; - on the other extreme is the institutional level which resembles the concept of open systems. This level relates the organization to its broad environment; in the middle is the managerial level which resembles the concept of natural systems. This level is more like a system of behavioural structure with enough flexibility to mediate tasks between the two extreme levels.

- P. Lawrence and J. Lorsch, who coined Contingency Theory (Scott, 1998), proposed that organizations face distinct degrees of differentiation and integration of activities. Differentiation of social structure and technology between and within the various divisions of the organization is contingent upon the distinct tasks environments that they face. Task environments vary along a continuous scale of complexity, subsuming market dynamics (innovation and variability of goods and services), uncertainty and predictability. For example, in some industries, research and development departments can face a more complex environment than do production units. However, differentiation requires integration. The greater the differentiation among the subtasks of the organization, the more complex is the integration in order to achieve successful completion of the whole task. Lawrence and Lorsch carried out empirical research with ten organizations in three industries. Not surprisingly, they confirmed their propositions and predictions about differentiation and integration.

Some other authors could join the list of contingency theorists, such as A. Chandler and R. Hall (Galbraith, 1973), and C. Perrow (Khandwalla, 1977). However, the conclusions would be almost the same: the best way to organize is contingent upon the uncertainty and diversity of the tasks performed by the organization and by its divisions (Galbraith, 1973).

Contingency theory plays an important part within the concepts introduced in Part II. Most of the contents of Part II about organization design are based on the work of Galbraith (1973, 1977 and 2002).

- **Organizational Learning School:** Organizational learning is a multi-disciplinary field of research which focuses on creation and management of knowledge (Dierkes *et al*, 2003). It has received contributions from diverse areas ranging from psychology, management science, sociology and anthropology to philosophy, history, political science and economics.

As recognized in the literature (Dierkes *et al*, 2003), the pioneers in the field of organizational learning include Argyris and Schön (1978), Cyert and March (1963) and March and Olsen (1975). However, this book puts forward the perspective that organizational learning was firstly touched upon in the work of Simon (1947) and March and Simon (1958) on organizations, administrative behaviour, decision-making and bounded rationality. The point of departure for such an assertion is that March and Simon (1958) also regarded the organization as a system with cognitive processes and with the ability to learn new routines and programs towards innovation.

Agents of organizational learning involve the participants within the organization and the relationships or social networks which they form. Learning in organizations is also supported by the goals, technology and social structure of the organization. Moreover, organizational learning is also influenced by inter-organizational processes and thus by the environment.

In psychology research, learning is defined as the process of making changes in the working of our mind, behaviour and understanding through experience (Bernstein *et al*, 1997; and Minsky, 1986). This book borrows such a definition to assert that:

Definition B.1: Organizational learning involves a process of making changes in the behaviour of the organization through experience.

A process of organizational learning involves an adaptive learning cycle which is in fact a concept borrowed from principles of feedback control and adaptive systems of the broad field of cybernetics and general systems theory (Buckley, 1968; and

Wiener, 1948, 1954 and 1961). This cycle operates as either single-loop learning or double-loop learning. On the one hand, with single-loop learning the organization identifies problems and makes corrections by using previous solutions and present procedures. On the other hand, with double-loop learning the organization identifies problems and makes corrections by changing present procedures, policies and processes (Daft & Noe, 2001).

Organizational learning is also synonymous with continuous process improvement (Paulk *et al*, 1994) and in such a way it plays an important part in the understanding of the industrial case results presented in Part V.

SUMMARY

Appendix B surveyed organization theory. It started by presenting a perspective on the history of organizations and it continued by describing the roles of organizations of today. It overlooked and reviewed some of the main the schools of organizations which emerged and developed during the 20th century.

Organizations and the practices of organizing emerged during ancient civilizations and the Middle Ages, and their development was paved by a revolution in thinking, supported by religious, political, economic and social transformations during the Renaissance and the Enlightenment Ages in Europe. Such transformations created the necessary conditions for the Industrial Revolution in Europe during the 18th century, and later in the United States of America during the 19th century. The gradual maturation of organizations was encompassed by: transformations of the perceptions, behaviour and motives of their participants; evolution and development of technology; the need for new organizational processes and structures with normative and behavioural parts; the human desire of pursuing more complex goals; developments in the social sciences, and most importantly in cognitive psychology research and general systems theory; and changes in the environment.

Modern organizations emerged after the Industrial Revolution and they were challenged by new political, economic and social contexts. Thus, schools of organizations and management were developed in order to support: the analysis of the new organization and the design of new organizational structures and processes. Such schools emerged in the first decade of the 20th century, giving rise (and maturation) to the discipline of organization theory. They started with theories of bureaucracy and principles of scientific management and administrative theory, and they received new insights from the experiments of the human relations school. However, organizations of today have been closer to the contributions provided by the schools of administrative behaviour (and decision-making), systems theory (including socio-technical systems), contingency theory and organizational learning.

Tracing back to the period of Industrial Revolution, organizations have developed from the concept of structures and agglomeration of people (with machines), to the principles of today which can be characterized by distributed cognitive processes for organizing and acting. Organization schools of today have given more attention to the concept of members of organizations (participants) as decision-makers and problem-solvers. Additionally, they understand that these participants have cognitive limitations and motives which differ from organizational goals. Thus, organizations have to provide them with inducements. Cognitive processes in organizations were mainly exploited by the administrative behaviour and decision-making school. Subsequently, more attention has been given to the environment, as recognised mainly with the schools of systems theory, contingency theory and organizational learning.

The Industrial Revolution introduced new members to modern organizations, in the form of machines. Such machines challenged humans by replacing their muscular activities with mechanical and electrical mechanisms, and also by providing people with economy of time and energy (i.e. physical and cognitive efforts). People then started to give more attention to the development of additional cognitive processes for organizing.

Organizations of today have been challenged by the advent of new machines in the form of computers, software programs and communication networks. These machines (when proper designed with the background of artificial intelligence, cognitive science and systems theory) can pursue capabilities to carry out cognitive tasks in organizations. As advocated in Chapter 1, such machines are emerging to act in the name of organizations, just like people do. Hence, they enter into the arena of organizations as additional elements of design which can replace human beings when performing technical and managerial activities. However, the use of such machines requests economic, social and political analysis.

REFERENCES

Argyris, C., & Schön, D. A. (1978). *Organizational Learning: A Theory of Action Perspective*. Addison-Wesley.

Barnard, C. I. (1938). *The Functions of the Executive*. Cambridge, Mass.

Bernstein, D. A. *et al* (1997). *Psychology*. Houghton Mifflin Company.

Blau, P. M. (1974). *On the Nature of Organizations*. John Wiley & Sons.

Blau, P. M., & Scott, W. R. (1963). *Formal Organizations: A Comparative Approach*. Routledge.

Bond, A. H., & Gasser, L. (1988). *Readings in Distributed Artificial Intelligence*. Morgan Kaufmann Publishers, Inc.

Buckley, W., (1968). *Modern Systems Research for the Behavioral Scientist*. Aldine Publishing Company.

Carley, K. M., & Gasser, L. (1999). Computational Organizational Theory. In G. Weiss (Ed.), *Multiagent Systems: A Modern Approach to Distributed Artificial Intelligence*, (pp. 299-330). The MIT Press.

Cyert, R. M., & March, J.,G. (1963). *A Behavioral Theory of the Firm*. 1st Ed. Blackwell Publishers.

Daft, R. L., & Noe, R. A. (2001). *Organizational Behavior*. Harcourt, Inc.

Delouche, F. (2001). *Illustrated History of Europe*. Cassell Paperbacks, Cassell & Co.

Dierkes, M., Antal, A. B., Child, J., & Nonaka, I. (2003). *Handbook of Organizational Learning and Knowledge*. Oxford University Press.

Easterlin, R. A. (2000). The Worldwide Standard of Living Since 1800. *The Journal of Economic Perspectives, 14*(1), 7-26.

Forrester, J. W. (1961). *Industrial Dynamics*. The MIT Press.

Forrester, J. W. (1973). *World Dynamics*. The MIT Press.

Galbraith, J. R. (1973). *Designing Complex Organizations*. Addison-Wesley.

Galbraith, J. R. (1977). *Organization Design*. Addison-Wesley.

Galbraith, J. R. (2002). *Designing Organizations - An executive guide to strategy, structure, and process*. Jossey-Bass.

George, C. S. Jr. (1972). *The History of Management Thought*. Prentice-Hall.

Gordon, R. J. (2000). *Does the New Economy Measure up to the Great Inventions of the Past? The Journal of Economic Perspectives, 14*(4), 49-74.

Grusky, O., & Miller, G. (1981). *The Sociology of Organizations: Basic Studies*. The Free Press.

Hall, A. D., & Fagen, R. E. (1956). Definition of System. In W. Buckley (Ed.), *Modern Systems Research for the Behavioral Scientist*, (pp. 81-92). Aldine Publishing Company.

Johnson, D. G. (2000). Population, Food, and Knowledge. *The American Economic Review, 90*(1), 1-14.

Khandwalla, P. N. (1977). *Design of Organizations*. Harcourt Brace Jovanovich.

March, J. G. (1994). *A Primer on Decision Making: How Decisions Happen*. The Free Press.

March, J. G., & Olsen, J. P. (1975). The Uncertainty of the Past: Organizational Learning under Ambiguity. *European Journal of Political Research, *(3), 147-171.

March, J. G., & Simon, H. A. (1958). *Organizations*. 1st Ed. John Wiley & Sons, Inc.

March, J. G., & Simon, H. A. (1993). *Organizations*. 2nd Ed. John Wiley & Sons, Inc.

Minsky, M. (1986). *The Society of Mind*. Picador.

Newell, A., & Simon, H. A. (1972). *Human Problem Solving*. Prentice-Hall.

Nobre, F. S. (2003d, July). *Organizations and Technology - Past, Present and Future Perspectives*. Seminar presented for the Artificial Intelligence Research Group of the Department of Computer Sciences in the Humboldt University of Berlin. Johann von Newmann-Haus, Berlin.

Nwana, H. S., & Azarmi, N. (1997). *Software Agents and Soft Computing: Towards Enhance Machine Intelligence*. Springer.

Parsons, T. (1960). *Structure and Processes in Modern Societies*. Free Press.

Paulk, M. C., & Chrissis, M. B. (2000, March). The November 1999 High Maturity Workshop. *Special Report CMU/SEI-2000-SR-003.*.

Prietula, M. J., Carley, K., & Gasser, M. (1998). *Simulating Organizations: Computational Models of Institutions and Groups*. AAAI Press / The MIT Press.

Pugh, D. S. (1997). *Organization Theory: Selected Readings*. Penguin Books.

Rabin, M. (2002). A Perspective on Psychology and Economics. *European Economic Review, 46*, 657-685.

Rao, M. *et al* (1993). *Integrated Distributed Intelligent Systems in Manufacturing*. Chapman & Hall.

Reed, S. K. (1988). *Cognition: Theory and Applications*. 2nd Ed. Brooks-Cole Publishing Company.

Reisberg, D. (1997). *Cognition: Exploring the Science of the Mind.* W.W. Norton & Company.

Richter, M. N. (1982). *Technology and Social Complexity.* State University of New York.

Scott, W. R. (1998). *Organizations: Rational, Natural, and Open Systems.* Prentice Hall, Inc.

Silverman, D. (1970). *The Theory of Organizations.* Heinemann.

Simon, H. A. (1947). *Administrative Behavior: A Study of Decision-Making Processes in Administrative Organization.* New York, NY: Macmillan.

Simon, H. A. (1977), *The New Science of Management Decision.* Prentice-Hall, Inc.

Simon, H. A. (1997a). *Models of Bounded Rationality: Empirically Grounded Economic Reason, 3.* The MIT Press.

Simon, H. A. (1997b). *Administrative Behavior: A Study of Decision-Making Processes in Administrative Organizations.* The Free Press.

Taylor, F. W. (1911). *The Principles of Scientific Management.* New York: Harper.

Trist, E. L. (1981). The Evolution of Sociotechnical Systems as a Conceptual Framework and as an Action Research Program, in Andrew Van de Ven and William Joyce (Ed.), *Perspectives on Organization Design and Behavior,* pp.19-75. New York: Wiley-Interscience.

Vecchio, R. P. (1995). *Organizational Behavior.* Harcourt Brace & Company.

Weiss, G. (1999). *Multiagent Systems – A Modern Approach to Distributed Artificial Intelligence.* The MIT Press.

Wiener, N. (1948). *Cybernetics.* 1st Ed. The MIT Press.

Wiener, N. (1954). *The human use of human beings: cybernetics and society.* 2nd Ed. London.

Wiener, N. (1961) *Cybernetics or control and communication in the animal and the machine.* 2nd Ed. The MIT Press.

Wren, D. A. (1987). *The Evolution of Management Thought.* 3rd Ed. John Wiley and Sons.

Zadeh, L. A. (1962). From Circuit Theory to System Theory. *Proceedings of the IRE, 50,* 856-865.

Zadeh, L. A. (1965). Fuzzy Sets. *Information and Control, 8*, 338-353.

Zadeh, L. A. (1973). Outline of a New Approach to the Analysis of Complex Systems and Decision Process. *IEEE Transactions on Systems, Man, and Cybernetics, 3 (1)*: 28-44.

Zadeh, L. A. (1994). Soft Computing and Fuzzy Logic. *IEEE Software, November*: 48-56.

Zadeh, L. A. (1996a). Fuzzy Logic = Computing with Words. *IEEE Transactions on Fuzzy Systems, 4*(2), 103-111.

Zadeh, L. A. (2001). A New Direction in AI: Toward a Computational Theory of Perceptions. *AI Magazine. Spring*: 73-84.

Zadeh, L. A., & Polak, E. (1969). *System Theory.* McGraw-Hill.

ENDNOTES

[1]   The subjects of systems and environment are further described in Part II. Nevertheless, we provide herewith a short definition of them as proposed in (Hall & Fagen, 1956): "A system is a set of objects together with relationships between the objects and between their attributes" (or properties). "For a given system, the environment is the set of all objects a change in whose attributes affect the system and also those objects whose attributes are changed by the behaviour of the system".

[2]   Span of control refers to the number of employees or subordinate roles which can be effectively supervised and coordinated by a first line manager or superior (Galbraith, 1977; and Scott, 1998).

[3]   The scalar principle states that the participants in an hierarchical organization are linked by single relations and the flow of decisions and authority should move from upper layers (of management) downwards lower layers (of workers) (Galbraith, 1977; and Scott, 1998).

APPENDIX C:
PERSPECTIVES ON ORGANIZATIONS

INTRODUCTION

This appendix presents perspectives on organizations. It starts with definitions on the elements which constitute the organization and it proceeds by introducing concepts of rational, natural and open systems which contribute to understand organizations from diverse points of view. It introduces some rationale for organizing into political, economic, and social contexts. It describes the benefits of organizations, the concept of organization theory, and its relation to the domains of analysis and design. It concludes by explaining the nature of organizations, the sources of diversity of theories of organizations, and the concept of formal organizations.

ELEMENTS OF ORGANIZATIONS

Organizations have received diverse and complex definitions in the literature. Hence, it may be helpful to establish a simplified model focusing on their major elements. The organizational model illustrated in Figure C.1 was firstly proposed by Leavitt (1965). Nevertheless, it was later stretched by Scott to include the environment as a separate factor which is regarded as an indispensable ingredient in the analysis of organizations (Scott, 1998).

   This book supports the definitions of the elements of this model as presented by Scott, and it also extends them in order to provide foundations for the scope of

Figure C.1. A model of the organization

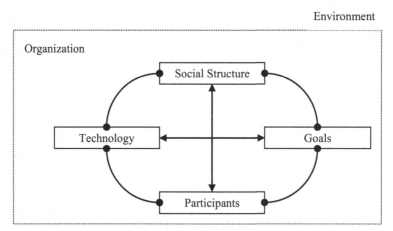

organizations and technology introduced in Chapter 1. Major extensions are pro-posed to the concepts of the participants in the organization since they include not only people, but also cognitive machines. The influence of new participants on the definitions of the other elements of the organization is also taken in consideration. Nevertheless, a better description of the subject of cognitive machines in organiza-tions is presented in Part IV.

Participants

The participants in the organization are agents and they include people, other orga-nizations and machines. People and other organizations are those individuals and social groups who, in return for a variety of inducements, make contributions to the organization (Scott, 1998). People can be synonymous, for instance, with em-ployees, managers, customers and stakeholders. By other organizations it is meant subcontractors, buyers, suppliers and other partners of the central organization.

Machines are agents which act in the name of organizations, as people do. Therefore, they fulfil roles in the organization ranging from muscular and repetitive activities to complex cognitive tasks. Hence, they can fulfil roles in organizations at the technical, managerial, institutional and worldwide level.

Social Structure

Social structure refers to the standards and regularized aspects of the relation-ships existing among the participants in the organization; it comprises two types of structure, called normative and behavioural structure (Scott, 1998).

• **Normative Structure:** A normative structure is an institutionalized set of rules which state what ought to be the behaviour of participants in the organization. Therefore, it provides reductionism and puts constraints on the behaviour of the organization. However, it can reduce the amount of uncertainty in the organization not only by channelling and equalizing information among its participants (March and Simon, 1993), but also by governing and patterning behaviour and decisions.

A normative structure includes norms, values and roles. Briefly, values are criteria used in selecting goals of behaviour; norms are rules governing behaviour which specify means, strategies and tactics for pursuing goals; and roles are ex-pectations of behaviour for the occupants of specific social positions[1]. Roles also represent similarities in the responses of different individuals to a common situation (Khandwalla, 1977). Therefore, in normative structures, values, norms and roles are organized to form a consistent set of prescriptive rules to govern the behaviour of participants.

Moreover, normative structures also play an important part in governing the processes of decision-making in organizations. Such decisions are synonymous with programmed decisions, since they are derived from detailed prescriptions which govern the sequence of responses of the organization (or divisions of the organization) to the environment (Simon, 1977).

- **Behavioural Structure:** Behavioural structure focuses on actual behaviour rather than on prescriptions for behaviour (Scott, 1998). Analysis of behavioural structure concerns those activities, relationships and emotions which exhibit some degree of regularity and similarity over a period of time. These can be among individuals, social groups and networks of organizations.

Behavioural structures also play an important role in processes of decision-making which belong to the class of non-programmed decisions (Simon, 1977). They are non-programmed because they are not governed by a set of rules and thus they have no specific prescriptions to deal with a situation like the one at hand. Instead, participants must use and exploit their general capabilities of cognition, intelligence and autonomy for decision-making, problem-solving and learning. Given a large spectrum of situations and problems, no matter how ill-structured and novel they are, man has a remarkable ability to solve them. The decision of a company to establish operations in a continent where it has not been before is an example of non-programmed decision. Nevertheless, non-programmed decisions also happen daily in people's life. Familiar situations where they are applied include parking a car, driving in city traffic, cooking a different meal, summarizing new stories, and so on.

Normative and behavioural structures of organizations are neither completely aligned nor totally independent of each other. Instead, they are better represented by an intermediate degree of compatibility and similarity of behaviour. Moreover, behaviour shapes norms just as norms shape behaviour (Scott, 1998).

Goals

Goals have received controversial opinions regarding their importance, and also different definitions in the literature of organizations (Scott, 1998). Nevertheless, goals constitute an important element within this book. Therefore, a definition is introduced in the following which is further discussed in the book.

Firstly, goals are ends, but they also can represent means to the achievement of other goals. Nevertheless, strategy and tactics are better definitions of means to the achievement of goals (Galbraith, 2002).

Secondly, goals can be applied to different levels of analysis of the organization. From a top-down path, these levels are environmental, institutional, managerial and technical systems.

Proposition C.1: The better the alignment of the strategic goals and sub-goals of the organization, from a top-down perspective, the greater is the probability to satisfy them.

Third, participants have goals which differ from those of the organization. Some authors call them motives (March & Simon, 1993), and they represent the desires of participants to join and to act in the name of the organization.

Fourth, if participants have motives and they include machines, then do machines have goals (motives)? The answer is yes if they are considered to carry people's desires, motives and general goals of the organization. It applies mainly for those machines which fulfil cognitive roles in organizations. A simple example is the elevator. It has the aim of transporting people from one floor to another according to a procedure of programmed decisions embedded in its digital memory. Another example, and more complex, requiring a higher level of cognition, is the application of electronic agents in the internet. They can fulfil the roles of searchers of information, buyers and suppliers of general services, and thus they can act in the name of the organization.

Technology

Technology is important and indispensable for organizations as the other elements. Organizations use technology in different ways and in distinct levels of application. They produce technology for their own consumption; they pass it to the environment; and they also consume it from the environment with the aim of survival, evolution and development. Appendix E surveys the subject of technology in the context of organizations and it also proposes definitions about this topic.

Environment

The environment of the organization comprises different levels of analysis and it involves technical and institutional aspects (Scott, 1998). The technical aspect is synonymous with production systems and the institutional aspect is synonymous with symbolic and cultural factors influencing the organization. The environment of the organization can also include ecological systems and some organizations exist to work for the preservation of nature and natural resources.

The literature of organizations have given special attention to an environment which is synonymous with networks of organizations, local and global economy, technology, cultural values, normative processes and regulative systems, institutions, etc. However, with some few exceptions (Simon, 1977), researchers of organizations have attributed little or no emphasis to the natural resources of the environment.

This book supports the literature about this subject and it asserts that the environment of the organization exists, evolves and develops according to economic, social and political contexts. The concept of environment is further defined in Part II.

ORGANIZATIONS AS RATIONAL, NATURAL AND OPEN SYSTEMS

The schools of organization theory, as developed during the 20th century, have proposed different definitions of organizations which lie in one of the perspectives among rational, natural and open systems (Scott, 1998). Additionally, some of these definitions can be better classified as a combination of such perspectives.

Rational Systems

Rational systems theorists assume that:

- Organizations are social systems of interacting agents.
- Organizations pursue specific goals.
- Organizations are based on high degrees of formalization.

These premises together classify organizations as special types of social systems which are characterized by goal specificity and formalization. Both characteristics are purposefully achieved by the processes of design.

Organizational goals are specified within the process of strategic planning and they provide the organization with direction and criteria of choice (among products and services, market of action, structure, processes and technology, participants, etc.).

Formalization is achieved with the specification and implementation of a normative structure which regulates the behaviour and decisions of the participants in the organization. Formalization requires the activities of specialization (distribution of roles), span of control (number of agents coordinated within a division or superior), hierarchy of power, centralization and departmentalization.

Rational systems theories comprise the concepts of design and redesign. The former can be understood as a mean for the achievement of efficient organizations, and the latter, for the improvement of organizational performance (including social, cognitive, institutional and economic factors).

Natural Systems

Although natural systems theories were developed to contrast the emphasis on rationality advocated by rational systems theorists, the former can be understood as a complementary perspective to the latter.

Natural systems emerge when the rational concepts of goal specificity and formalization are relaxed and extended to a more complex definition which asserts that:

- Organizations are social systems of interacting agents.
- Organizations pursue multiple goals.
- Organizations evolve informal and behavioural structures.

Like rational systems, natural systems theorists do consider organizations as a class of social systems, but of a different kind from that of rational systems. Emphases are played on goal complexity and informal structure, rather than on goal specificity and formalization.

Goal complexity characterizes the multiple goals and interests of the agents (or participants) of the organization. Although organizations may have specific goals, the behaviour of their participants may be governed by their own motives. Among them there exist common and divergent interests, and thus cooperation and conflict phenomena.

Informal structure emerges from social relationships and coalitions among the participants in the organization; and it evolves to a patterned behavioural structure which differs from the rules prescribed within the normative structure.

Natural systems theorists also advocate that rationality constrains the creativity of the participants in the organization, since it regulates behaviour and decisions. Most importantly, they view the organization as an indispensable resource which evolves and adapts to particular situations according to internal forces; moreover, the organization attempts to survive and to support the interests of its participants. However, if survival is under threat, then new patterns of behaviour emerge among the participants and their individual and collective interests suppress the specified organizational goals.

Open Systems

The open systems perspective plays emphasis on both: the dynamics of the organization and the relation between the organization and the environment. It assumes that:

- Organizations are social systems of interacting agents.
- Organizations are dynamic systems coupled with the environment.
- The environment shapes organizations (and vice-versa).

Open systems theories extend the perspectives of rational and natural systems to a broader concept of organizations as systems connected with major systems (or supra-systems). The definition of the organization becomes more complex because: the border between it and the environment is more a less vague and fuzzy; the elements of the organization are dependent upon each other, and a change in one of them influences the whole organization; agents join the organization and participate in the activities of the organization if they can reach satisfactory bargains; and as the organization is open, it is subject to the uncertainty of the environment. However, the environment is viewed as a source of resources for the organization which is necessary for its evolution, development and survival.

Open-Rational Systems

The open systems perspective motivated some authors to review their original theories on (closed) rational systems, and influenced other researchers to develop theories on (opened) rational systems. Such a fusion of perspectives gave origin to the concept of open-rational systems. Among the theories which can be classified within open-rational systems are administrative theory (or bounded rationality), comparative structural analysis, and contingency theory (Scott, 1998).

Open-Natural Systems

Similarly, open-natural systems represent a fusion of the perspectives of natural and open systems. Among the concepts within this perspective are those of: evolutionary processes, adaptation, survival, natural selection, institutional and social stability, and belief networks (Scott, 1998).

RATIONALE FOR ORGANIZING: POLITICAL, ECONOMIC AND SOCIAL CONTEXTS

Organizations are important for many reasons, and perhaps the most ancient rationale for organizing was the one stated by Aristotle (384-322 B.C.), i.e. "the whole is more than the sum of its parts" (Wren, 1987).

Broadly speaking, organizations provide people with processes. These processes support them in the achievement of complex goals. Such complex goals have political, economic and social facets (Nobre, 2005 and 2003d).

Political Facet

Organizations provide people with power - in the form of legitimate or informal authority (Scott, 2001). Power resides in people's dependencies (Kipnis, 1990), and organizations gain in power as people depend on them, says, information, goods, services, wages, rewards and so on. It can be created in diversified forms: by agglomerating muscles as explored during the prehistoric era, ancient civilisations, Middle Ages and later in lesser scale after the Renaissance; and also by assembling individual and collective cognitive processes in order to achieve complex information-processing systems to cope with the uncertainty of the environment. The latter has been increasingly explored after the apogee of the Industrial Revolution in Europe and in the United States of America. Nevertheless, it started to receive more attention and new insights from the last fifty years only, empowered by the advances in computers, communication networks and artificial intelligence research.

Economic Facet

Organizations provide people with efficient costs of production and transactions - the transfer of goods and services from one individual to another (Milgrom & Roberts, 1992). This facet supports the latter by providing organizations with capabilities to create incentives to people, to the market and to other organizations.

Social Facet

Organizations provide people with sociability, societal status, knowledge, satisfaction, physical and mental health, and general well-being. The economic facet supports this one since the history has shown that the emergence of the new organizations after the Industrial Revolution has provided people with better standard of life and with longer expectation of life (Johnson, 2000; Easterlin, 2000; and Wren, 1987).

Nevertheless, such positive effects were also supported by other transformations like in the transport, urbanisation, sanitation and medical affairs. The social part plays important roles in both political and economic facets. Through charisma and status for instance, people may relate to, and infiltrate into political and economic decisions.

People join organizations for different reasons and motives, which may have political, economic and social facets. The facets briefly presented in this section form a framework to support a rationale for people to participate in organizations.

BENEFITS OF ORGANIZATIONS

Organizations can benefit people politically, economically and socially, as discussed in the previous section. Moreover, organizations benefit people if they are considered as means to overcome some limitations of their individual agents. Such limitations are classified as cognitive, physical, temporal and institutional (Carley & Gasser, 1999), and they can also be extended to include *spatial limitation*, as introduced here.

Cognitive Limitation

Firstly, agents have cognitive limitations according to the definition of bounded rationality (Simon, 1997a and 1997b; and March & Simon, 1958). Organizations can improve such limitations by providing them: with the support of additional cognitive processes of other cooperative agents; with a social structure to support decision-making and problem solving; with common goals and strategies in order to simplify choices and alternatives; with division of work and problems, through departmentalization and decentralization for instance; with the formation of channels of communication to spread and share knowledge; and with technology which provides automation of cognitive tasks - like those of communication, computation, storing and memory, decision-making and problem solving - and other technologies - like those of process improvement and quality programs - to name some but a few of them.

Physical Limitation

Secondly, agents have physical limitations due to their physiology. Agents cannot carry weight as much as they may need; they cannot move as fast as they may want; and they cannot handle as many things as they may desire. Organizations can provide them with technology and coordination in order to support their physical capabilities.

Temporal Limitation

Thirdly, agents have temporal limitations and therefore they have to organize themselves together to achieve goals which transcend the lifetime of any one agent.

Institutional Limitation

Fourthly, Agents are legally or politically limited and therefore they have to attain organizational status in order to act as a corporate actor rather than as an individual one.

Spatial Limitation

Fifthly, agents are spatially limited because they cannot be in different locations at the same time. Therefore, organizations can provide them with distributed resources, and also distributed capabilities of cognition and action in the form of a multi-agent system.

Organizations also provide intelligence to the connections or relationships between their agents. Such intelligence cannot be found with one agent only, and neither by simply putting together some agents.

Organizations as a whole pursue robustness. They can still keep the same behaviour and performance even when one or more of their agents are replaced with others.

THE DISCIPLINE OF ORGANIZATION THEORY

Organization theory concerns the analysis and design of organizations. Analysis is the activity used to examine something in detail. It provides knowledge on the elements (or parts) of the organization; on the relations between the elements; and also on the whole organization. Organization design involves a continuous process of decision used to provide coherence among the elements of the organization. Such a process involves choices of: goals and strategy; social structure; technology and processes; reward systems; and policies of human resources.

In such a way, analysis and design are complementary tasks where the former plays an important role by providing designers with approaches to create or to change organizations.

Galbraith proposed a framework to support people in the activities of selecting alternative organization forms and assessing the likely consequences of their choice (Galbraith, 1977 and 2002). This book views design according to his framework.

NATURE AND DIVERSITY OF ORGANIZATIONS

Organizations have been widely defined in the literature with divergent, complementary and common perspectives. Ironically, Perrow has compared organizations to a zoo with a bewildering variety of specimens (Perrow, 1974). The differences in perspectives can vary according to the following three factors of diversity (Scott, 1998).

The first is the diversity of organizations, which is characterized for instance by their type, size and shape, the culture into which they are immersed, and their purpose. The church, firms, profit and non-profit institutions, public and private industries, universities, trade unions and hospitals are organizations whose features differ from each other. Nevertheless, divergences can also be found with the analysis of organizations of the same class. Firms of different sizes can have different social structures for instance, and thus they can provide different perspectives. A study about particular aspects of different classes of organizations is found in (McKinlay, 1975; and March, 1965).

The second is concerned with the interests and the background of the researchers, which can vary for instance from political scientists, economists, sociologists, psychologists and anthropologists to engineers and computer scientists. A tutorial about different writers of organizations is presented in (Pugh, 1997; and Pugh & Hickson, 1997).

The third is related to levels of analysis which can vary from a micro to a macro view. They are the social psychological, structural and ecological levels of analysis. The social psychological level focuses on individual participants and their interrelations, and it tries to explore the impact of environment, technology and social structure on the behaviour of individuals. At the structural level, the concern is to investigate the characteristics of organizational forms and design, to explain structural features, processes and the technology of organizations. At the ecological level, organizations and networks of organizations are analyzed as collective actors operating in larger and interdependent systems of relations, constituted by other organizations and their environment. These three levels of analysis are presented in (Scott, 1998) and covered in (March, 1965; and Khandwalla, 1977).

FORMAL ORGANIZATIONS

Degree of Formality

Formal organizations have received distinct definitions spanning perspectives of economics (Milgrom & Roberts, 1992) and sociology (Blau & Scott, 1963). Milgrom and Roberts define formal organizations as entities of independent legal identity which can sign contracts in their own name and seek court enforcement of those contracts. Blau and Scott differentiate formal organizations from social organizations stating that the first constitutes entities deliberately established for the explicit purpose of achieving certain goals, while the second emerges whenever men are living together. Despite distinct, such perspectives complement each other. The former provides the second definition with the ability of the organization to exercise contractual rights and legitimate power, while the second provides the former with the conception of organization design.

This book supports both definitions and it extends them to the principle that the frontier between informal (or social) and formal organizations is a matter of degree which depends on the choice of criteria of analysis on formalization. For example, if performance and achievement of goals are the criteria defined to measure formality among a body of organizations, then it is not possible to assure that organizations holding contracts are more formal than those which have none. Nevertheless, it may be asserted that organizations which are deliberately designed according to some criteria have higher probability of satisfy such criteria, and hence they are more formal than other organizations.

SUMMARY

Appendix C introduced diverse perspectives on organizations. It started with definitions on the elements which constitute the organization and it proceeded by introducing concepts of rational, natural and open systems which contribute to understand organizations from diverse points of view. It introduced some rationale for organizing into political, economic and social contexts. It describes the benefits of organizations, the concept of organization theory and its relation to the domains of analysis and design. It concluded by explaining the nature of organizations, the sources of diversity of theories of organizations, and the concept of formal organizations.

Organizations are coordinated according to their social structures of normative and behavioural parts and they comprise goals (subsuming survival and development), participants and technology. Furthermore, they depend on the environment and vice-versa.

Organizations resemble cognitive systems and distributed minds. Minds are synonymous with individual agents, teams, departments or divisions; systems are synonymous with levels of analysis (e.g. technical, managerial, institutional and worldwide systems). Organizations process, manage and exchange information between their distributed parts and also between them and the environment.

The literature has provided organizations with divergent, complementary and common definitions. Diversity exists because of the different types and shapes of organizations; because of the various backgrounds of the researchers; and due to the different levels of analysis which can focus on social psychological, structural and institutional organizational issues. However, the concepts of rational, natural and open systems have provided organization theory with more precise perspectives on the borders that separate the various definitions of organizations. These concepts together represent a general framework for the analysis of organizations; they also contribute for the classification of organization theories into the perspectives of rational, natural and open systems.

Organizations have political, economic and social facets, and thus they can provide people with power, wealth and status. Organizations are also means to overcome and to extend the limits of individual agents; such as cognitive, physical, temporal, institutional and spatial limitations. Hence, organizations benefit people in various ways.

Organization theory concerns the analysis and design of organizations. Analysis is the activity used to break something down in a minute examination of its parts. It provides knowledge of the elements (or parts) of the organization; on the relations between the elements; and also on the whole organization. Organization design involves a continuous process of decision in order to provide coherence among the elements of the organization. Such a process involves the choice of goals, social structure, technology and the participants in the organization. Organization theory has received contributions mainly from the disciplines of social sciences, including theoretical and empirical results of economics, political science, sociology and social psychology. Engineering and computer science have provided organizations with mathematical and computational tools to support the activities of analysis and design, and also to explore and to exploit organization theories.

The distinction between formal and informal organizations is just a question of degree, and thus the transition from one to another type is gradual, rather than abrupt.

REFERENCES

Blau, P. M., & Scott, W. R. (1963). *Formal Organizations: A Comparative Approach*. Routledge.

Carley, K. M., & Gasser, L. (1999). Computational Organizational Theory. In G. Weiss (Ed.), *Multiagent Systems: A Modern Approach to Distributed Artificial Intelligence* (pp. 299-330). The MIT Press.

Easterlin, R. A. (2000). The Worldwide Standard of Living Since 1800. *The Journal of Economic Perspectives, 14*(1), 7-26.

Galbraith, J. R. (1977). *Organization Design*. Addison-Wesley.

Galbraith, J. R. (2002). *Designing Organizations - An executive guide to strategy, structure, and process*. Jossey-Bass.

Johnson, D. G. (2000). Population, Food, and Knowledge. *The American Economic Review, 90*(1), 1-14.

Khandwalla, P. N. (1977). *Design of Organizations*. Harcourt Brace Jovanovich.

Kipnis, D. (1990). *Technology and Power*. Springer-Verlag New York Inc.

Leavitt, H. (1965). Applied Organizational Change in Industry: Structural, Technological and Humanistic Approaches. In J. March (Ed.), *Handbook of Organizations* (pp. 1144-1170). Rand McNally & Company.

March, J. G. (1965). *Handbook of Organizations*. Rand McNally & Company.

March, J. G., & Simon, H. A. (1958). *Organizations*. 1st Ed. John Wiley & Sons, Inc.

March, J. G., & Simon, H. A. (1993). *Organizations*. 2nd Ed. John Wiley & Sons, Inc.

McKinlay, J. B. (1975). *Processing People: cases in organizational behaviour*. Holt-Blond Ltd.

Milgrom, P., & Roberts, J. (1992). *Economics, Organizations & Management*. Prentice-Hall Inc.

Nobre, F. S. (2003d, July). *Organizations and Technology - Past, Present and Future Perspectives*. Seminar presented for the Artificial Intelligence Research Group of the Department of Computer Sciences in the Humboldt University of Berlin. Johann von Newmann-Haus, Berlin.

Nobre, F. S. (2005). On Cognitive Machines in Organizations. *PhD Thesis*, 343 pages. University of Birmingham / Birmingham-UK. Birmingham Main Library. Control Number: M0266887BU.

Perrow, C. (1974). Zoo story or Life in the organizational sandpit. In C. Perrow (1974), *Perspectives on Organizations*. The Open University Press. ISBN 0335015689.

Pugh, D. S. (1997). *Organization Theory: Selected Readings*. Penguin Books.

Pugh, D. S., & Hickson, D. J. (1997). *Writers on Organizations*. Penguin Books.

Scott, W. R. (1998). *Organizations: Rational, Natural, and Open Systems*. Prentice Hall, Inc.

Scott, W. R. (2001). *Institutions and Organizations*. SAGE Publications.

Simon, H. A. (1977). *The New Science of Management Decision*. Prentice-Hall, Inc.

Simon, H. A. (1997a). *Models of Bounded Rationality: Empirically Grounded Economic Reason*, *3*. The MIT Press.

Simon, H. A. (1997b). *Administrative Behavior: A Study of Decision-Making Processes in Administrative Organizations*. The Free Press.

Wren, D. A. (1987). *The Evolution of Management Thought*. 3rd Ed. John Wiley and Sons.

ENDNOTE

[1] A social position is a location in a system of relationships (Scott, 1998).

APPENDIX D:
DISCIPLINES OF ORGANIZATION THEORY

INTRODUCTION

Organization theory is a multi-disciplinary field. Most of the contributions it has received are borne from the disciplines of social sciences. This Appendix represents a summary of the main body of disciplines which have supported organization theory.

ECONOMICS

Economics is concerned with economic decision-making, and thus with the efficient allocation of relatively scarce resources to satisfy the needs of human beings. It involves principles of maximization of outcomes through a minimal input of resources. Nevertheless, efficiency of outcomes (and allocation) is not the main concept for the study of economic organizations. Instead, economists are also concerned about the efficiency of the organizations themselves. So, the discipline of economics provides organization theory with approaches to the analyses of different arrangements and forms of organizations, and also to the design of organizations which pursue economic goals.

Organizations as the Whole Economy

Economists have defined organizations as created entities within and through which people interact to reach individual and collective economic goals (Milgrom & Roberts, 1992). At the highest level of economic analysis, organizations are represented by the whole economy, which consists of networks of people, organizations, institutions and regulative processes with the market, and general transactions.

Agency Theory and Organizations

At the next level, which concerns principles of agency theory (Clark, 2000), the organization is viewed as a nexus of contracts among individuals who belong to the classes of principal and agent. Principal is equivalent to owner, and agent is the person or worker who acts on behalf of the principal. At this level, organizations are regarded as formal entities having independent legal identity, which enables them to enter biding contracts, and thus to seek court enforcement of those contracts. Owners seek to maximize their return on investment by the most efficient use of the organization (including the workers). Agents, on the other hand, seek to minimize their efforts and maximize their remuneration. To protect their interests, principals will use various forms of contracts and organizing to ensure that agents carry out their jobs.

Transaction Costs Theory and Organizations

Another level of analysis in economic organization theory is the transaction - i.e. the transfer of goods or services from one individual to another (Milgrom & Roberts, 1992; and Williamson & Masten, 1999). Such transactions involve costs that take place inside and outside the organization. Such costs of running the organization are mainly originated by the activities of coordination of markets and motivation of people - including transactions between owners and managers, managers and subordinates, suppliers and producers, and sellers and buyers. Transaction costs depend on the nature of the transaction and on the way it is organised. Therefore, organization design at this level is concerned with the choice of organizational structures which better minimizes on these transaction costs.

Both agency and transaction cost perspectives view the primary reason for organizing as being the reduction of uncertainty that exists in typical transactions. Economists have also provided organizations with theories supported by analytical approaches, mainly with contributions received from the discipline of game theory (Gul, 1997). Table D.1 summarizes such organizational economic perspectives.

POLITICAL SCIENCE

Political scientists have tailored general principles of political science for organizations.

The chief concern of political scientists is the study of power, politics and political parties within the whole society and its derivatives - like government, institutions and unions (Khandwalla, 1977). In its short definition, power is the ability of

Table D.1. Organization economic theories

Level of Analysis	Components	Perspectives
Economics	The whole economy	Organizations are created entities within and through which people interact to reach individual and collective economic goals.
Agency Theory	Principal and Agent	Organizations are nexuses of contracts.
Transaction Costs	Firms and markets.	Organizations are firms that coordinate costs associated with internal and external exchanges.

agents to allocate and control resources to the ends they favour, by legitimacy, i.e. legitimate power, by charisma, or by force (Scott, 1998). Politics involve the study of strategies employed by agents - individuals and organizations - to the pursuit of power. Political party means the political organization of a body of people under a governmental system which reflects an ideology, a set of values and beliefs about what the governmental system ought to be.

Political science has been primarily studied through philosophical, institutional and behavioural approaches.

Philosophical Approach

Political philosophy emerged with ancient civilizations, and it received new contributions passing through the periods of the Middle Ages, Renaissance, Enlightenment, and Industrial Revolution up to now. Aristotle (384-322 B.C.), Socrates (469-399 B.C.) and Plato (427-347 B.C.) were distinguished pioneer philosophers with political contributions during ancient civilizations, and also in more recent centuries were Niccolò Machiavelli (1469-1527), Thomas More (1478-1535), Thomas Hobbes (1588-1679), John Locke (1634-1704), Jean-Jacques Rousseau (1712-1788), Thomas Paine (1737-1809), Karl Marx (1818-1883), Frederick Engels (1820-1895), Mao Tse Tung (1893-1976) and Rosa Luxemburg (1871-1919) - among others (Delouche, 2001). Among their contributions are the studies of alternative forms of government and organizing a society; the origin of a state and the genesis of regulative processes; and the implications of different forms of politics for a state and society.

Institutional Approach

Institutional approaches to political science were dominant in Europe and in United States of America during the second half of the 19th century and the first half of the 20th century (Scott, 2001). Institutional analysis was based in constitutional law, bureaucracies and moral philosophy. Particular attention was given to the study of governmental structures, their functioning and the normative processes within them.

Contemporary Approach

Contemporary political science has advanced from the study of political philosophy and institutional aspects of government to political economy and behaviour. The latter involves the analysis and design of economic political systems, and also the studies of conflicts of interest among agents, relationships between normative and behavioural structures of political systems - including organizations and general political parties - and the influence of normative structures on the behaviour of citizens, and vice-versa - i.e. the influence of citizens on the normative structure of a democratic state by voting for instance. Such studies have given genesis to the research of other subjects related to organizations such as individual (personality, attitudes, perception, learning and motivation), interpersonal (group and team behaviour, conflict and negotiation, leadership and communication) and organizational (decision-making and design, change and culture) processes (Hellriegel *et al*, 2001). This has led political scientists to integrate sociological, anthropological and psychological concepts such as hierarchy and bureaucracy, culture and socialisation into their background.

Political Science and Organizations

Organizations comprise politics and political parties - i.e. authority systems - and they hold distributed power among agents within their hierarchical structure. Organizations influence the environment through power, and the environment also influences them by the same means, i.e. power. Agents within the organization may have power because of their ability to reward and to punish others; because of their legitimate position in the organizational hierarchy; because of their charisma and social relation with others; or because they posses more knowledge than others on the domains of both the organization and its environment. Moreover, as important as knowledge, are the special cognitive skills that agents have for decision-making and problem solving. The latter ability, on knowledge and cognition, plays the most important role in organizations of today.

Concepts of power, authority, legitimacy, hierarchy of authority and bureaucracy - among others - were firstly introduced into the context of the structure of organizations by Max Weber (1864-1920) (Scott, 1998). Weber qualified in law and then he became a member of the staff of Berlin University. He had also interest in the broad fields of philosophy, historical development of civilizations, sociology of religion and economy. Nevertheless, those of his writings which have been translated into English have established him as a major contributor to organizational sociology

Table D.2. Political analysis of organizations

Topics of Analysis	Tailoring to Organizations
Power	Analysis of sources of power, distribution of authority, and the implications of power on individual and organizational behaviour.
Politics	Design of strategies and tactics to the achievement of organizational goals, and to the motivation of participants with inducements.
Political Parties	Design of normative structures and analysis of their implications on individual and organizational behaviour.

(Pugh & Hickson, 1997). Table D.2 summarises the tailoring of political analysis to organizations.

SOCIOLOGY

Sociology concerns the study of systems of social actions, social phenomena and social life. Social action is non-instinctual human behaviour to satisfy needs. Social phenomena emerge from human behaviour and interrelations existing within a social system. The subject of social life ranges - to name but a few of them - from the intimate family to the hostile mob; from organized crime to religious cults; from the divisions of race, gender, wealth categories and social status to the shared beliefs of a common culture; and from the sociology of work to the sociology of organizations. Sociologists investigate the structure of groups, organizations and institutions, communities and societies, and how people interact within these contexts. In fact, few fields have such broad scope and relevance for research, theory and application of knowledge (Khandwalla, 1977).

Organizations resemble miniature societies, and thus they are strong candidates for sociological studies (Blau, 1974; Etzioni, 1969; Grusky & Miller, 1981; Perrow, 1974; and Silverman, 1970). Researchers have provided the literature with sociological perspectives and social processes of prominent contributions to the analysis and design of organizations (Khandwalla, 1977).

Sociological Perspectives

Sociological perspectives encompass the subjects of stability and order, disorder, continuity and change.

- **Social Stability:** Social stability and order are supported by the equilibrium model of society which resembles the concepts of homeostasis and self-regulation. In organizations, stability and order can assume various definitions, and they can also be achieved by different means. Nevertheless, stability and order can be synonymous of equilibrium, and thus of a theory on organizational equilibrium (March & Simon, 1958). Organizational equilibrium is essentially a theory of motivation which concerns the alignment of organizational goals with participants' motives. Organizational goals are expected to govern the decisions of the participants in the organization, and motives are individual goals (or expectations) which govern the participants' decision to join and to remain in the organization (Scott, 1998). Such an alignment can be satisfied, or maximized, by designing inducements - i.e. incentive and reward systems - to the organization (Dunnette & Hough, 1992: 1009-1055). In such a field, agency theory plays an important role to support economic analysis of organizations (Gibbons, 1998). Nevertheless, we may need to design a control system within the organization in order to assure such an alignment (Anthony *et al*, 1984).

- **Social disorder:** Social disorder is supported by explanations of the conflict model of society. Disorder can be synonymous with lack of harmony and organization among different segments of a society. Within organizations, disorder can emerge from diverse factors like from dispute of power; from disagreements of agents with organizational normative structures; from distortions between agents' motives and organizational goals; from the lack of resources; from the lack or inefficiency of incentive and reward systems; from intra-individual and group conflicts (March & Simon, 1993); and from conflicts between the organization and its environment - which can include technical (e.g. technological requirements and standards), managerial (e.g. coordination of buyers and suppliers), institutional (e.g. regulative systems within the market) and environmental (e.g. natural resources) levels of conflicts. In these cases, sociologists might assume that such phenomena of disorder arise because agents have a high need for power, differentiation in perceptions and limits of cognition. Hence, the roles, the hierarchy of authority, the communication systems, and the strategic reward systems within the organization should be reviewed and redesigned to provide it with stability. In such a way, sociologists avoid having to focus on the particularities of the personality of the agents. Nevertheless, they do not necessarily ignore the nature of personality and human needs.

- **Continuity:** Continuity refers to the study of survival of a society and social patterns of behaviour within this society over time, despite the turnover of its members. It can be argued that a society persists and continues to exist with its social life when it is supported by structures which represent the means whereby it satisfies the needs for its survival. In such a way, Parsons developed an approach which identifies the primary functions that all social systems must perform if they are to survive and to persist (Parsons, 1960). Such functions defined by him are: adaptation (the search and acquisition of resources); goal attainment (the setting and achievement of goals); integration (cooperation and coordination among the parts of a system); and latency (the creation, preservation and transmission of values and culture of a system). Similarly to societies, organizations also have functional needs and structures. However, more than many other types of social structures, organizations are designed to persist over time by supporting complex tasks which go beyond the limits of individual agents. Organizations, when well designed, possess robust structures with capabilities to adapt to both internal and external demands;

with abilities to accommodate and to coordinate a broad diversification of activities; with ability to motivate their participants; with flexibility to change their members, technologies, structural features, processes and even goals; and with agility to respond to their environment. In such a way, stability and order play a fundamental role in the survival of organizations, while disorder, viewed as pathology, can lead organizations to instability and extinction.

- **Change:** Change concerns the broad study of social evolution and it has received contributions mainly from Darwinian theories of natural selection, evolution and processes of evolution (Huxley *et al*, 1958; and Huxley, 1974). Social evolution has inspired researchers to the study of evolution of organizations - i.e. the study on how organizations evolve and adapt to their environment (Cummings & Staw, 1990; and Singh, 1990) - and also on the emergence of new organizational forms among a population of other organizations (Scott, 1998). In such a way change plays a fundamental role to the continuity and survival of organizations.

Social Processes

Social processes involve a series of activities within a society that when performed lead us to the achievement of ends. Some examples of social processes include classification or stratification of people into status and wealth categories, and deviant behaviour such as crime. In organizations, stratification can be synonymous of division of labour and specialization; departmentalization; delegation of authority or distribution of power; centralization of decisions; promotion of agents according to their qualifications and skills; and so on. Deviant behaviour is likely to take the forms of strikes, conflicts and general disorder. In order to survive, evolve and develop, organizational processes also have to be continuously analysed, designed and redesigned. If structure is thought of as the anatomy of the organization, processes are its physiology or functioning, and thus information and decision processes cut across the organizational structure (Galbraith, 2002). Organizational processes can be classified as having two foci. The first is concerned with the allocation of scarce resources - like funds and talents - and they encompass activities of planning and budgeting for instance. The second refers to work flows within the activities of requirement management, project and product development - among others.

Sociology and Organizations

Sociology plays an important role in the process of designing organizations by providing people with means (knowledge and technology) to select a candidate among a set of alternatives of organizational forms which better satisfy specific

Table D.3. Sociological contributions to organizations

Sociological Perspectives	Application to Organizations
Stability and Order	Design of inducements, and thus incentive and reward systems; alignment of individual motives and organizational goals.
Disorder	Analysis of conflicts and organizational redesign; design of communication systems to equalise individual perceptions.
Continuity	Design of robust organizational forms.
Change	Evolution, adaptation to the environment, and redesign of organizations.
Social Processes	Application to Organizations
Stratification	Analysis of specialization, departmentalization, and delegation of authority.
Deviant behaviour	Analysis of conflicts and general disorder.

criteria. What is remarkable in the study of organizational sociology is the emphasis on uncovering the structural factors shaping the functioning of organizations. It is because of the sociological preoccupation with structural explanations and with the study of the whole organization, rather than of just groups and individuals within it, that sociologists have sought to explain the structure and functioning of organizations in terms of their elements (like environment, social structure, technology, participants and goals), and also considering their size, shape, age and purpose for instance (Scott, 1998).

Table D.3 summarises the tailoring of sociological perspectives and social processes to organizations.

SOCIAL PSYCHOLOGY

As derived from the Latin, *psyche* means mind, and *ology* means study, and thus psychology is the science of the mind which studies human behaviour and thinking. The mind involves mental processes, functions and issues like emotions, sensations, thoughts, dreams, consciousness, imagination, perception (among others), which cannot be observed through the physical senses of seeing, hearing, smelling, tasting and feeling. Hence, psychologists have opened three main directions of research called introspection, behaviourism and cognitivism (Reisberg, 1997). Although such schools share similar goals, i.e. the study of human behaviour and mental processes, they differ in the strategy or approach to the achievement of such goals.

From Introspection and Behaviourism to Cognition

The introspection school was intensive in the late 19th century and it was aimed to explain mental concepts as perception, emotion and consciousness by examining our own thoughts.

The behaviourist school emerged in the early 20th century as an alternative approach to the lack of scientific basis within the introspection research. Behaviourism is concerned with scientific methods which pursue to provide researchers with the analysis of objective data, i.e. information that can be observed or measured by others. Hence, behaviourism was oriented to stimulus-response and reward theories of human behaviour, learning and intelligence. Nevertheless, although providing the literature with approaches to deal mainly with empirical and observable aspects of human behaviour, the behaviourist school underestimated the study of human mental processes like perception. This was the point of departure for the emergence of a new direction of research called cognitive psychology.

The transition from behaviourism to cognitivism was paved by the school of gestalt psychology in the first half of the 20th century. Gestalt scientists were extensively concerned with the study of human perception through the use of animals (as well as humans). Cognitive psychology is oriented to the study of high mental processes which govern human behaviour, learning and intelligence, and thus it investigates theoretical models and those concepts underlying the functioning of the human mind, like perception, attention, categorization, knowledge representation and organization, memory, language, decision-making and problem solving. However, greater advances in cognitive research were paved by the development of the digital computer and the discipline of artificial intelligence around the 1950's. These gave power to the emergence of new theories and models of the human mind. Among these models are information-processing systems (Newell & Simon, 1972) and others on multiple human minds as distributed computational agents (Minsky, 1986; and Carley & Gasser, 1999)

The schools of introspection, behavioural and cognitive psychology have also provided new insights to the research and understanding of human evolution and development (Butterworth *et al*, 1985; and Heyes & Huber, 2000). Lefrançois provides a complete overview about these schools, and he also presents a clear analysis on the transition and re-orientation from introspection and behaviourism to cognitivism (Lefrançois, 1995).

Psychology and Its Social Context

Social psychology is a branch of psychology which comprises introspective, behaviourist and cognitive theories, but extended to individuals in a social context. Social

psychology investigates those phenomena which emerge within interpersonal relations. It focuses on how human behaviour and mental activities - and thus personality, attitudes, motivation, emotions, beliefs and also perception, attention, learning,
decision-making and problem solving processes of individuals - are influenced by
other people, technologies, machines, groups and teams, organizations, normative
and regulative processes, and by any other social factor.

Social psychology includes different and complementary orientations like
gestalt, field theory, reinforcement, psychoanalytic and role theory (Khandwalla,
1977).

- **Gestalt Psychology:** Briefly, the gestalt orientation provides analysis on how
  individuals' perception, beliefs and cognitive processes are influenced by the
  presence of others.
- **Field Theory Orientation:** Field theory, as influenced by gestalt conceptions, has been concerned with the dynamics of human motivation, and thus
  needs and goals. It asserts that people's motivations, attitudes, opinion and
  hence behaviour can change due to the influence of others. Hence, field theory
  provides analyses on conflict, cooperation and coalition among agents and
  groups.
- **Reinforcement Learning:** Reinforcement is a branch of learning theories and
  it is synonymous of behavioural change. It asserts that behaviour is a product
  of conditioning imposed by external forces. In such a way humans are viewed
  as passive instruments whose behaviour is regulated by the environment. The
  main principles of regulation of behaviour are those of rewarding and punish-
  ing, and also the frequency of reinforcements.
- **Psychoanalytic Research:** The psychoanalytic orientation received most of
  its contribution from Sigmund Freud (1856-1939). Psychoanalysis has provided
  social psychologists with studies on personality formation and change, and
  also on authoritarian and pathological behaviour (including stress, anxiety,
  frustration, conflict and tension).
- **Role Theory:** If personality is synonymous with similarities in the responses
  of an individual to different situations, role represents the similarities in the
  responses of different individuals to a same situation. So, in a given culture,
  a role is synonymous with prescribed behaviour associated with a given
  status or position. Role theory investigates the influence of roles on shaping
  personality and vice-versa, and also role conflict and deviant behaviour. Role
  conflict can arise because of incompatibilities between the personality of an
  individual and the roles he has to fulfil, and also because of incompatible and
  high demands of different roles on the same individual. Deviant behaviour
  emerges when individuals do not play their appointed roles.

Table D.4. Social psychology perspectives on organization: analysis and design

Perspectives	Analysis	Design Issues
Social Psychology (Gestalt, field theory, reinforcement, psychoanalytic, and role theory orientations)	Organizations are viewed as arenas of interpersonal relations with interlinked mental processes and behavioural phenomena.	Alignment of: normative and behavioural structures; organizational goals and individuals' motives; roles and personalities. Use of reward and control systems. Incentive to communication and problem solving.

Social Psychology and Organizations

In the context of social psychology, organizations are viewed as arenas and networks relationships with interlinked mental processes and behavioural phenomena which shape their structure, functioning and also the behaviour of their participants. Therefore, social psychology plays an important part into the domain of organization behaviour and management science (Carley & Gasser, 1999; and Hellriegel *et al*, 2001).

Table D.4 presents a summary on the perspectives of social psychology within the context of organizations, and on how such perspectives are viewed in organizational analysis and design.

While sociologists place emphasis on structural and functional conditions which shape events within organizations (similarly to a top-down approach moving from macro to micro level of analysis), social psychologists try to explain and predict macro-level behaviour, such as overall organizational performance, from the analysis of micro-level behaviour which emerges from complex interactions among the participants in the organization, towards a bottom-up approach.

ENGINEERING

Engineering has contributed to the field of organizations with disciplines and methodologies of systems analysis and design. Among such disciplines are industrial and systems engineering, operational research, and engineering economics and management.

Industrial and systems engineering, and operations research, traditionally focus on the analysis and design of manufacturing and service systems for the efficient production and distribution of goods and services. Engineering economics concerns the application of principles of economy and engineering to the analysis and design of systems. Therefore, it involves trade-offs between economical and technical deci-

Table D.5. Engineering and organizations

Subjects	Concerns
Industrial and Systems Engineering, and Operational Research	Analysis and design of manufacturing and service systems, and their integration to other parts. They provide tools for searching optimal and efficient solutions.
Engineering Economics	Economical and technical decision analysis of projects and organizational forms.
Engineering Management	Fulfil the gap between technical and managerial tasks. It provide tools for optimizing managerial processes like operational research.

sions. The role of engineering management is to bridge the gap between engineering and management activities. It provides engineers with principles of organizations and management. On the other hand, it provides managers with engineering tools which pursue the optimization of managerial and organizational processes through the use of scientific methods, like those within operational research and artificial intelligence. Therefore, it is also synonymous of industrial engineering. Table D.5 summarises the contributions of engineering to organizations.

COMPUTER SCIENCE

Computer science has provided organization theorists with new principles and tools to the analysis and design of organizations. Computational modelling for instance has provided researchers with models of organizations which are synonymous of theories (Cohen & Cyert, 1965). By simulating such models in computers, theories can be explained and tested, organizational behaviour can be predicted under new assumptions, and additional propositions can be derived to constitute new theories. Moreover, computational simulations can be used to support organizational design by determining for instance which among several alternatives of organizational forms are best suited to satisfy specific goals as settled to the organization.

Table D.6. Computer science and organizations

Subjects	Concerns
Computational Modelling	Design of organizational models.
Computational Simulation	Analysis of organizational forms; analysis of organizational behaviour, decisions and theories; it provides evidence for theories and it makes possible the proposal of new theories from massive data analysis.
Computational Organization Theory (COT)	A new discipline for modelling and simulating organizations as distributed computational agents. It has been largely studied at the Carnegie Mellon University.

Computer science has also provided new approaches to the analysis of organizations by resembling them to the principles of information processing systems, distributed computational agents (Blanning & King, 1996; and Carley & Gasser, 1999) and artificial life (Langton, 1995). However, it shares such contributions mainly with the disciplines of psychology, artificial intelligence and biology. Table D.6 summarises the contributions of computer science to organizations.

SUMMARY

Appendix D summarized some of the contributions that the disciplines of economics, political science, sociology, social psychology, engineering and computer science have provided to the development of organization theory.

REFERENCES

Anthony, R. N., Dearden, J., & Bedford, N. M. (1984). *Management Control Systems*. Richard D. Irwin, Inc.

Blanning, R. W., & King, R. K. (1996). *AI in Organizational Design, Modeling, and Control*. IEEE Computer Society Press.

Blau, P. M. (1974). *On the Nature of Organizations*. John Wiley & Sons.

Butterworth, G., Rutkowska, J., & Scaife, M. (1985). *Evolution and Developmental Psychology*. The Harverster Press.

Carley, K. M., & Gasser, L. (1999). Computational Organizational Theory. In G. Weiss (Ed.), *Multiagent Systems: A Modern Approach to Distributed Artificial Intelligence* (pp. 299-330). The MIT Press.

Clark, P. A. (2000). *Organizations in action: competition between contexts*. Routledge.

Cohen, K. J., & Cyert, R. M. (1965). Simulation of Organizational Behavior. In J.G. March (Ed.), *Handbook of Organizations* (pp. 305-334). Rand McNally & Company.

Cummings, L., & Staw, B. (1990). *The Evolution and Adaptation of Organizations*. Jai Press Inc.

Delouche, F. (2001). *Illustrated History of Europe*. Cassell Paperbacks, Cassell & Co.

Dunnette, M. D., & Hough, L. M. (1992). *Handbook of Industrial and Organizational Psychology, 3*. Consulting Psychologists Press, Inc.

Etzioni, A. (1969). *A Sociological Reader on Complex Organizations*. Holt, Rinehrt and Winston, Inc.

Galbraith, J. R. (2002). *Designing Organizations - An executive guide to strategy, structure, and process*. Jossey-Bass.

Gibbons, R. (1998). Incentives in Organizations. *The Journal of Economic Perspectives, 12*, 115-132.

Grusky, O., & Miller, G. (1981). *The Sociology of Organizations: Basic Studies*. The Free Press.

Gul, F. (1997). A Nobel Prize for Game Theorists: The Contributions of Harsanyi, Nash and Selten. *The Journal of Economic Perspective, 11*(3), 159-174.

Hellriegel, D., Slocum, J. W., & Woodman, R. W. (2001). *Organizational Behavior*. South-Wester College Publishing.

Heyes, C., & Huber, L. (2000). *The Evolution of Cognition*. The MIT Press.

Huxley, J., Hardy, A., & Ford, E. (1958). *Evolution as a Process*. George Allen & Unwin Ltd.

Huxley, J. (1974). *Evolution: The Modern Synthesis*. George Allen & Unwin Ltd.

Khandwalla, P. N. (1977). *Design of Organizations*. Harcourt Brace Jovanovich.

Langton (1995). *Artificial Life: An Overview*. The MIT Press.

Lefrançoies, G. (1995). *Theories of Human Learning*. Brooks Cole Publishing Company.

March, J. G., & Simon, H. A. (1958). *Organizations*. 1st Ed. John Wiley & Sons, Inc.

March, J. G., & Simon, H. A. (1993). *Organizations*. 2nd Ed. John Wiley & Sons, Inc.

Milgrom, P., & Roberts, J. (1992). *Economics, Organizations & Management*. Prentice-Hall Inc.

Minsky, M. (1986). *The Society of Mind*. Picador.

Newell, A., & Simon, H. A. (1972). *Human Problem Solving*. Prentice-Hall.

Parsons, T. (1960). *Structure and Processes in Modern Societies*. Free Press.

Perrow, C. (1974). Zoo story or Life in the organizational sandpit. In C. Perrow, *Perspectives on Organizations*. The Open University Press. ISBN 0335015689.

Pugh, D. S., & Hickson, D. J. (1997). *Writers on Organizations*. Penguin Books.

Reisberg, D. (1997). *Cognition: Exploring the Science of the Mind*. W.W. Norton & Company.

Scott, W. R. (1998). *Organizations: Rational, Natural, and Open Systems*. Prentice Hall, Inc.

Scott, W. R. (2001). *Institutions and Organizations*. SAGE Publications.

Singh, J. V. (1990). *Organizational Evolution: New Directions*. SAGE Publications.

Silverman, D. (1970). *The Theory of Organizations*. Heinemann.

Williamson, O. E., & Masten, S. E. (1999). *The Economics of Transaction Costs*. Edward Elgar Publishing, Inc.

APPENDIX E:
TECHNOLOGY

INTRODUCTION

This appendix surveys the subject of technology. Furthermore, it fits technology into the domain of organizations. The chapter starts by presenting a perspective on the genesis of technology, and by proposing a definition of technology. It explains the benefits of technology to organizations, and it also proposes some rationales for technology into a political, economic, and social context. It explains the scope of technology in organizations, which ranges from different levels of analysis to distinct elements of application. Additionally, it explains why cognitive machines represent a challenge for scientists of organizations and technology. This appendix concludes by proposing that the Industrial Revolution has already turned its emphasis from energy to information-demanding technologies.

A PERSPECTIVE ON THE GENESIS OF TECHNOLOGY

Humans have needs, but even when they satisfy their needs, they want more and more. Perhaps at first it was to obtain more food, or to find better shelter. Nowadays, however, the desires of humans seem endless. People want to cure diseases, to explore continents, the sea and the universe, to reshape nature and to build artificial habitats like cities and airports, to replace muscular and cognitive tasks with machines, and even to live longer and longer (Kipnis, 1990).

Most of human needs are created by conditions imposed by the environment on them. They answer by imposing changes on the environment. Most animals survive by adapting to the environment. However, although humans do the same, they also survive by adapting the environment to themselves.

The genesis of technology resides in the human ability to search knowledge. Humans transform knowledge in identifiable ends. Ends have economic, social and political facets, and they can be ends by themselves or even other means used to achieve more complex goals. Moving upwards from means to ends there exist sub-goals, goals and more complex goals at upper levels. Therefore, technology can also be conceived as processes of hierarchical order and control.

A DEFINITION OF TECHNOLOGY

Technology is a broad discipline which has received diverse definitions in the literature. However, all of them include knowledge as a common element (Anthony & Gales, 2003; Goodman, 1990; Richter, 1982; Scott, 1998; and Simon, 1977). Similarly to the definition of organizations, the conception of technology within this section avoids any divergence from the literature. Moreover, it represents a synthesis aligned to the book scope.

Technology represents means deliberately employed by humans for attaining practical outcomes. Technology encompasses knowledge, and furthermore, processes to produce, to process and to manage knowledge. It also includes tools, practices and even other technologies.

In such a way, science plays an important part in the conception of technology, since it is defined as the use of scientific methods to search knowledge. Science can be classified in natural and artificial forms (Simon, 1996). In summary, the former is knowledge about natural objects and phenomena, and it is concerned with analysis and discoveries - like the Newton's law of gravitation for instance. The latter is knowledge about artificial (and synthetic) objects and phenomena; it is concerned with engineering and inventions, man-made things, and thus with design - like knowledge on agriculture, medicine, machines and organizations for instance.

BENEFITS OF TECHNOLOGY TO ORGANIZATIONS

Technology reduces the amount of uncertainty in the attempt to solve practical problems, and it increases the probability of occurrence of events as wanted by power-holders (Kipnis, 1990; and Perrow, 1967).

This book supports this statement and extends it to the next chain of propositions which were discussed in (Nobre, 2003d) and latter stated in (Nobre, 2005):

Proposition E.1: Technology increases the level of complexity of the organization, and it relatively reduces the level of complexity of the environment.

Firstly, Proposition E.1 assumes by definition that the higher the level of complexity of the organization, the higher its degrees of cognition, intelligence and autonomy. Secondly, it does not mean that the level of complexity of the environment reduces, but it says that such a level of complexity is relatively reduced when compared to the growth in the level of complexity of the organization. Therefore, we can proceed by stating that:

Proposition E.2: The higher the level of complexity of the organization, the higher are its degrees of cognition, intelligence and autonomy.

Proposition E.3: The higher the degrees of cognition, intelligence and autonomy of the organization, the lower is the relative level of complexity of its environment.

Proposition E.4: The lower the relative level of complexity of the environment, the less is the relative amount of uncertainty.

Similarly, proposition E.4 says that the amount of uncertainty in the environment is relatively reduced with an increase in the degrees of cognition, intelligence and autonomy of the organization. Therefore, we can deduce the next theorem from the previous chain of propositions:

Theorem E.1: Technology increases the level of complexity of the organization, and it relatively reduces the amount of uncertainty of the environment.

These propositions are further discussed in Parts II and IV.

RATIONALES FOR TECHNOLOGY: POLITICAL, ECONOMIC AND SOCIAL CONTEXTS

Among the major achievements of humans through technology is the progressive economy of time and energy that we must devote to any given activity, including both physical and mental tasks. By creating technologies of automation, humans can direct their effort upward into more complex tasks.

To think about technology as synonymous with machines and processes only is to reject its broad significance and implications for the society. As organizations do, technology emerges from political, economic and social contexts. Therefore, technology can provide humanity with general improvements as well as with reverse and negative results in these contexts. Consider for instance the expansion of Europe between the 15th and 18th centuries, which was empowered by the dominance of the colonizers in navigation and army technologies. Their overseas discoveries and actions brought about a revolution in the history of humanity, resulting in good, negative and controversial results of political, economic, religious, and social facets for the new world (Delouche, 2001). Apart the contributions of technologies of today, they can also be viewed under the perspectives of destruction, caused by nuclear wars, and total automation, caused by the efficient and materialist world, where man is eliminated from the economic world system and replaced with machines.

Political Context

The most important political facet of technology is power (Kipnis, 1990; and Scarbrough & Corbett, 1992); technology provides people with it. These people are named power-holders when they control the technology. Power-holders pursue the achievement of complex goals and practical outcomes by exercising control over the environment, and thus by overcoming the resistance of nature and people who are target of control - e.g. workers, consumers, citizens, etc. Therefore, technology can give those who govern the technology control over others, either by taking away some of their alternatives or by constraining them to particular choices. A hierarchy of power-holders is then synonymous with a hierarchical process of decision control.

Economic Context

Technology also emerges from economic reasons and needs, and it feeds back new outcomes to society. The economic facet of technology concerns the efficient production of goods and services. Therefore, technology is supposed to provide people with better standard of life and wealth. However, power-holders are who control the distribution of economic outcomes.

Social Context

On the one hand, some studies on technology have demonstrated that it can provide people with better standard of life and other social outcomes (Easterlin, 2000; and Johnson, 2000). Consider for instance the advent of communication systems with the radio, the television, the telephone and the internet. With such technologies we can meet (or get in contact with) people from any continent; get more and more knowledge, faster than in any period of the human history; and even work in home with the benefit to spend more time with the family. On the other hand, some authors advocate that technology, and thus the use of power, transforms social relations between the more and the less powerful (Kipnis, 1990). Other authors (orthodox Marxists) say that technology (and in particular automation) may provide massive unemployment and societal pathologies, like alienation, inequity, social stratification, etc.

This book asserts that new technologies may force people to move from one kind of job to another. The new jobs will be carried out by more complex mental tasks and they will require greater mental efforts than before. However and foremost, unemployment will have to be managed between transitions of technologies. Additionally, institutional processes will have to play a prominent part to regulate and to intermediate consensus between organizations and their employees; and broadly speaking, between organizations and the environment.

THE SCOPE OF TECHNOLOGY IN ORGANIZATIONS

Technology is a discipline which encompasses distinct elements of application and different levels of analysis. Elements of technology vary from machines to normative and regulative processes. Similarly to organizations, levels of analysis of technology range from technical, managerial and institutional to worldwide systems. These systems comprise technologies of machines and cognitive processes in the respective levels of analysis of the organization and they form a major cognitive system.

The technical level refers to the set of possible arrangements of machines and processes employed to produce desired outcomes, goods and services. The literature calls it technical system (Scott, 1998). Furthermore, this level also encompasses the technology of the machines, characterized by their structure (anatomy) and processes (functioning or physiology). This latter refers to the processes embedded in machines and those processes (or protocols) of communication used to connect the machines to a network. Hence, such processes play a preponderant part in the design of cognitive machines, by providing them with capabilities to carry out high mental tasks in organizations.

Additionally, such cognitive machines are also used to carry out activities and cognitive tasks at the managerial, institutional and worldwide levels. However, as we move from technical towards worldwide level of analysis, the processes within these machines and systems become more complex. At upward levels, goals, problems, and decisions become more complex, uncertainty increases, and the predictability of consequences of choices and outcomes diminishes.

Perspectives of the organization defined as hierarchic cognitive systems along with the concept of organizational levels of analysis are presented in Part II.

A CHALLENGE FOR TODAY: COGNITIVE MACHINES IN ORGANIZATIONS

Consider for instance a technical system constituted by machines. The interdependence among its parts is such that their behaviour is highly constrained and limited to the prescriptions of a normative structure. This structure is relatively rigid and the system of relations determinant. Such a normative structure of technical systems and machines includes programmed and non-programmed decisions. An overview on programmed and non-programmed decisions is found in (Simon, 1977). By contrast, in social systems such as organizations, the connections among the interacting parts are somewhat less constrained, providing them with more flexibility of response. Moreover, organizations have a structure of normative and behavioural parts. The latter part focus on actual behaviour rather than on prescriptions for behaviour, and thus it provides organizations with a more complex behaviour – where in this particular case complex behaviour is synonymous with unpredictable outcomes. Therefore, the elements of social systems, and the relationships between them, hold higher levels of complexity than those of technical systems. Social systems such as organizations possess emotions along with higher degrees of cognition, intelligence and autonomy.

Nevertheless, artificial systems of high levels of complexity (and thus possessing high degrees of cognition, intelligence and autonomy) have been developed with the advances in technologies of machines. This includes software programs, computers and communication networks, and also developments with the advent of the disciplines of artificial intelligence (Luger & Stubblefield, 1998; and Zadeh, 1999 and 2001) and soft computing (Zadeh, 1994 and 1997). Such systems have started to play a fundamental and an increasing role in the society of today, by supporting individual and distributed cognitive tasks in organizations (Blanning & King, 1996). Therefore, the integration of these systems into organizations of today constitutes a subject of challenge for researchers of technology and social sciences.

There is no doubt that technological principles of the past and the present have contributed with brilliantly successful applications in many areas of organizations, such as in manufacturing and management (Simon, 1977). But these successes should not obscure the fact that the world is changing, that high machine intelligence is becoming reality (Zadeh, 1996b), and that methods which have proved to be successful in the past may not provide the right tools for addressing the problems of the future.

THE INDUSTRIAL REVOLUTION: FROM ENERGY TO INFORMATION

In discussing technological transformations paved by the Industrial Revolution, it is relevant to distinguish two polar phases in the extremes of this continuous period of the history. These extremes are characterized by energy-based technologies and information-based technologies (Simon, 1977).

At one end, we have energy-based technologies which are characterized by machines with capabilities to replace mainly intensive muscular tasks in organizations.

Figure E.1. Relative demand of energy and information over time

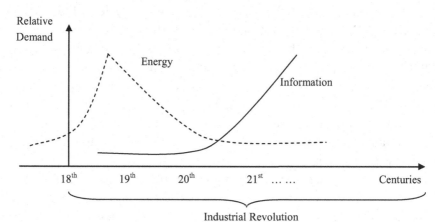

At the other end, we have information processing-based technologies which are those machines carrying knowledge on how to produce and to manage information more effectively and efficiently. Moreover, they are consumers of a quite modest amount of energy and materials - like modern computers.

Of course we can find technologies of all shades of grey along the continuum between these two extremes of black and white. Machines that autonomously[1] transform one type of energy in another represent the first extreme. Thus, we can assert that they have already been designed mainly after the beginning of the Industrial Revolution in the 18th century.

The other extreme is represented by machines which posses levels of cognition, intelligence and autonomy comparable with humans. These extreme machines have not been completely designed yet, but man has been continuously moving towards the design of them along a continuous path of revolution.

Figure E.1 illustrates two symbolic functions which represent the demands of machines for energy and information, when we move from the beginning of the Industrial Revolution, up to now, to its continuous development.

Moving along the continuous period of Industrial Revolution, on the horizontal line, it can be observed that information is increasingly demanded, produced and managed by machines, and thus it becomes relatively more important than energy for organizations of today. Nevertheless, machines at shop floor still demand a great amount of energy, but not greater than the demand required by those machines of similar purpose as designed in the first phase of the Industrial Revolution.

Therefore, Figure E.1 does not mean that energy is being less consumed nowadays in the world than before, but it does assert that nowadays each unit of machine demands less energy and more information[2] than those machines of similar purpose which were designed in the past.

SUMMARY

Appendix E overviewed the subject of technology, and it fitted technology into the domain of organizations. It started by presenting a perspective on the genesis of technology and by proposing a definition of technology. It explained the benefits of technology to organizations and it also proposes some rationales for technology into political, economic and social contexts. It introduced the scope of technology in organizations, which ranges from different levels of analysis to distinct elements of application. Appendix E continued by explaining why cognitive machines can represent a challenge for scientists of organizations and technology. It concluded by analysing the transition of attention from energy to information in the continuous period of Industrial Revolution.

Technology encompasses knowledge, and furthermore, tools, practices, processes and other technologies to produce, to process and to manage knowledge.

Concerning the subject of technology in organizations, the book's point of departure is twofold. Firstly, it asserts that organizations expand what people can achieve. Secondly, it states that technology expands what organizations can do. Despite being slightly distinct, such premises complement each other. Organizations and technology are complementary means which extend people capability for the achievement of more complex goals.

Technology arises from the human ability to search knowledge in order to transform it in identifiable ends for their own well-being. It provides humans with means deliberately used for attaining practical outcomes.

Technology can reduce the amount of time and energy which people must devote to any given activity, including both physical and mental tasks.

Technology plays an important part in connecting organizations to the environment. Technology can increase the level of complexity of the organization by improving the organization's powers of cognition, intelligence and autonomy. Hence, technology in one sense relatively reduces the amount of uncertainty in the environment.

Technology emerges from political, economic and social contexts and it provides people with power, economic use of resources and social outcomes such as wealth and well-being. However, it simultaneously provides power-holders with control over the environment. Hence, technology can also give those who govern the technology control over others, either by taking away some of their alternatives or by constraining them to particular choices. These steps form a hierarchical process of decision control.

Analysis of technology ranges from technical, organizational and institutional to worldwide levels, and its elements vary from machines to normative and regulative processes.

The advent of machines pursuing high levels of complexity, and thus high degrees of cognition, intelligence and autonomy, represents a challenge for researchers of organizations and technology. Such machines are coming to play an increasing role in organizations of today as decision-makers and problem-solvers, and they are emerging to work in the name of organizations, just like people do.

The Industrial Revolution proceeds with continuous transformations. It has been moving towards new directions to rationalize energy and to provide man with the design of cognitive machines. Such revolution has already shifted its emphasis from energy to information-demanding machines.

REFERENCES

Anthony, R. N., Dearden, J., & Bedford, N. M. (1984). Management Control Systems. Richard D. Irwin, Inc.

Blanning, R. W., & King, R. K. (1996). AI in Organizational Design, Modeling, and Control. IEEE Computer Society Press.

Delouche, F. (2001). Illustrated History of Europe. Cassell Paperbacks, Cassell & Co.

Easterlin, R. A. (2000). The Worldwide Standard of Living Since 1800. The Journal of Economic Perspectives, 14(1), 7-26.

Goodman, P. S. (1990). Technology and Organizations. Jossey-Bass Inc.

Johnson, D. G. (2000). Population, Food, and Knowledge. The American Economic Review, 90(1), 1-14.

Kipnis, D. (1990) Technology and Power. Springer-Verlag New York Inc.

Luger, G. F., & Stubblefield, W. A. (1998). Artificial Intelligence: Structures and Strategies for Complex Problem Solving. The Benjamin/Cummings Publishing Company, Inc.

Nobre, F. S. (2003d, July). Organizations and Technology - Past, Present and Future Perspectives. Seminar presented for the Artificial Intelligence Research Group of the Department of Computer Sciences in the Humboldt University of Berlin. Johann von Newmann-Haus, Berlin.

Nobre, F. (2005). On Cognitive Machines in Organizations. PhD Thesis, 343 pages. University of Birmingham / Birmingham-UK. Control Number: M0266887BU.

Perrow, C. (1974). Zoo story or Life in the organizational sandpit. In C. Perrow (1974), Perspectives on Organizations. The Open University Press. ISBN 0335015689.

Richter, M. N. (1982). Technology and Social Complexity. State University of New York.

Scarbrough, H., & Corbett, J. M. (1992). Technology and Organization - Power, meaning and design. Routledge.

Scott, W. R. (1998). Organizations: Rational, Natural, and Open Systems. Prentice Hall, Inc.

Simon, H. A. (1977). The New Science of Management Decision. Prentice-Hall, Inc.

Simon, H. A. (1996). The Sciences of the Artificial. 3rd Ed. The MIT Press.

Zadeh, L. A. (1994). Soft Computing and Fuzzy Logic. IEEE Software, November: 48-56.

Zadeh, L. A. (1996b). The Evolution of Systems Analysis and Control: A Personal Perspective. IEEE Control Systems, June, 95-98.

Zadeh, L. A. (1997). The Roles of Fuzzy Logic and Soft Computing in the Conception, Design and Development of Intelligent Systems. In Nwana & Azarmi (Ed.), Software Agents and Soft Computing: Towards Enhancing Machine Intelligence (pp. 183-190). Springer.

Zadeh, L. A. (1999). From Computing with Numbers to Computing with Words – From Manipulation of Measurements to Manipulation of Perceptions. IEEE Transactions on Circuits and Systems, 45(1), 105-119.

Zadeh, L. A. (2001). A New Direction in AI: Toward a Computational Theory of Perceptions. AI Magazine. Spring, 73-84.

ENDNOTES

[1]   In this context, autonomous means independence of the intervention of human muscles for the transformation of energy. Therefore, old mills - for instance - are not autonomous machines.

[2]   The term "demand of information" means the capability of machines to create, to process, and to manage information.

APPENDIX F:
DEFINITION OF THE PERFORMANCE FACTORS

INTRODUCTION

This appendix presents definitions of the state variables (X) of the organization process as applied throughout the industrial case study in Part V. These variables are denotations of performance factors of the organization process and they comprise project schedule (T), project cost (C), and project requirements completeness (R).

Project Schedule (T)

It is concerned with the periods of time or dates associated with the completion of the activities of a project. It is classified into planning and actual schedule.

Planning Schedule (T_o)

It represents the expected period of time or date for the completion of a project and it is estimated during the phase of project planning. T_o may also be defined in terms of the project's milestones or according to other specific granularities of the schedule.

Actual Schedule (T_A)

It represents the actual period of time which was expended for the completion of a project. Similarly to T_o, T_A may also be defined in terms of the project's milestones or according to other specific granularities of the schedule.

PROJECT COST (C)

It is concerned with the financial investment put in a project and it is classified into planning and actual costs.

Planning Cost (C_o)

It represents the expected cost of a project and it is estimated during the phase of project planning.

Actual Cost (C_A)

It represents the actual cost of a project computed at time T_o.

PROJECT REQUIREMENTS COMPLETENESS (R)

It is concerned with measures that indicate the degree of completeness of the requirements of a project as it is expected and ordered by the customer. The completion of the project requirements will result in the final product of the customer. This variable is classified into planning and actual requirements completeness.

Planning Requirements Completeness (R_o)

It represents the total number of requirements of a project as it is expected and ordered by the customer.

Actual Requirements Completeness (R_A)

It represents the number (or subset) of requirements of a project which were successfully achieved at time T_o.

SUMMARY

Appendix F introduced definitions of the state variables (X) of the organization process as applied throughout the industrial case study in Part V.

APPENDIX G:
MENTAL MODELS OF THE COGNITIVE MACHINE

INTRODUCTION

This appendix presents the linguistic descriptions of mental models of the cognitive machine designed in the chapter X of the Industrial Case Study. The mental models were embedded into fuzzy rule bases and represented by linguistic statements about Customer Satisfaction (CS) and Project Management Quality (PMQ), where CS and PMQ denote performance indexes of the organization process. Such mental models were written according to the experience, knowledge and perception of the participants (designer, engineers and manager) in the TMN Section of NEC of Brazil (NOB) to the pursuit of excellence in customer satisfaction as well as in software project management.

LINGUISTIC STATEMENTS ABOUT CUSTOMER SATISFACTION

(1) IF R is *empty* THEN CS is *very low*
OR
(2) IF R is *almost empty* THEN CS is *low*
OR
(3) IF R is *partial* THEN CS is *medium*
OR
(4) IF R is *almost full* THEN CS is *high*
OR
(5) IF R is *full* THEN CS is *very high*

LINGUISTIC STATEMENTS ABOUT PROJECT MANAGEMENT QUALITY

(1) IF C is *cheap* AND R is *empty* THEN PMQ is *bad*
OR
(2) IF C is *cheap* AND R is *almost empty* THEN PMQ is *moderate*
OR
(3) IF C is *cheap* AND R is *partial* THEN PMQ is *good*
OR

(4) IF C is *cheap* AND R is *almost full* THEN PMQ is *very good*
OR
(5) IF C is *cheap* AND R is *full* THEN PMQ is *really good*
OR
(6) IF C is *not so cheap* AND R is *empty* THEN PMQ is *very bad*
OR
(7) IF C is *not so cheap* AND R is *almost empty* THEN PMQ is *bad*
OR
(8) IF C is *not so cheap* AND R is *partial* THEN PMQ is *moderate*
OR
(9) IF C is *not so cheap* AND R is *almost full* THEN PMQ is *good*
OR
(10) IF C is *not so cheap* AND R is *full* THEN PMQ is *very good*
OR
(11) IF C is *expensive* AND R is *empty* THEN PMQ is *really bad*
OR
(12) IF C is *expensive* AND R is *almost empty* THEN PMQ is *very bad*
OR
(13) IF C is *expensive* AND R is *partial* THEN PMQ is *bad*
OR
(14) IF C is *expensive* AND R is *almost full* THEN PMQ is *moderate*
OR
(15) IF C is *expensive* AND R is *full* THEN PMQ is *good*

SUMMARY

Appendix G presented the linguistic descriptions of mental models of the cognitive machine designed in the Chapter 10 of the Industrial Case Study. The mental models were embedded into fuzzy rule bases and represented by linguistic statements about Customer Satisfaction (CS) and Project Management Quality (PMQ). Such mental models were written according to the experience, knowledge and perception of the participants (designer, engineers and manager) in the TMN Section of NEC of Brazil (NOB) to the pursuit of excellence in customer satisfaction and software project management.

APPENDIX H:
BOUNDARIES AND CONVERGENCE OF THE
COGNITIVE MACHINE

INTRODUCTION

This appendix is concerned with boundary studies and the proof of convergence of the output variables of the cognitive machine designed in the Chapter X of Part V. It complements the studies of quantitative analysis by demonstrating Theorem 10.4.

The state space of the cognitive machine designed in this chapter can be broken down and classified into the following regions or intervals of operation.

REGIONS OF OPERATION OF THE COGNITIVE MACHINE

State Space of (R → CS)

Region 1: $(0 \leq R_A \leq 0.6Ro)$
Region 2: $(0.6Ro < R_A \leq 0.7Ro)$
Region 3: $(0.7Ro < R_A \leq 0.8Ro)$
Region 4: $(0.8Ro < R_A \leq 0.9Ro)$
Region 5: $(0.9Ro < R_A \leq Ro)$
Region 6: $(Ro < R_A \leq \eta$, for $\eta < \infty)$

State Space of (C AND R→ PPQ)

Region 1: $(0 \leq C_A \leq Co)$ and $(0 \leq R_A \leq 0.6Ro)$
Region 2: $(0 \leq C_A \leq Co)$ and $(0.6Ro < R_A \leq 0.7Ro)$
Region 3: $(0 \leq C_A \leq Co)$ and $(0.7Ro < R_A \leq 0.8Ro)$
Region 4: $(0 \leq C_A \leq Co)$ and $(0.8Ro < R_A \leq 0.9Ro)$
Region 5: $(0 \leq C_A \leq Co)$ and $(0.9Ro < R_A \leq Ro)$
Region 6: $(0 \leq C_A \leq Co)$ and $(Ro < R_A \leq \eta)$
Region 7: $(Co < C_A \leq 1.25Co)$ and $(0 \leq R_A \leq 0.6Ro)$
Region 8: $(Co < C_A \leq 1.25Co)$ and $(0.6Ro < R_A \leq 0.7Ro)$
Region 9: $(Co < C_A \leq 1.25Co)$ and $(0.7Ro < R_A \leq 0.8Ro)$
Region 10: $(Co < C_A \leq 1.25Co)$ and $(0.8Ro < R_A \leq 0.9Ro)$
Region 11: $(Co < C_A \leq 1.25Co)$ and $(0.9Ro < R_A \leq Ro)$
Region 12: $(Co < C_A \leq 1.25Co)$ and $(Ro < R_A \leq \eta)$
Region 13: $(1.25Co < C_A \leq 1.5Co)$ and $(0 \leq R_A \leq 0.6Co)$
Region 14: $(1.25Co < C_A \leq 1.5Co)$ and $(0.6Ro < R_A \leq 0.7Ro)$

Region 15: $(1.25\text{Co} < C_A \le 1.5\text{Co})$ and $(0.7\text{Ro} < C_A \le 0.8\text{Ro})$
Region 16: $(1.25\text{Co} < C_A \le 1.5\text{Co})$ and $(0.8\text{Ro} < C_A \le 0.9\text{Ro})$
Region 17: $(1.25\text{Co} < C_A \le 1.5\text{Co})$ and $(0.9\text{Ro} < C_A \le \text{Ro})$
Region 18: $(1.25\text{Co} < C_A \le 1.5\text{Co})$ and $(\text{Ro} < R_A \le \eta)$
Region 19: $(1.5\text{Co} < C_A \le \eta)$ and $(0 \le R_A \le 0.6\text{Co})$
Region 20: $(1.5\text{Co} < C_A \le \eta)$ and $(0.6\text{Ro} < R_A \le 0.7\text{Ro})$
Region 21: $(1.5\text{Co} < C_A \le \eta)$ and $(0.7\text{Ro} < C_A \le 0.8\text{Ro})$
Region 22: $(1.5\text{Co} < C_A \le \eta)$ and $(0.8\text{Ro} < C_A \le 0.9\text{Ro})$
Region 23: $(1.5\text{Co} < C_A \le \eta)$ and $(0.9\text{Ro} < C_A \le \text{Ro})$
Region 24: $(1.5\text{Co} < C_A \le \eta)$ and $(\text{Ro} < R_A \le \eta)$, for $\eta < \infty$

MATHEMATICAL ANALYSIS

The regions of operation of both CS and PPQ can be described mathematically by the application of the results of Theorems 10.2 and 10.3 respectively. As shown in the following, Theorem 10.2 is applied to describe the analytical equation that describes the region of operation 2 of customer satisfaction (CS): $(0.6\text{Ro} < R_A \le 0.7\text{Ro})$.

$$CS(t) = -\frac{10}{R_o}(R_A - 0.7R_o).0 + \frac{10}{R_o}(R_A - 0.6R_o).2.5 \qquad \text{(H.1)}$$

$$CS(t) = \frac{25}{R_o}(R_A - 0.6R_o) \qquad \text{(H.2)}$$

By calculating the limits of *CS(t)* in the boundaries of the region 2, it is found that:

$$\lim_{R_A \to 0.6R_o} CS(t) = 0 \qquad \text{(H.3)}$$

$$\lim_{R_A \to 0.7R_o} CS(t) = 2.5 \qquad \text{(H.4)}$$

It can be concluded that the value of CS in the region of operation 2, as modelled by the equation H.2, converges to a bounded real value in the interval [0,10] as the input variables C and R tend to the limits of operation defined to this region. The same results can be concluded to the overall regions of operation of CS and PPQ. Therefore, the output variables of the cognitive machine are bounded and they converge to real values in the interval [0,10] defined to their respective universes of discourse.

SUMMARY

Appendix H demonstrated boundary studies and convergence proof for the output variables of the cognitive machine designed in Chapter X of Section V. It complemented the studies of quantitative analysis after having demonstrated Theorem 10.4.

APPENDIX I:
THE CMM MATURITY LEVELS

INTRODUCTION

This appendix presents an overview about definitions and characteristics of the five maturity levels of the CMM (The Capability Maturity Level).

MATURITY LEVELS OF THE CMM

The CMM framework involves five levels of maturity as illustrated in Figure I.1. They form an evolutionary path to support continuous process improvement and organizational learning practices (Paulk *et al*, 1994).

Level 1: The Initial Level

At level 1, the organization process is characterized as ad hoc and unstable. Success in organizations at level 1 depends on the competence and heroics of their participants and cannot be repeated unless the same competent individuals are assigned to the next projects. Capability is a merit of the individuals, but not of the organization.

At level 1, the organization process is poorly defined and amorphous – like a black box – and visibility into the process is limited. Hence, managers have difficult to identify the status of the activities of the projects and customers can only assess whether the product satisfy requirements when it is delivered. Figure I.2 illustrates an organization process at level 1.

Level 2: The Repeatable Level

At level 2, the organization process is specified along with basic management practices which comprise requirements management, project planning, tracking and oversight, subcontract management, quality assurance and configuration management. Success is achieved with discipline and experience accumulated with similar projects. The organization process is specified and divided into successive black boxes as illustrated in Figure I.3. Hence, managers have better visibility into the process. They can track the status of projects and products at transition points (milestones) of the organization process.

Figure I.1. The CMM maturity levels

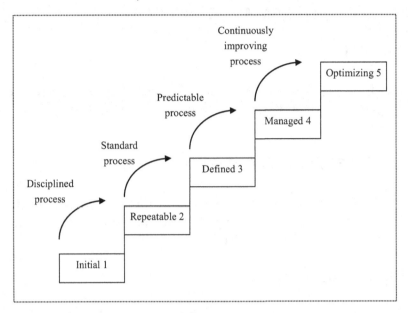

Figure I.2. Visibility into the organization process at level 1

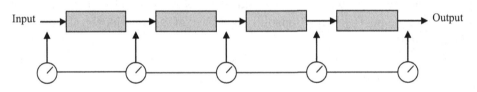

Figure I.3. Visibility into the organization process at level 2: repeatable

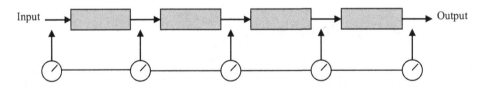

Level 3: The Defined Level

At level 3, the organization process is defined, standardized, institutionalized and used across the organization. It comprises engineering and management practices. This process is referred by the CMM as the organization's standard software process (OSSP). The projects of the divisions and units of the organization tailor the OSSP

Figure I.4. Relation of the OSSP and PDSP at level 3

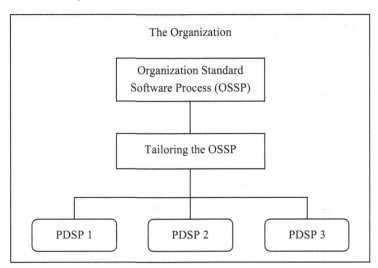

and develop their own software process. A tailored process is called a project's defined software process (PDSP). Figure I.4 illustrates the relation between the OSSP and the PDSP of three divisions of an organization.

Moreover, at level 3, managers have clear visibility into the organization process and into the internal structure of the boxes (stages) which form the project's process. Hence, the relation between management and engineering activities are understood, and the status of the project and products can be accurately updated and controlled. The integration of different project's defined software processes (PDSP) across the organization provides the organization's standard software process (OSSP) with new practices and thus with organizational learning. The best practices within the PDSP are recognized, standardized and institutionalized within the OSSP. Figure I.5 illustrates such a process at level 3.

Level 4: The Managed Level

At level 4, the organization establishes quantitative criteria and measures for software products and processes. Management and engineering decisions are based on quantitative measurements and they provide the organization with improvements in predictability, control and effectiveness. Hence, managers have visibility into the organization and project's processes and also access to measurements such as quality and productivity. Figure I.6 illustrates the organization process at level 4.

Figure I.5. Visibility into the organization process at level 3: defined

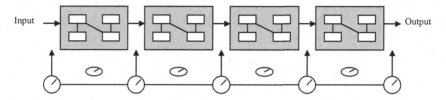

Figure I.6. Visibility into the organization process at level 4: managed

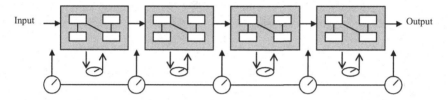

Figure I.7. Visibility into the organization process at level 5: optimizing

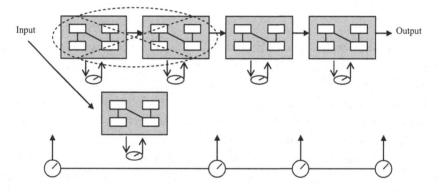

Level 5: The Optimizing Level

At level 5, the organization focuses on continuous process improvement principles for defect prevention along with the management of process and technology change. Managers are able to predict and to control the implications of change and innovation of processes, products and technology for the organization and projects quantitatively. Technology change and process improvement are planned and managed as ordinary activities in the organization. Figure I.7 illustrates the organization process at level 5.

SUMMARY

Appendix I complemented Chapter IX by presenting definitions and characteristics of the five maturity levels of the CMM framework.

REFERENCES

Paulk, M. C. *et al* (1994). *The Capability Maturity Model: Guidelines for Improving the Software Process*. Addison Wesley Longman, Inc.

Glossary

Cognitive Information Systems (CIS): are Information Management Systems (IMS) that pursue high degrees of cognition, intelligence and autonomy. They are particular classes of cognitive machines, and they are deliberated designed to participate in the organization by performing cognitive tasks and by fulfilling managerial roles in all the levels and layers of the whole enterprise.

Cognitive Machines: (1) are necessary when we need to extend the human boundaries of computational capacity along with knowledge and uncertainty management to more advanced models of cognition or information processing. (2) cognitive machines are agents whose processes of functioning are mainly inspired by human cognition. Therefore, they have great possibilities to present intelligent behaviour.

Cognitive Machines (designer of): (1) the designer (which involves the manufacturer) of a cognitive machine is the person (or entity - organization) responsible for the cognitive abilities and the behaviour of the machine. Such a kind of designers can have independent legal identity which enables them to make contracts and to seek court enforcement of those contracts if necessary. (2) Designers can use technologies for automatic design and generation of cognitive machines. Genetic programming for instance is a paradigm which has provided a profound impact on the design of software programs capable of generating tangible replicas and with enough ability to perform at least similar functions (Koza, 1992). Such technologies are classified as artificial designers and they cannot ask for, nor answer, a formal contract. Therefore, their first designer (a person or an organization) is the agent who is able to make it.

Computational Organization Management Networks (COMN): organizations whose structure, processes, participants, goals and technologies are designed according to the concepts of Functional Layers which comprise Element Layer, Network Management Layer, Service Management Layer and Business Management Layer. COMN pursue high degrees of organizational cognition and their main participants comprise Cognitive Information Systems (CIS) and cognitive machines.

Emotional Intelligence: the ability to use emotional and cognitive processes in order to understand ourselves (i.e. intra-personal intelligence) and relate with others (inter-personal or social intelligence).

Immersiveness: represents the ability of the organization to interact with its customers (either humans or machines) in a friendly way, by immersing them into the organization's operations through approaches such as virtual reality, simulation or via real world protocols; in order to satisfy customers by capturing their exact needs, by customizing and managing the design, engineering and production of their goods and services, and by delivering their products with efficacy and effectiveness.

Machine Consciousness: the awareness of its designer in relation to the cognitive processes and abilities that the machine carries on during task execution.

Management Threshold Principle: the gradual transition of manufacturing organizations from mass and batch production systems to customer-centric models - which are characterized by a continuous growth in the level of customization - will reach a threshold where customers will be part of the design, production and management of their own needs – resulting in the generation of highly personal and customized services and goods.

Organizational Threshold Principle: the gradual transition of manufacturing organizations from mass and batch production systems to customer-centric models - which are also characterized by a continuously growth in the levels of organizational and environmental complexity - will reach a threshold where current (and dominant) models of organizing will found their limits of contribution.

Rational Intelligence: the ability to use cognitive processes in learning, decision-making and problem-solving.

Socio-Technological Threshold Principle: the gradual transition of organizations from mass and batch production systems to customer-centric models - which are also characterized by a continuous growth in the degrees of flexibility and agility

- will reach a threshold where the current (and the dominant) technological state of the art will found their limits of contribution.

Uncertainty: (1) the difference between the total amount of information that the organization needs to have in order to perform a task, and the amount of information that the organization has already possessed. (2) the difference between the degree of cognition that the organization needs to have in order to perform a task, and the degree of cognition that the organization has already possessed.

About the Authors

Farley Nobre is founder and director CEO of Innovation Technology Enterprise, Brazil. He earned a PhD by The University of Birmingham UK (2001-2005) with research experience in the fields of organizations, information management systems, and artificial intelligence. Nobre was guest researcher with the Institute of Organization Theory and the Artificial Intelligence Research Group of the Humboldt University of Berlin (2002-2003), where he also participated in the Socionics Project. In the industry (NEC, 1997-2000), he worked on software process improvement, project management and software development for telecommunication management networks. Nobre participated in the implementation of The Capability Maturity Model in NEC of Brazil where he was awarded in 1998 with the Industrial Honor Prize for his contributions in the areas of productivity and quality.

Andrew Tobias is senior lecturer in operations management at the University of Birmingham, UK. His early work involved providing systems engineering support to business development task forces within Lucas Industries, and later relocating and restructuring solenoid manufacture into Magneti Marelli. He moved to Birmingham in 1988 to work in management systems, organizational dynamics and corporate strategy. More recently he joined the Birmingham Centre for Railway Research and Education to specialize in network capacity. To date, Dr. Tobias has over 50 publications to his name, several being in co-authorship with David Walker and two having attracted international conference prizes.

David Walker is senior teaching fellow at the Business School of the University of Birmingham UK, where he has taught since 1995. Previous to this he was professor of marketing, head of the Marketing Department and director of business research at Wolverhampton Business School. He commenced his academic career at Aston

Business School where he completed his doctorate in marketing as a Foundation for Management Education research fellow. He has throughout his professional life founded and managed several extensive companies in the industrial cleaning and chemical industries, besides current appointments as an external examiner at the Chartered Institute of Marketing, Southampton Business School, Westminster Business School, Northampton Business School and Brighton Business School. He has published extensively in numerous business and management journals both individually and in co-authorship with Dr. Andrew Tobias over many years.

Index